The Bible constantly reiterates that "divine" intervention lifted stumbling mankind into the light. Can it be that starmen have been the "angels" and emissaries of God, in an indirect way, with the mission of creating human life on Earth?

Are we the "Sons of God" by virtue of colonization? Colonization by a people so highly advanced in morals, ethics, intelligence, and spiritual wisdom, that it is part of a Greater Plan than we know?

MANKIND
CHILD OF THE STARS

By

Max H. Flindt & Otto O. Binder

Foreword by Erich von Däniken

P.O. Box 754
Huntsville, AR 72740
WWW.OZARKMT.COM

Library of Congress Cataloging-in-Publication Data
Flindt, Max H., 1915 -
Binder, Otto O., 1911 - 1974
        Mankind - Child of the Stars, by Max H. Flindt & Otto O. Binder
        Scientific evidence that supports the theory that mankind did not evolve naturally, but was the product of hybridization. Evidence supporting the Ancient Astronaut Theory. Foreword by Erich von Däniken. Includes extensive index and footnotes of references.
        1. Ancient Astronaut Theory. 2. Evolution. 3. Archeology.
        4. Anthropology. 5. UFOs & Aliens.
I. Flindt, Max H., 1915 - II. Binder, Otto O., 1911 - 1974   III. Title
Library of Congress Catalog Card Number: 99-075843
ISBN: 1-886940-06-1

Cover Design: Tom Cannon
Book Set in : Times New Roman, Arial
Book Design: Tom Cannon
Published By

P.O. Box 754
Huntsville, AR 72740
WWW.OZARKMT.COM

Printed in the United States of America

To my wife, *Elfriede,* for her patience, and to *George Higer,* without whose intellectual aid this book would have been impossible. And to all others who encouraged me in presenting this new theory.

— MAX H. FLINDT

To my wife, *Ione,* for her many secretarial aids, and to my collaborator, *Max Flindt,* whose brilliant new concept of mankind's origin inspired me in coauthoring this book.

— OTTO O. BINDER

"The proper study of mankind is man."
— ALEXANDER POPE

To the Authors

We search with humbled thoughts and reeling brains
For stellar footprints, cosmic legacy,
For signs of visitors from distant lanes
Who bred this race in dim prehistory,
And wonder if these watchers of the earth,
These strange observers from a stranger port,
Evolved us from the brutes to foster mirth,
Created us in fancy and in sport.
The mighty structures of a dateless age
That hold their stories thoughtfully concealed
May still become an open lamplit page
In which these riddles show themselves revealed;
And we, who strive to open and to rob
The secrets, face the laughter of the mob.

— WADE WELLMAN

Table of Contents

ACKNOWLEDGMENTS

(Many of the following received Max Flindt's original pamphlet, *On Tiptoe Beyond Darwin,* and kindly gave the author encouragement in producing this expanded book).

With deep gratitude to the late President-Lyndon B. Johnson (who sent us his new book in return); to Nobelists Dr. Glenn Seaborg, Dr. Edward Teller, and especially to Dr. Melvin Calvin for his warm personal interest. We take this opportunity to express our appreciation to these faculty members at their respective universities: Professor Emeritus Percy Baumberger, Professor White, Dr. Olds, Dr. Krupp, Dr. McClenahan. Dr. Borovsky, Dr. Sowers, Dr. Alvarez, Dr. Milleron, Dr. Leong, Dr. Voelker, Dr. & Mrs. Carroll Berryman, Dr. & Mrs. Davenport, Dr. Elizabeth McComb. Thanks also to Dr. John Foster, Department of Defense, and to the Honorable Richard Marriot, mayor of Sacramento.

Very especially, Erich von Däniken has been a fabulous pillar of strength, believing that this book's anthropological and his archeological approach together strongly bolster our common theme of extraterrestrial visitation of significant proportions in mankind's past.

Credit for various aids and approving comments must also go to Arthur C. Clarke of England, and to Phil and Kathy Diacanoff, Mr. & Mrs. Francis McCarthy, Addie and Cray Lange, Pat Pope, Mr. & Mrs. Raymond Feagans, William Ruehie, William Phillips, Mr. Garden, Bernie Ellis, Mr. Bartlett, Henry Ponleither, Miss Tremaine, Dick James, Wes Barry, Cledith Jones; and finally to our parents, various relatives and friends, and dozens of others. Those not mentioned for lack of space *(you know who you are)* nevertheless merit our thanks too.

In no way are any of the above named responsible for the final contents of this book. All the ideas, theories, and conjectures are solely those of the two authors, and must not be construed as being endorsed by any person to whom we've extended our thanks for encouragement, information, and scientific comments.

Foreword

by Erich von Däniken

What exactly is a scientist? A person who has run the course of a prescribed education and then belabors a certain discipline with scientific methods. The scientist becomes a specialist in his particular field when he engages in certain activities for several years, remains informed in his area of research, and, if possible, publishes something of his own in it.

The flow of information is so immense in the age of the media that every scientist is obliged to specialize. No one can any longer be sufficiently informed about everything. On the one hand, specialization leads to magnificent results, such as computer technology, landings on the moon, nuclear fusion. On the other hand, however, it harbors the danger of a simplistic perspective that, with the abundance of directed information, can lead to apparently well-founded yet erroneous conclusions.

Anthropology and prehistory are closely linked. The preparations for both branches of human knowledge run parallel up to the borderline that separates the specialists. The goals are well defined, the outcome predetermined by the training. The literature of predecessors to be consumed remains erratic while pointing the way to be taken. Where, then, is a well-ordered, concentric search for truth to be found?

Our historical past is composed of indirect knowledge. Discoveries of bones and tools, cave drawings, and so on, are incorporated into a research hypothesis. The jigsaw puzzle then becomes an impressive, interesting mosaic; but it is based on a preconceived notion into which all parts can be fitted —although the putty is at times all too clearly visible. Either, or . . . there is but one way. And that is it. But there we are; if one is willing to accept it, that is exactly the way it was supposed to be.

The scientific community is, in many respects, a secretive society. Its individual members "know" something, but they are not at all concerned about the fact that their one-sided information may merely give them the impression of being knowledgeable. And if their knowledge is ever attacked, familiar human defense reactions are set in motion: ridicule, arrogance, and the struggle for respect. After all, it is impossible that both parties could be right, assailant and assailed. And who wants to admit that he is wrong?

In this regard, the famous "scientific community" is actually a rather disjointed conspiracy. It has a restraining and destructive effect on new, possible truths. An unbiased attitude and objectivity are certainly promised but not practiced. Not one of us is ever completely objective, neither prosecutor nor defender. Specialization has made both camps far more subjective.

This book provides detailed evidence for the fact that Homo sapiens is not the product of natural evolution, and that human intelligence is not the result of a spontaneous mutation. Traditions, religions, and myths do, in fact, enable us to deduce that unknown beings — gods — created man "in their image." Gilgamesh, in the Sumeric epic, is two-thirds human, one-third god. Noah, the biblical survivor of the Deluge, was, according to the Lamech scroll found near the Dead Sea, "the Guardian of Heaven (of the Skies)." The patriarch Enoch, who lived before the Deluge, unmistakably establishes this relationship between gods and men (Book of Enoch, Chapter 15):

> Say unto the Guardians of Heaven... why have you forsaken the high, holy heaven above, lain with women, soiled yourselves with the daughters of man, taken wives as did the sons of the earth and sired giants?... You have ... lusted for the blood of man and brought forth flesh and blood as do those who are mortal and perishable.

Can one, *objectively* speaking, overlook such crystal-clear passages? And around the globe, mythologies are filled with similar evidence.

I am one of those who must daily face arguments denying a visit by gods from our galaxy. The attacks are formulated in a "particularly reasonable" fashion, and behind them lurks knowledge as profound as gaping gullets. For scientific depth is one-dimensional. Its counterarguments are rooted in *previous* (literally, up-till-now) learning, *previous* translations, *previous* archeology, *previous* paleontological findings, *previous* dating methods, *previous* space travel. Interrelationships between all fields of knowledge and the easily anticipated technological future are never established.

In my correspondence, and in public, I debate with scientists. Our verbal battles are fair and honest. Yet they are not objective. Paleontologists generally know too little of man's record. And what they have never heard of they are not interested in. Myths and old books are rejected as fairy tales. They are terribly sure of themselves.

Can we, from an objective standpoint, simply ignore the old scriptures? Science should always get as close as possible to the truth. In the case here presented, the discovery of truth is rendered impossible by the mania for specialization. Thus, scientists can be accused of holding a channeled view — *vide* their lack of knowledge in mythology.

And should someone raise the objection that our primitive ancestors saw God in nature — in clouds, lightning, thunder, earthquakes, volcano eruptions, the sun, the stars, and natural catastrophes — this comfortable view in no way rhymes with the cave paintings that make no gods of natural events. And how dare chroniclers assure us that the gods created man "in their image"? If God was believed to be a natural event, the most stupid of our ancestors could not have thought of himself as "God's image." And those who thousands of years ago mastered the art of writing were not of the dumbest kind.

May the debates evoked by this book make tumultuous waves. I know of no work since Darwin's that deserves as much attention regarding the evolution of man.

Translated by Dr. CONRAD BOROVSKI

Introduction

A Step Into the Future

This book is concerned with the strong possibility — almost a probability, in our measured opinions — that mankind on Earth may have had superintelligent ancestors from outer space. Man may therefore be a hybrid, partly of terrestrial origin, partly extraterrestrial. There exist an incredible number of amazingly persuasive "proofs" in support of this theory, which are duly presented in the pages ahead.

We sincerely feel we have dramatic evidence — very nearly proof — that will hopefully make a never-to-be-forgotten impact on the mind of the reader. An impact that will even affect scientific opinion, eventually.

Those proofs or evidence of the theory's validity will be found virtually everywhere around us — in our bodies, our brains and minds, our histories, our archeological and anthropological pursuits, and in many other unexpected areas of the humanities and sciences.

This book might very well be titled *On Tiptoe Beyond Darwin,* for we have in reality "extended" Evolution beyond the limited scope of natural selection on Earth, to an expanded concept that might be called *AstroEvolution,* or Evolution from the stars.

We wish to state at the outset, however, that we do *not* condemn or recommend casting aside the great Theory of Evolution. We believe, along with any biologist or scientist, that its basic premise apparently explains the whole progression of life on Earth, from its earliest beginnings in primeval times to the amazing proliferation of creatures today — with one notable exception.

That exception, that one damning exception, is the creature called Man.

He, alone of all species, plagues the Theory of Evolution and, in fact, shakes its foundations. For by no stretch of available facts (or even imagination) can human beings be products solely of orthodox Evolution and its classic rules.

Starting with Alfred Wallace, codiscoverer of Evolution with Darwin, many anthropologists, naturalists, and biologists frankly admit that mankind is an *anomaly,* a maddening "misfit," in the grand sweep of survival of the fittest. His physiological body might have evolved from lower forms of animals, but his amazing brain — never.

Just how large a stumbling block this is to Darwin's theory will be fully explained and explored in this book, resulting in our boldly advancing a new theory — the concept of *Hybrid Man* and the *Earth Colony.*

Yet, we reiterate that Darwin's theory seems to cover adequately all other animate life on Earth. It only fails, and fails dismally, in explaining you and me.

We wish to take up another subject that may bother the reader from the start. How do two nonprofessionals in the field dare to assail Evolution? How can two "amateurs" so crassly defy the well-trained anthropologists, biologists, paleontologists, archeologists, and all the other types of scientists concerned with Man's origin?

In answer to that, let us quote from a recent book titled *Darwin Retried,*[1] in which the following words appear (with our italics):

"Darwin was an *amateur.* He did not teach in a university or work in a laboratory. He 'did' science in his own house with no trained staff and very little [fossil] equipment."[2]

Thus, we see that all the later adherents of Evolution, most of them very eminent scientists, were in truth only following the theory of an *amateur,* an unskilled (in academic terms) nonprofessional with an "untrained" mind in comparison with the later experts and authorities who took up his tremendous basic idea with the fervor of zealots.

We are amateurs and Darwin was an amateur.

That, in a sense, "equates" us as having the same full right as nonprofessional Darwin to exercise our studied viewpoints on Evolution. And to present — as *Darwinlike amateurs,* if you wish — a wholly new theory as to the origin of Man.

We are *not,* however, equating ourselves or our concept with Darwin, but simply pointing out that our "amateurism" should not in any sense be allowed to stand in the way when our theory is being evaluated. We only ask that authorities in Evolution give our theory the same due respect and on-merit-only analysis as all the world's authorities have for a century accorded to the theory of that great amateur — Charles Darwin.

Along with this goes a final thought. "Science today," writes a female professor of philosophy at the State University of New York,[3] "is divided neatly into compartments and niches (specialties) *quite unlike the real world.* The true universe," she continues, "is fused in *oneness* and cannot be successfully analyzed or treated in *fragmentary* form."

"If each science specialty," she concludes, "restricts itself to its own selected subject matter, with no serious regard for the relevance of other specialties and with no real effort toward synthesis," what chance is there for any "coherent and integrated master theory" ever emerging?

The key word is *synthesis,* and her plea is for an *inter-disciplinary* approach to all major theorizing. And this is precisely what that controversial figure, Dr. Immanuel Velikovsky, has done with his small-theory-shattering concepts in order to bring forth a "unified" theory crossing all scientific lines and binding them into a whole that reflects the true *oneness* of the universe and its phenomena.

Though utterly and savagely refuted, even castigated, by the scientific fraternity in 1950, when his first book came out, Velikovsky today has been vindicated over and over by new scientific discoveries he *predicted* through his Catastrophism Theory. Notably, he predicted the planet Venus to be unbearably hot and was subsequently, and astonishingly, proved right by the Venus space-probes of NASA.

Velikovsky had this to say about the Theory of Evolution:[4] "Most controversial is the evolutionary question. I have done a great deal of work on Darwin and can say with some assurance that Darwin did not derive his theory from nature but rather superimposed a certain philosophical world-view on nature and then spent 20 years trying to gather the facts to make it stick."

It is documented that, to date, Velikovsky's scientific predictions *have never once been proved wrong.* Thus, his disparaging viewpoint on Evolution must be taken seriously. He might also, be it noted, blast our theory in this book, if he saw it, but at least we do not have to make a sacred cow out of Darwin's theory as if fully "established."

Veikovsky had a telling answer for his success, to the scientific fraternity,[5] that when one looks at *all* the evidence, without restricting oneself to the limited number of so-called "facts" usually considered so by one group of specialists, it becomes possible to make a strong case for catastrophism. *Or any other revolutionary concept.*

And we think this would indeed apply to our Hybrid Man theory also, for we have examined a wide range of evidence involving many science disciplines — anthropology, paleontology, biology, genetics, archeology, astronomy, anatomy, physiology (the full list is even longer) — and believe we have found a miraculous "common denominator" in all their phenomena of anomalies. We are thus using the above-recommended "interdisciplinary" system, with the aim of presenting a "coherent" theory that will stand the tests of concerted research by others, and thereby let science take one more step forward — as it always must.

The "oneness" of the universe, and of life everywhere — that is what we have striven to bring to light by our new theory of Hybrid Mankind being part of a colony largely established by extraterrestrial beings of a humanoid type. Perhaps a truly shocking theory, as shocking as when Copernicus wrenched Earth out of the center of the universe.

But has truth, through the ages, ever been less than shocking?

MAX H. FLINDT & OTTO O. BINDER

1

EVOLUTIONARY
CLUES

In 1925, at Dayton, Tennessee, there occurred one of the most dramatic trials in courtroom history. John T. Scopes, a schoolteacher, was charged with teaching Darwin's "new" Theory of Evolution. In fundamentalist Tennessee, this was illegal. Clarence Darrow, his lawyer, was unable to win an acquittal against the fierce oratory of William Jennings Bryan. In essence, the court said — "Man is not descended from the monkeys."

Nevertheless, the theory of Evolution eventually became universally accepted around the world. But the battle is not yet over. In November 1969, the California State Board of Education declared that new textbooks must include all other theories of the origin of Man, including that of the Biblical Creation; and children will also be allowed to learn the spontaneous-generation concept of Aristotle, the panspermia (spores from space) theory of Svanté Arrhenius, and others.

The significant point here is that Darwin's Theory of Evolution has apparently failed, in more than 100 years, to establish itself without question.

Why?

Is it time now for a new theory to replace, or at least significantly modify or expand, Darwin's Evolution theory? Decidedly so, the authors of this book feel. There are various categories of "clues," which shall constitute the chapters in this book.

Since Evolution's debut, many new discoveries have been made in every field of science. It is now possible, in light of these discoveries, to develop a new leap forward in Evolutionary Theory — a leap as fantastic as was Darwin's in its time.

But before delving into the new and revolutionary two-part theory presented in this book, let us briefly examine some of the perplexing unknowns about earthly life that today remain unexplained by science, and that we hope to explain through application of this new theory, which "Tiptoes Beyond Darwin."

1. *The explosive beginnings of life on Earth, 500 million to 600 million years ago.*

We do not know how to explain the fact that we have no fossil record of the beginnings of the primary classifications of early marine life (which preceded dry-land life): sponges, sea lilies, starfish, worms, water fleas, brine, shrimp, clams and others. These genera (groups of related species) appear *suddenly* in the sedimentary record. We cannot find any fossils that reflect their step-by- step evolutionary development. Why don't these fossils exist?

The following paragraph is from current authoritative literature.[1]

The ... still deeper mystery concerns the advent of life itself, the initial rung on the evolutionary ladder. Paleontologists still wonder why fossil evidence of life on Earth appears abruptly in rocks of the Cambrian period 500,000,000 [to 600,000,000] years ago. Why are there so few traces of life in the Pre-Cambrian which lasted 1.5 billion years, [almost one-third] of the total age of the Earth? Cambrian life was not merely incipient; it had already evolved into most of the primary classifications known today.

The above deals with early invertebrate life only. The oldest vertebrate fossil found so far is in the form of footprints (pawprints) only, discovered in southeastern Australia.[2] The vertebrate creature who made them existed in Devonian times, some 350 million years ago.

Only two primitive types of floral life that existed in the Pre-Cambrian era have left a fossil record. One is algae, the most primitive of plants, dated as of 1.7 billion years ago, found in 1971 by Preston Cloud of the University of California.[3] The second type is fossil microorganisms located in rocks 2.5 billion years old and, possibly though less certainly, in rocks dating back 3.6 billion years.[4]

Are they the progenitors of every later earthly species of life? But what happened to all in-between fossil forms, which became progressively more complex during the awesome stretch of multimillions of years in the Pre-Cambrian era? Why are all these evolutionary life-steps missing, until there abruptly appear comparatively highly organized species at the start of the Cambrian era, only a half-billion years ago?

From mere one-celled creatures (including algae) to worms, sponges, starfish, and clams is quite a jump. The latter cannot be a second generation of species, but a thousandth or millionth generation. And all the generations in between are the "missing links" of marine life.

Darwin himself was bedeviled by this baffling riddle: "To question why we do not find rich fossilliferous deposits belonging to these assumed earlier periods prior to the Cambrian system, I can give no satisfactory answer."[5]

One hundred years later, a noted newspaper wrote that the "chief puzzle" in the life record of ancient earth is how, 600 million years ago, the basic divisions of species of the plant and animal kingdom had already "suddenly appeared."[6] There being no earlier fossil record, this meant "the first part of evolutionary history is missing."

Obviously, we have a great biological discrepancy here, one that cuts at the roots of the Theory of Evolution. If no orderly ladder of life can be found through some 3 billion years since the first genesis of primary living cells, all further evolutionary patterns in the Cambrian era and onward tend to be undermined.

The "laws" of Evolution, it seems, have fallen down right at the inception of all Earthly life. We will later give a daring explanation for the missing fossils and the abrupt emergence of highly developed species of marine life.

2. *Why is it that an analysis of the six spreading movements of primitive Man indicates that three of these spreading movements have come from Asia Minor?*[7]

Why are there Men with white, yellow, brown, red, and black skin? Why is mankind a mixture of breeds, in his outward form, almost as diverse as the breeds of dogs, whereas all wildlife is relatively uniform within its own species?

3. *Unexplained greater size of brain of prehistoric Man, compared to Modern Man.*[8]

The race (Aurignacian or Cro-Magnon Man) that possibly swept away Neanderthal Man approximately 35,000 years ago in Europe had a larger brain-case by 100 cubic centimeters than modern Man. Yet there is nothing whatsoever to indicate that Aurignacian Man (Cro-Magnon) had more intelligence than Modern Man. And where, in the first place, did this huge brain-case, three times the volume of a gorilla's, come from?

4. *Lack of explanation for Man's greater intelligence arising out of strict Evolution.*

All of the lesser animals — the dog, cat, horse, elephant, and others — had the same number of years in which to develop — by Evolution's natural selection or mutations, or both — the surpassing intelligence possessed by Man. Yet Man alone achieved this.

Why? How? The evolutionists don't know.

An illustration of this dilemma, taken from current literature, follows:

"And two great mysteries of Evolution remain. The first involves the origin of Man — the unique, tempestuous, rational, passionate, esthetic, irascible, proud, anxious, toolmaking, troublemaking animal that has dominated the planet for the last half million years. To the anthropologist, the evolutionary line of descent leading from Man's dark beginnings down to *homo sapiens* seems physically continuous, held together here only by a segment of skull, there by a crumbling jawbone. Yet the point of Man's emergence as a human being, the threshold he crossed to enter the realm of self-awareness, the moment of his attainment of personality and spirit — these are still shrouded in the shadows of the prehistoric past.[9]

5. *Lack of explanation for Man's greater brain weight compared to other animals.*

Although all the other warm-blooded inhabitants of Earth have been evolving as long as we humans, not one of them has a brain that is over a hundredth (1/100) the total weight of his body. The sole exceptions are the hummingbird, one-twenty-ninth (1:29), and the chimp, one-seventy-fifth (1:75). Man's brain on the other hand is one-thirtieth (1:30) of his total weight. Where did this great discrepancy come from?

6. *Why is it that Man is unique in so many ways among all primates that roam the world?*

Man possesses relatively no body hair, nothing compared to the thick pelts of gorillas, chimps, and monkeys. This is not the result of wearing apparel, for aboriginal tribes such as the Australian bushmen, who have existed for geological eras, wear virtually no clothing and yet are as hairless as modern Man.

In turn, why does Man alone have a topnotch of hair that is never exhibited by the great apes?

Also, why is Man, alone of all Earthly creatures, able to shed copious tears?

Why can only he speak words?

Why is the human female, unlike all anthropoids as well as other animals, "in heat" uninterruptedly?

Why can humans alone smile?

Why does only our species of naked ape have no diastemata (spaces between teeth)?

And why does Man display 312 distinctive physical traits that set him utterly apart from his so-called primate cousins?

7. *The tool riddle.*

Why were shaped tools invented and used solely by all species of early ape-men (Hominids) but never by any other animals, including the Pongids (true apes)?

8. *The civilization mystery.*

Why did the *homo* branches of both Neanderthal Man and Cro-Magnon, who had brain-cases *larger* than modern Man, never, through a period of 60,000 years, create civilization, living instead as brutes?

9. *The intelligence enigma.*

Why did civilization spring up with an abruptness, in Sumeria ca. 10,000 B.C., that makes all archeologists and anthropologists gasp to this day? How could mankind change from a neolithic savage who was a nomadic hunter to a social being with villages and agriculture? Overnight, so to speak?

What can explain the skilled map-making art prior to Columbus, exemplified by the astonishing Piri Reis map that shows accurate detail of South America and of Antarctica? Of Antarctica, mind you, *before* the last Ice Age some 10,000 years ago?

Where did the ancients, as long as 2,000 years ago, learn an advanced form of mathematics that allowed calculations of the Earth's size, and pinpoint the eclipses of the sun and moon?

What accounts for the fact that the Mayan calendar of 1,000 years ago is the most accurate ever known, even more precise than our present calendar?

How could machineless mankind in B.C. and early A.D. times perform incredible engineering feats, such as building the pyramids and other stone structures so huge they would tax even modern machinery to duplicate?

10. *Mental phenomena in Man.*

Why is it that no ape brain, according to exhaustive tests,

displays the fantastic higher qualities of Man's brain, such as genius, imagination, scientific inspiration, and less flatteringly, schizophrenia?

11. *The thinking puzzle.*

Why do human beings alone, apart from any animal, have religion? The exploratory instinct sparked by curiosity alone? The sense of high destiny? The feeling that life has a meaning?

12. *Mythological enigma.*

And now, perhaps the most important ancient puzzle about mankind — why does the mythology of *every one of Earth's cultures* in the past tell the same general tale, that the human race either came from the stars, or that "gods" visited Earth and helped us launch civilization?

Now that we have briefly examined twelve major unanswered mysteries of Evolution, biology, anthropology, archeology, anatomy, and such, we are ready to answer the big question: Can we develop a mutually compatible and single over-all solution to these frustrating mysteries? A solution that takes into account many new discoveries of science? In short, a solution that is a new leap forward in evolutionary theory, a leap as monumental as was Darwin's?

In this book we offer such a theory, which will be treated and discussed as a mutually dependant two-part theory.

However, we must stress at this point that the reader will be shocked and perhaps angered by the boldness and seeming irreverence toward religion and orthodox science inherent in this theory. Fortunately, this irreverence will, by the end of the book, be revealed as nothing more than a mirage.

Briefly, this new theory proposes that mankind is a hybrid between early men on Earth and men from another world.

And, second, that Man and much of life on Earth may comprise a colony, an intentional colony, put here and nurtured by persons unknown, who came from outer space.

The amount, variety, mutual compatibility and persuasiveness of the evidence in support of this theory, we believe, is nothing short of startling as we apply it point by point.

Can Man be such a star-crossed Hybrid? If so, what sense is he a Hybrid?

The first precept of this theory is that Man is somewhat like a cross between a buffalo and a cow (a cattalo), or a turkey and a chicken (a turken). In the case of Man, it is proposed that modern humans are descended from a crossbreeding or several crossbreedings that occurred many thousands or millions of years ago, between superintelligent travelers from outer space and early men.

We have a strong clue in the Bible itself (Genesis 6: 2):

"And it came to pass, when men began to multiply on the face of the Earth, and daughters were born unto them, that the sons of God saw the daughters of men that they *were* fair, and they took them wives of all which they chose."

Who were the "sons of God"?

One meaning instantly lifts universal mythology and religious writings of the past from mere legend and superstition to stunning historical truth — that starmen visited Earth and mated with early females (perhaps Hominids) to sire the modern human race of Homo sapiens.

The moment we provisionally accept this proposal, we at once have solutions for topic headings from numbers 3 through 12. Several mysteries of Man's anatomical developments, three anthropological riddles, three archeological puzzles, and various psychological and philosophical enigmas, are logically cleared up.

Surely, a theory that can answer so many major riddles of the past simultaneously deserves closer examination.

Here's how, for example, this theory explains the question raised under topic heading 3. Many anatomists agree that Man, in evolving from the present day onward, will probably have a larger and larger head and brain in the future. Presumably, 500,000 years from now, we could have 1,800 cubic-centimeter-brain-cases instead of our current 1,300 cubic centimeters.

Since Stars and Men, by Dr. Harlow Shapley, explains how perhaps half of the inhabitants of the universe have been civilized and more completely evolved than we, by millions of years. The assumption is that space travelers, successfully crossbreeding with early Homo or Hominid species (by virtue of medical knowledge a million years ahead of ours), would bring to Earth larger heads and brains, plus the potential for the development of a relatively vast intellect.

Further, this explains why Man's brain is much larger in weight ratio to the rest of his body, as compared to the brain-to-body weight ratio of the lower animals — the latter but not the former conforming to the classic pattern of Evolution.

At this point in the unfolding of our new theory, it seems wise to indicate that nothing now known about Man or his history *precludes* his arriving at his present state of intellectual and physical development via the *hybrid* route, as compared to the currently accepted evolutionary route. In fact, we know of nothing in genetics that can produce so many sudden, rapid, and tremendous changes (mutations) in a species as have occurred in Man — except *enforced* hybridization.

It may be instructive now to review Darwin's Theory of Evolution and see where it fails to cover the many anomalies that block the way in discovering the origin of Man on Earth. We believe the failure hinges on Man's development alone, and that it is possible to show that, in the past 500,000 years or more, Man continually gave strong evidence of being a hybrid rather than a strict evolutionary product.

Man has been the only animal on Earth that showed dramatic biological and evolutionary development in the last half-million years, even in the past 50,000 years. It is strange that this occurred *only* to Man.

Couldn't it far more logically have been hybridization instead of normal evolutionary development?

Let us go back to the time when Charles Darwin was at last ready to publish his revolutionary *Theory of Evolution*. It was the year 1858.

He received a letter from his friend Alfred R. Wallace, who was in the East Indies.[10] This letter must have been a devastating blow to Darwin. In it, Wallace stated that he had developed, after long thought and observation, a Theory of Evolution that had the concept of *natural selection* as its central theme.

By himself, Wallace had discovered the grand concept that Darwin felt was his own singular contribution to science.

In deference to Wallace, Darwin concluded that the only proper thing to do was to withdraw his own paper, so that Wallace would get credit for the original discovery. Darwin apparently had an essentially sterling character.

His friends were upset at what they considered to be a self-imposed miscarriage of justice, and they prevailed upon Darwin to change his mind. The problem was finally solved by having Darwin and Wallace present their papers at the same meeting of the Linnaean Society of London. They were then published together in the society's *transactions* for 1858. But subsequently and gradually, for various reasons, Darwin was credited as the "father" of Evolution.

Darwin and Wallace remained good friends throughout their lives. Wallace conceived of the great theory independently of Darwin and denied any claim upon it simply out of regard for his friend.

There is one aspect of this strange tale of the friendship between these two gifted men that bears directly upon our argument that Man may be a hybrid. Darwin believed that Man, like all other animals, was a product of natural Evolution.

Wallace, however, finally concluded that Man was an exception to the orderly operation of biological laws.[11]

The principle of natural selection or its corollary, survival of the fittest, did not fit mankind.

These words have thunderous implications now. Here were two intellectual giants who simultaneously developed one of the greatest theories in scientific history. Yet, one of these two men believed that human beings were an *exception* to the rule that all living things developed by means of natural selection (survival of the fittest) from lower forms of life.

How did Wallace conceive that Man was an exception to the rules of Evolution, and did his arguments leave room for the concept advanced within this book, that Man may be an Earthman/starman hybrid?

Very definitely! For one of Wallace's explosive statements was "that some intelligent power has guided or determined the development of Man."

Either he meant God and his divine power, or he was thinking of an unknown force — which leaves it wide open that *something* influenced mankind's Evolution. And that "something" could very well be the starmen.

One very important fact must be pointed out before we proceed. Though having doubts himself, Darwin decided *not* to go along with Wallace in the latter's belief that Man represented a departure from the laws of natural selection.[12] As Darwin gradually assumed the major credit for his survival-of-the-fittest concept, he also assumed the great burden of attempting to prove to the world that his theory was correct, inviolable, without fault or exception.

This burden inevitably caused Darwin to lose some scientific objectivity. He became a champion instead of a scientist. He championed one of the greatest and most disturbing concepts since the birth of Christ, and he fully appreciated the importance of his role.

Small wonder, then, that he chose to ignore the many ways in which Man himself deviated from the otherwise perfect workings of the great theory. In bypassing the anomaly of Man by providing less than perfect explanations based solely upon his theory, Darwin was able to convince large segments of the scientific community that his theory was, by and large correct.

But actually, he was not at all at ease with the explanations that he had devised to explain some of Man's deviations from the rules that obviously *did govern all the rest of the animal kingdom.*[13]

For instance, he was at a complete loss to come up with a truly satisfactory answer to the amazing phenomenon of why Man alone is relatively hairless.

Just as it is true that Darwin lost scientific objectivity by assuming the burden of champion, it is also true that Wallace was thereby given the role of using ultimate objectivity. He had nothing to prove to the world and consequently could be, if anything, more objective than before.

So Wallace, the naturalist, was able to analyze the available data more searchingly and dispassionately than Darwin. He was able to take the first hesitant (if unknowing) step toward the concept, rather shocking at first glance, that is being proposed in this book.

Wallace noted some strange facts about Man that caused him to conclude Man was a contrary exception to the classic workings of the laws of Evolution.

In an alarming number of ways, man's great brain and mind, for instance, did not fit into the laws of natural selection. Nowhere in the animal kingdom was there to be found anything like the quality of mathematical or scientific capabilities of the human race. Moreover, nothing could be found in the environment of Man that could, by the inexorable laws of natural selection, produce any sort of genius in any individual.

Wallace put it down in black and white — "Nature never overendows a species beyond the demands of everyday existence."

Further, Wallace knew that Man had desires and esoteric yearnings that were never observed in the mind or behavior of other animals.

The most revealing is Man's need for religion, a need to feel that he is not alone, but a part of a larger and more important order in the plans of a creator. This order assures Man that he, and he alone, has "connections" — what might be called "cosmic connections" — with God and the lesser gods of the vast universe. There is nothing in human environment that could cause Man, by natural selection, to develop in such a way that a need for religion would be "natural."

If anything, Man has less need than any other animal to devise religion.

Man is dominant over all other animals. He is king of all he surveys.

Why is it, then, that he feels a need to be *assured* that he was, and is, a part of some much greater scheme of things — all of divine origin?

Wallace knew these things and he also knew that Man had a greater gross brain-weight than any other animal except the dolphin, elephant, and the whale. He felt sure that Man was an exception to the rule that all living things grew from one primal living cell.

Wallace may also have know that Man is the only primate that cries "emotional" tears. A small thing, but still a great barrier when no explanation for this odd and irreconcilable fact could be derived from the principles of natural selection.

He knew, too, that the unbelievably advanced cultures of the ancient Sumerians and Egyptians had sprung up overnight, apparently without cause, certainly without counterpart in the animal or primate world.

Wallace knew that the laws of natural selection could not explain the sudden explosion of those ancient cultures without also insisting that the cultural advance should go *forward*. This had not happened, and Wallace knew that the failure of cultural advance to continue to new heights was of great importance in the story of mankind.

Does Wallace's belief surprise you? Namely, that mankind has not really progressed — except technologically — since earliest civilized times?

Outside of arrogant and egotistic scientists among the establishment leaders of today, many sober scholars and thinkers see undeniable evidence that all the basic rules of ethics, morals, philosophy, social structure, and religion — everything important to mankind as a whole — were laid down long, long ago, starting with the Sumerians around 10,000 B.C.

Peaks of human thought were already reached in B.C. times, particularly in Greece and Rome. And we will see in a later chapter that there is strong evidence for believing that there were more geniuses per capita in ancient times than today. The advent of modern science and technology has not changed or "advanced" the fundamental rules and precepts of human nature and human society, no matter how much we would like to think ourselves "superior" to our ancestors.

Will anybody deny that there is much unrest in the current world, much searching of souls, dissatisfaction, doubt, and uncertainty over what the "meaning" of life is? We are really less secure today than the well-enlightened people of certain B.C. eras. Our vaunted "advancement' is largely illusory, based on pure materialism.

Wallace knew that there was a logical explanation for the cessation of forward movement in human affairs, and that, without doubt, Man was therefore an exception to the otherwise universal law of natural selection and its relentless drive for *improvement* in all creatures.

This great man, freed as he was from the responsibility of proving the Evolution theory to be correct, could dispassionately analyze the available facts.

He came to the inescapable conclusion that Man was *not* the result of natural selection by itself but was the result of natural selection plus some other *unknown variable*.

That unknown variable, which we propose will solve the mysteries that plagued Wallace and even Darwin, is the concept that Man is a hybrid and Earth a colony of starmen.

During the past 500,000 years, Man has particularly given evidence that he is a hybrid of only half-earthly heritage. His tools of shaped stone are the only tools produced deliberately by any animal that lasted through the ages. Wallace knew about these tools and knew they were mute evidence that years ago, somewhere, mankind had undergone some *change* that forever set him aside from the other animals.

Wallace knew that Man was not the result of Evolution alone, but if he guessed the truth as to the probability of *hybrid* humans, he dared not voice it.

There are many other voices that at times have pointed out the "holes" in the Evolution Theory. Not so much in the case of other creatures, for whom the laws of natural selection and survival of the fittest seem to apply quite well, but most definitely in the case of the human species.

At times, very peculiar fossils of the lower animals are found, associated with ancient human or subhuman bones, as pointed out in an authoritative compendium of anthropology.[14]

In 1924, the Taung Baby (child specimen of *Australopithecus africanus*) was unearthed by anatomist Raymond Dart of Johannesburg, South Africa, and later examined by Robert Broom, a South African anthropologist. Animal fossils were also found among the ape-man child's bones, no less than fifteen different creatures.

But, amazingly, *not one of these extinct animals had been previously known.*

Even more mystifying was the discovery the late Louis Leakey and his wife, Mary, noted anthropologists, made in the 1950s at the Olduvai Gorge dig in northern Tanzania. Associated with Australopithecine skeletons were the fossil bones of *several hundred* extinct animals new to palentology.

The appearance of great groups of unknown fossils, centered around or near subhuman bones, has a peculiar ring to it. Almost as if the starmen were bringing new species from their world and introducing them on Earth. In order to give early Man more game to hunt? Or perhaps the species are mute and startling evidence of certain hybridizing experiments among lower animals that were carried on by starmen biologists. Later, we will give more attention to this distinct possibility.

In a book that attempts to present a sweeping and over-all picture of what the cosmos is all about, a question is asked: "Granting the truth of Evolution's quantitative development here on earth, what about Evolution's *qualitative* development — these periodical appearances of new genera and new species, or even of new varieties in these species so radically different as to cause science, *unable to account for their source,* to call them 'mutations.'" (Italics added)[15]   The author goes on to state that we know only "half of Evolution" and that "mutations" into unexpected species must come from "someplace beyond earth-life."

A noted biologist first points out that the elephant or buffalo, when trying to escape a hunter, will cannily go upwind, while the

rhino may blunder downwind in panic. He then states: "If
Darwin was right — which I do not believe — that only the fittest
survive, it is a miracle that this prehistoric idiot [the rhino] exists,
unless by fitness Darwin meant only physical fitness, which is
absurd." [16]

The biologist goes on to affirm that he staunchly supports the
"whole notion of Evolution" as being a natural process. *But:* "I
could name hundreds [of species] that don't appear to be fit for
anything." He is obliquely referring to the idea of survival of the
fittest. He concludes: "Maybe they evolved by natural selection
but the point is how have they managed to survive?"

Natural selection and the survival-of-the-fittest concept are
both sore points among various evolutionist factions, since they
are hard put to account for sudden, strange mutations that thumb
their nose at the orderly progressions of classic Evolution.

Biologists today often create their own mutations, among fruit
flies and guinea pigs in general — in *laboratories.* Were
mutations in the long sweep of Evolution also created in the
laboratories of the starmen? And was their most notable mutation
Homo sapiens, the creature with superior intelligence beyond the
scope of natural selection or survival of the fittest as it applied on
Earth?

Gunther Rosenburg, scholar and researcher into human
origins, states that "Man is a unique animal. He stands out like
a sore thumb when comparisons are made with his cousins, the
apes. The differences are more numerous than the similarities.
Darwin's Theory of Evolution is simply unproven."

This doubt seems to be shared by other scientists. Vernon L.
Gross, a physicist, recently remarked that "Creation and
evolutionary theories are not necessarily mutual exclusives.
Some of the scientific data may best be explained by a creation
theory, while other data substantiate a process of Evolution."[17]

Also, we noted before that the California Board of Education
decided that the biblical Creation theory of Man's origin would
have equal parity with the Evolution Theory. Shades of the
Tennessee Scopes trial!

But, obviously, much more enlightened investigation and

evaluation went into the decision to demote the Evolution Theory — because it could only lamely explain the origin of Man — and therefore to place it on equal terms alongside the old standby of biblical Creation.

However, this "sharing" of theories to explain a single phenomenon hardly constitutes an advance in solving the mystery and leaves it more unexplained than ever. It means that a single, all-embracing theory remained to be found.

And that single, all-embracing concept, in all its pristine simplicity, is what this book hopes to supply. We might say that, even if Darwin's theory wins out to scientific minds against the vagaries of divine creation, it still cannot compete, we believe, with the sheer logic of Hybrid Man's creation by starmen. In the following chapters, we will try to solidify this *homo hybrid* concept as fully as possible in the *scientific way.*

The need for a new theory to supplant the Evolution Theory (but for Man only, *not animals*) is highly apparent from the following quotes:

An authoritative book on primates candidly admits that "Unfortunately, the early stage of Man's evolutionary progress along his own individual line remain a total mystery."[18]

Another paleoanthropological work states forthrightly, as follows (italics added):

"Man is not just another species of animal. He is the first in the history of the world who at last understands something of his place in it and of the laws that govern his own activities here."[19]

The voice of an esteemed Soviet anthropologist adds to the chorus: "Some scientists maintain that our planet is not old enough for intelligent beings to have spontaneously developed on it, from the protozoans to the present day species *[of man]."*[20]

Most significant of all is a quotation from a recent book exploring the relationship between mythology and Man's origin:

Man's alleged ascension from anthropoid to human being remains unproven simply because the famed "missing link" is so elusive. Sober scientists have declared that the bones of this ape-human will never be found because they simply do not exist. The "missing link" could have been a shipload of space travelers from another world.[21]

Starmen as the "missing link" of Man's baffling evolutionary history! Despite its rather "romantic" flavor (and with little factual data to back it up), no other statement could express so briefly and succinctly what this book is about and will attempt to prove viable in a scientific way.

2

Space Clues

The previous chapter reviewed the various shortcomings of Darwin's theory in regard to explaining Man — the "misfit" of Evolution — and investigated the strong evidence that Man may be a star-crossed hybrid of two worlds.

Now we take up the second part of the theory — that mankind is a colony. And that we humans are a colony of the starmen by conscious design or plan that is still being withheld from Earth people.

Why the colony and the secrecy?

Perhaps it would be best to explain with a brief tale:

Many millions and perhaps billions of years ago — and no human on Earth knows how many light-years away — Man evolved on a distant planet. They were people as human as we are. In a short space of time, say 100,000 years after his early ancestors, Starman arrived at our present state of development. For something like one to five hundred thousand years more, he continued to develop socially, politically, and scientifically.

Then, in time, his planet became too small, too cold or too crowded for him, and he colonized one or more young nearby planets. Eventually, perhaps millions of years later, he had to move again. His planet was losing its atmosphere, or perhaps population pressure was the cause.

But then came the saving discovery: Starman's mind was marvelous and highly developed, far beyond the capabilities of our present-day Earthling minds. At the same time, unfortunately, Starman's body was totally inadequate for pioneering jobs on other planets.

This discovery forced Starman to make a momentous decision.

Mankind, as a race, would henceforth be divided into two branches, as a means, the only means, of preserving the race. There would be the ancestral race, the keepers of wisdom and knowledge, the pursuers of scientific inquiry. And the other race, the hybridized colonial race, would always be physically more able, but also always mentally inferior to the ancestral race.

And so, time passed while the starmen spread. Planet after planet was colonized, then discarded in the course of time as its atmosphere drifted away or as it became cold or otherwise unsuitable. Many millions of years passed. The system of colonizing became standardized and very successful.

Scientific progress continued. The search for ever stronger physical specimens with which to colonize the planets gradually grew into the system we are partly aware of here on Earth today, which we call "Evolution" but which is in reality, a part of colonization: namely, *planned Evolution through artificial hybridization.*

Contact between the ancestral race and each interstellar colony was never permitted in the beginning, in the sense that no colony was ever allowed to know it had been created. However, when the colony evolved into a sufficiently mature form and ventured into space under its own impetus, conscious contact was at last permitted.

The reason for this apparently unreasonable procedure of secrecy was as follows:

Man learns best that which he learns for himself, in his own good time. (And this is just as true for the Earth today and its problems as it is for one of our youngsters growing up.)

So the colonies on other worlds grew politically, scientifically, philosophically, and in other ways important to the ancestral race. They grew along these paths by trial and error, learning and gaining mental stature, just as we have done for several thousands of years here on Earth.

When the time arrived for the colony to become aware of the presence of other intelligences throughout the universe, and to begin the process of probing outward to meet or communicate with these other people *(we are close to that position today)*, then at last the first knowing contact could be made between the ancestral race and the colony.

From then on, for some period of time, the new world gasped in wonderment at the seemingly endless succession of marvels that came to bless its scientific and cultural life.

Gradually, the purpose of the colony became clear to its inhabitants.

The colony was to act as a host to the ancestral race. A willing host, because, in return for doing the spadework desired by the ancestral race, the colony was given the marvelous superscientific knowledge gleaned through eons of time — the philosophical wisdom, the social achievements, the political astuteness, and all such finer benefits.

Thus, the colony fulfilled its destiny and became one more of the endless succession of planets chosen to be the home of original interstellar Man. And there the tale ends.

This is not meant to be an authentic version of how original Man — or Starman — spread through the universe. Naturally, it must be mainly guesswork. But certain fundamentals are presented that we believe are true — that Man evolved elsewhere in space, that he in time colonized many other worlds, and that on each he used some form of crossbreeding or biogenetic manipulation literally to create rational life ahead if its slow, evolutionary time.

We now see that this second, colonization part of the theory, along with the first, hybrid part, offers explanations for all the topic headings in Chapter 1.

It would be wise to note that the main attraction of this story and the theory it gives rise to, is that it reinforces mankind's strong feelings of "special destiny," his sense of "preordained superiority" among living things.

Therefore, this theory tends to be relatively compatible with Darwin's work, at the same time partly removing the one feature of his theory the public found repulsive in the extreme: that "Man has descended from monkeys."

This hybrid theory proposes that Man is not quite as bestial as that phrase implies. And, in fact, that Man *ascended* from the apes, through the crossbreeding program of the wise, ultra-intelligent planet-hoppers who visited Earth long ago.

Further, not quite as obvious but equally as important, is the implication that if we can only get out into space, meet our ancestors, acquire their knowledge and their timeless, surpassing wisdom, then perhaps "Peace on earth, good will to Man" can be ours forevermore.

But all of the preceding, of course, hinges on one looming question — *is* there life and intelligence elsewhere in the universe? Is the rest of the cosmos filled only with dead planets whirling around their fierce suns? Or are there other worlds propitious to life, where living things sprang up as they did on Earth?

And where does life come from in the first place, on any ripe planet?

Did the primeval atmosphere of Earth, containing several gases— hydrogen, methane, ammonia, carbon dioxide, among others — act as a giant chemical laboratory and accidentally toss together atoms to make molecules? Did these molecules shuffle around in violent waters under fierce heat and radiation until they formed the first organic compounds? Then, finally, did those compounds further unite to form amino acids, the basic units of protein — which is living matter?

Such is one theory of life's genesis on Earth.

And it could happen on any other world similar to Earth and with comparable conditions.

In fact, biologists and biochemists almost unanimously agree that such Earthlike planets could *not* remain sterile. That life *must* spring up on them, given sufficient atoms and molecules that are basic to life — hydrogen, oxygen, nitrogen, sulfur, phosphorus, carbon dioxide — and billion-year stretches of time for random forces to juggle them together into the first bits of living protein.

More importantly, the process can no longer *stop* there, by theory.

It continues until the first primitive one-celled creatures are formed in the condensing seas of the planet, making an "organic soup." Now the classic process of Evolution — building up of life forms — takes over, and the tiny single cells form larger aggregates that become increasingly complex as nature stirs the brew. Invertebrates, fishes, amphibians, reptiles, birds, mammals — it may all be a sort of inevitable "pattern" that occurs on any and all Earthlike worlds.[1]

However, another theory of life's origins has recently sprung up, tied in with cosmology, so that the Evolution of the material universe and of life itself become strangely interwoven.

This theory is, in reality, a revival of a concept a century old, when Svanté Arrhenius, the famed nineteenth-century chemist, propounded his theory of *panspermia.* In brief, he envisioned tiny life-buds, or virus-like spores, that were wafted through space by the pressure of light waves from star-suns. If they landed on a "ripe" world ready for life, the spores came out of their suspended animation and formed one-celled life, which then again launched the whole climb of species up the evolutionary ladder.

Oddly enough, this seemingly "way-out" theory has recently been taken up and expanded upon by serious scientists. John A. Ball of Harvard brings forth a peculiar fact, well known to evolutionists, that spontaneous generation of new life has utterly stopped for ages, as if evolution itself had come to an abrupt halt.[2] He then offers an astounding conjecture: "Most evolutionists believe that it [life] was generated long ago *but perhaps it never was.*"(Italics added.) "Perhaps the Earth was infected from elsewhere [in the beginning]."

Two other leading lights in biological science published a paper in which they suggest that living spores did not merely drift through space, but came as colonies of micro-organisms *sent* in a protective (unmanned) spacecraft by intelligent beings elsewhere, and deliberately aimed at Earth.[3]

There are two strong points favoring this concept. One is that all life on Earth has a uniform genetic code in its most basic DNA form, from amoeba to man. If life had formed spontaneously on Earth, it seems more than likely several kinds of genetic codes would have arisen.

The universal genetic code, say the scientists, could be compatible with the idea of a *single ancestral source* — such as ancient microorganisms dumped on Earth by a spacecraft, thus "seeding" our planet with life.

The second odd point is that molybdenum, a very rare metal, plays an important role as a trace element in the physiology of all Earth creatures. It is surprising, therefore, that life so dependent on a rare metal should arise on a molybdenum-poor world like Earth, rather that on some world rich in that metal— a world from which, perhaps, the "microseeding" originated.

What has excited astronomers and cosmologists in the past ten years is the amazing discovery of *organic gases* in "empty" space, existing as gigantic clouds along with dust and debris between the stars. They are extremely attenuated gases, so that space is still almost "empty," but our galaxy is so huge in volume that the total aggregate of the scattered atoms and molecules runs into staggering tons almost beyond count.

Radio-telescopes were the first to detect the spectral lines of hydrogen gas in the open areas of space, thus opening a new branch of science called *molecular astronomy.*

As of May 1974, some twenty-nine different substances had been detected in outer space.[4] There will probably be more by the time you read this. Among the detected substances are such organic radicals (parts of organic molecules) and pre-organic molecules (which make up living matter) as water, ammonia (NH_3), formaldehyde (H_2CO), methyl alcohol (CH_3OH) and acetaldehyde (CH_3CHO).

Biochemists must be utterly astounded that such complex organic substances can exist in the cold, empty reaches of space itself. For by a variant of the panspermia theory, organic chemicals rather than spores can descend on any planet whirling through the space cloud to have its seas saturated with the building blocks of protoplasm.

"The discovery of an increasing number of organic molecules in interstellar space," reports *Science News*, "has led a number of scientists to suggest that the first chemical steps in the evolution of life may have taken place in the interstellar clouds."[5]

Another fascinating hypothesis is that of Dr. J. Mayo Greenberg of New York State University, who set up a laboratory experiment in which he produced "grains" of chemical debris comparable to the estimated size of grains of space dust.[6] He then arranged for the grains to collide under ultraviolet light (rampant in space) and found he could produce molecules of high molecular weight. He thinks this mechanical accretion-process, in giant interstellar dust clouds, could produce grains of a size and composition similar to *viruses.*

His conclusion is that here may be the very *origin of life itself* — out in the colossal chemical laboratory between the stars. Hence, according to this theory, every planet in the universe is floating through this thin "space soup," which can trigger off life in the warm seas of any and all suitable planets.

Life is, then, not the exception but the rule, throughout the myriad of star-families of planets.

An entirely different clue leading to this same deduction comes from the examination of the "Murchison Meteorite," which fell to Earth in 1970. Scientists of the Ames Research Center of NASA have found definite traces of amino acids (building blocks of living protein) in the meteorite, substantiated later by the researchers of two universities.[7]

Two scientists of Arizona State University independently examined another meteorite that fell near Murray, Kentucky, in 1950, and detected the presence of all eighteen of the known amino acids. They also found two pyrimidines that are basic ingredients of the nucleic acid vital to living cells.

Significantly, those meteoric amino acids and pyrimidines have a molecular structure *different* from Earthly types in various esoteric ways, such as "left" or "right" configurations.

Hence, they are living matter *not* of this Earth, and almost a dead-sure clue to extraterrestrial life.

The consensus is that these findings *enormously increase the likelihood of life elsewhere in the universe.*

Even before the great breakthrough discovery of organic compounds in no longer "lifeless" space, astronomers and cosmologists were convinced by other evidence, not only that living worlds were widespread throughout the galaxy, but also that an immense number of them had evolved thinking beings who might be "signaling" their brother worlds.

Back in 1960, at the National Radio Astronomy Observatory of Green Bank, West Virginia, Project Ozma, under the leadership of Dr. Frank Drake, attempted to pick up intelligent signals from two nearby stars, Tau Ceti and Epsilon Eridani.

Results were negative but now in the works is Project Cyclops, an international endeavor including Russia and the United States, which may cost up to $5 billion and involve no less than 10,000 radio-telescope dishes and antennae.

Purpose? "Its mission would be to add a new dimension to cosmology. It might establish the science of biological cosmology." Namely, set up communications between intelligent biological beings on different worlds.

If top-notch, sober scientists boldly ask for the enormous sum of $5 billion to set up apparatus to contact other civilizations in outer space, *then surely they must be going by more than flimsy clues that such civilizations exist.*

And they may, in time — to their own surprise — receive a staggering message from the very starmen who colonized Earth long ago and created Hybrid Man!

Hence, the discovery of organic-space clouds was only a confirming factor in a belief that scientists have almost unanimously held for a quarter century. This belief is based on certain astronomical data about stars that statistically indicate more than half of them must have planets revolving about them, as our sun with its family of planets.

One of the first famed astronomers to speculate about the presence of life on other planets in the outer universe was Dr. Harlow Shapley, former head of the Harvard University Astronomy Department, who in his famous book *Of Stars and Men* states:

Exactly where these other life-bearing planets are we cannot now say; perhaps we never can, lost as they are in the glare of their stars, isolated as we are in space, and equipped with sounding apparatus that is still, we hope, primitive (and will improve). Although not seen or photographed, those planets are deduced as statistical probabilities. There must be at least 100,000 of them in our galaxy, if we accept the frequency the writer prefers.[8]

This estimate of Dr. Shapley's is so conservative that it amounts to not more than one populated star per million in our galaxy.

He ignored in that paragraph the rest of the universe, and we know that the universe contains ten billion other galaxies.[9]

More recent estimates are truly mind-staggering.

We find in one publication the statements of Dr. Harrison H. Brown of the Division of Geological Sciences, California Institute to Technology, Pasadena.[10] He estimates that virtually *every* star in our galaxy has a planetary system, in each of which from two to four planets might have an Earthlike environment and chemistry that encourages our kind of life to exist. He gives the enormous figure of 100 billion stars with planets in the Milky Way galaxy alone.

That would mean 200 to 400 billion planets like Earth, or

perhaps Mars, on which life would almost certainly arise.

He also makes another startling observation: that, because a large part of the theorized mass of the universe is "missing," there may exist innumerable "dark stars," or suns that have burned out and are thus invisible to our optical telescopes.

Dr. Shiv S. Kumar of the Goddard Institute for Space Studies, New York City, has also speculated along this line and hypothesizes that the "invisible" or dark stars may outnumber the visible stars by twenty to one.

Dr. Harlow Shapley himself did not ignore this possibility and also spoke of many millions of tiny unseen stars sprinkled through the vast reaches of space, hanging between the giant burning suns we see. He added boldly that it was not impossible that life would exist on the surfaces of these dark and cool stars, which would be in the nature of large planets, but circling no sun.

And some of these "living" stars would by statistical certainty be *between* the Earth and Alpha Centauri, the so-called "nearest" star, which is somewhat over four light-years away (about 25 trillion miles).

It is quite a mind-boggling thought that small dark-sun planets that have given rise to life may be close "neighbors" within a mere light-year or two of Earth, making the possibility of alien visits even more likely. Because, as we have seen, any planet that first spawns life at all almost certainly will produce intelligent beings, simply because Evolution cannot stop at any point — or because the colonizing starmen have visited those dark-sun planets too.

Dr. Shapley bring forth a really earthshaking idea when he states: "There is no reason not to believe that the biochemical Evolution on ... one-half of the suitable planets has equaled or attained much greater [technological] development than here [on Earth].

This means that more than half of his estimated 100,000 inhabited planets in our galaxy are occupied by people who are chronologically, and thus (according to Darwin) intellectually, *more advanced* that we are.

Obviously, since we have already started an astronautics program, space flight has been known by the inhabitants of some of these planets for thousands or millions of years. Now, the mystery here is — at least the mystery to orthodox science — why have we not been visited?

The answer is — we probably *have* been visited! That neatly solves the mystery, if the science establishment will only accept it.

No, this is not a reference to the controversial "flying saucers" and Unidentified Flying Objects that have been in and out of the news for more than fifty years, although we shall take up that subject later in some detail.

UFOs aside, even hard-nosed scientists believe we may have had at least one space visitor in recent times.

A very huge and puzzling "meteorite" fell thunderously in Soviet Siberia on July 30, 1908. It fortunately fell in a remote uninhabited woodland, but peasants heard the awesome explosion as far as 620 miles away. A large area of forest was flattened as if an immense object had fallen.

It was put down as a giant meteorite until several Soviet expeditions began exploring the site from 1921 on. They found a series of strange mysteries. No remnants of the alleged meteorite could be found anywhere underground.

Second, radioactivity had initially been released in enormous amounts. Third, the general destruction showed that the energy released had been far greater that the mere impact of a falling stone, no matter how huge.

Most significantly, the aerial path of the falling object had not been uniform but had seemingly *changed* during descent.

Various Soviet scientists then put forth an amazing theory — that it had been a *spaceship*, driven by intelligent beings and loaded with great power from a nuclear powerplant, which had exploded through some accident.

Or, a variant of this was that an *antimatter* spaceship had attempted to land on Earth and had met the fate of antimatter particles when they meet norm-matter particles — instant annihilation.

However, most scientists are dubious about any recent visits by starmen, preferring to consider that this happened only in ancient times (why?). Dr. Albert Einstein, for instance, stated that he was in complete sympathy with the idea of a visit by spacemen back in prehistoric times.

Then we come to the words of an internationally acclaimed scientist of today, Dr. Carl Sagan, planet sciences expert of Cornell University. In a monumental book jointly written with a Soviet scientist,[12] Sagan estimates that super-technological starmen with interstellar spaceships may have visited Earth — hold your breath! — some 5,000 times since life first proliferated on Earth 500 million years ago.

Five thousand times! But if we divide that into 500 million years, we get one visitation every 100,000 years. So he is not suggesting a constant flow of starships back and forth.

The reason he suspects visitations from space is to account for the sudden uprise of civilization in Sumeria, ca. 8000 - 10,000 B.C. There are "legends" he cites as almost direct evidence that starmen landed there and launched mankind on the road to civilization.

And Sagan's speculations, of course, immensely bolster the theory of Hybrid Man as a star-colony — even if unwittingly on his part.

In a talk before the American Rocket Society in 1962, Sagan also gave the more accepted figure of how many civilized worlds should exist in our galaxy alone: one million as a *minimum*.[13]

Now, an odd thought arises — how many of those inhabited worlds are also colonies of the starmen who colonized our Earth?

This brings up a new picture about the origin of life throughout space. Perhaps life did not spring up independently on each and every world. We can assume that one, or several, planets were among the earliest to form out of the amorphous condensing galaxy, between 10 and 25 billion years ago (cosmologists do not yet agree on the age of the macro-universe).

If life first arose — whether earth-bred from primary biochemistry or from space-cloud organic chemicals is not relevant — on just a few worlds and flowered into human or human-like intelligences, then they may have achieved space travel and eventually explored the entire galaxy.

Not waiting for the slow process of life arising spontaneously from "organic soup" or "life clouds," they may have "seeded"any planets with primeval life.

And, as in the planet-hopping theory given before, they then "colonized" other worlds, including Earth.

Whatever the true answer is, many scientists have stated their belief, like Sagan, that our galaxy (as well as all others, inevitably) simply teems with life and with super-technological worlds. Many of them talk of vast organizations of "United Worlds" who cooperate with their neighbors in stupendous projects like galactic exploration and colonization.

Our starmen who produced Hybrid Man on Earth may thus actually be a group of advanced worlds who jointly colonize other planets. These are profound revelations we may not be told for some time to come — when we can withstand the shock without blowing our minds.

But orthodox (and opinionated) science as yet is not ready to accept any such radical explanation for the genesis of intelligent life on Earth. However, the real joker is that they still unconsciously supply grist for our mill in their general beliefs about the cosmos.

Soviet scientists have taken a step beyond other scientists in their attempts to contact the postulated civilizations in outer space.

Their huge, radio-telescope assemblies — both radial dishes and linear antennae — have for several years been trying to pick up nonrandom or patterned signals, which would instantly indicate other sentient beings deliberately sending such signals.

Several times, Soviet radio-astronomers tentatively announced exciting signals that seemed apart from natural ones, especially in connection with pulsars — stars that peculiarly pulsate in the radio spectrum with an intricate set of frequencies that are so utterly precise they seem man-made.

But theory indicated (rather shakily) that pulsars could send such "patterns" purely by natural nuclear processes.

But that did not discourage the Soviet searchers, and on October 16, 1973, *Tass* the official bulletin of the Soviet Union, "jubilantly announced" that their scientists had definitely picked up alien signals from other intelligent beings.[14] The feat was performed by three top-grade Russian astrophysicists, who said, "We have been receiving radio signals from outer space, in bursts lasting from two to ten minutes. Their character, their consistent pattern, and their regular transmissions leave us in no doubt that they are of artificial origin — that is, they are not natural signals, but have to be transmitted by civilized beings with sophisticated transmission equipment."

If you doubt their word and think they are over-excited visionaries, it would be like doubting the word of Dr. Edward Teller and Dr. Harold Urey of the United States, or any of our top-flight scientists. Vsevolod Troitsky is Director of the Research Radiological Institute in Gorky. Nikolai Kardashev is Laboratory Chief at the Institute of Space Research of the USSR Academy of Sciences. Higher than that you can hardly get in Russia. Samuel Kaplan is also eminent as chief astronomer at Gorky University.

But with their electrifying revelation came a baffling, and perhaps significant, mystery. In their own words, "So far, we have not been able to establish exactly from where the signals emanate, but we can say the source is located in our solar system."

Not from a distant star, but *from within our own solar system*?

That would place the alien transmitter somewhere within 3.5 billion miles, the orbit of Pluto, our outermost planet. But even more startling were their peculiar qualifying words: "It is possible that they [the signals] come from the upper layers of the atmosphere."

That would place the source far closer to Earth, depending on what is meant by "upper layers of the atmosphere." An immediate thought comes up, but relax, the Soviets stated positively, "For the moment, one thing is sure — the signals do not come from satellites launched from Earth."

One always has to read between the lines of any tightlipped Soviet report, and that last phrase is again peculiar — not from any *Earth*-launched satellite, they say. Which leaves it open that it could be from an *alien* satellite within Earth's vicinity, and that would tie in with the signals coming from the "upper atmosphere."

What is the answer to this riddle? What are the Soviet scientists trying to say, without giving too much away? Do they imply that a robot *probe* sent from a distant star is orbiting withing the solar system and sending us messages?

Or — is it *a UFO*?

Like the U.S. government, the Soviet government has taken great pains to deny the existence of the many reported UFOs, or flying saucers. Are they too ashamed now to admit that they were wrong and that their radio-telescopes picked up UFO signals? More likely, they are too canny to call it a UFO, because they need stronger evidence.

Though the Russians seem positive about the signals, there has been no confirmation yet from any U.S. or European scientists, as of this writing. Before you read this, however, the signals may have been corroborated, with worldwide scientists tuning them in and no doubt trying to translate them with computers.

And that would mean the theory of Hybrid Man and colony Earth is boosted high in probability.

But even more of a boost comes from one of those three scientists. Listen to the arresting words of Professor Nikolai Kardashev, of the Soviet Space Institute: "I also believe there is intelligent life elsewhere but, unlike most of my colleagues, I think there is *only one other civilization in our galaxy, a supercivilization.* It would be millions, even a billion years older than we are and fantastically more developed (scientifically). To the beings of this civilization we would be insects."[15] (Italics added.)

Or a colonial anthill?

Why would Professor Kardashev make such a peculiar statement? Surely he does not believe that only Earth independently developed civilization *besides* that single supercivilization. Unvoiced in his opinion, for fear of ridicule, no doubt, must be the implied belief that the original great civilization then spread out and *populated* or colonized the rest of the galaxy.

If his suspicions are based on any sort of clues at all in his astronomical work, then certainly the theory of a colonized Earth, if not Hybrid Man, is bolstered at a top level of science.

Now another problem enters the picture. Even if there are civilized worlds, how could their spaceships ever have reached Earth? By the law of averages, the nearest inhabited worlds might be at least 100 light-years away, and more likely over 1,000 light-years.

A light-year, of course, is the distance light travels in a whole year at the fantastic speed of 186,300 miles per second, making a total of just under 6 trillion miles. If light is the "fastest thing in the universe" (according to Einstein's relativity), then starmen would require 100 or 1,000 or even 25,000 years to get to Earth. Such trips would, in short, occupy *lifetimes.*

This seems to make the Earth-colony concept untenable, but only at first glance. *If* the light-speed barrier cannot be broken, let us list some of the possibilities:

1. The starmen are long-lived, with lifetimes of 1,000 years or more. (Why not, if the Bible lists its Methuselahs living for centuries on end?) In that case, a trip from a star within 100 light-years would take only one-tenth of their lifetime, comparable to some of the years-long sailing trips unhesitating made by Magellan and others to explore Earth.

2. The starmen put themselves into "hibernation," or suspended animation, for the bulk of the trip. Thus, they could lie blissfully asleep for a century or even 100 centuries and wake up only upon arrival on Earth. And remember, such a major project as colonizing another distant world would call for those or similar heroic measures.

3. The "time dilation" angle to Einstein's relativity points out that the closer the spaceship gets to light-speed itself, the

more time "slows down" for the crew aboard. There have been many examples given in literature of how space travelers going at 99 percent of the light-speed would only age ten or twenty years, while the planet of departure would experience ages going by. Though a rather unsatisfactory solution to long-range space travel, with the penalty of returning to their home planet to find it an age ahead, determined starmen could be willing to come and colonize Earth under those conditions.

But the answer may be far simpler than that, *if the light-speed barrier of unknowing Earth science is fallacious.*

And just as scientific orthodoxy at one time rather recklessly said that aircraft could never fly, that the sound barrier could not be broken, that rockets could never reach to the moon, so today the science establishment opposes the possibility that the light barrier can be broken.

It would, however, seem safer to say that a world of science-technology a million years old *could* have found the golden way to speed through space at fantastic rates measured in multi-lightspeeds and reach any world they wish.

We will drop the matter there as too nebulous to pursue. If the starmen have been and are here, does it matter *how* they got here?

However, making it possible for starmen to go faster than light in their vast planet-hopping project is of interest only if the starmen truly exist. And that brings us back to the question of whether there is life, and particularly intelligent life, in the universe. A question that may soon be solved.

There is a sort of "exobiology race" going on today. Exobiology is the embryo science of extraterrestrial life, or life anywhere else in the universe than on Earth. So far, it is almost entirely theory, with little empirical (experimental or material) proof.

The radio-astronomers are racing to pick up the first provable intelligent signals.

The space-cloud bioastronomers are seeking to nail down the existence of life molecules between the stars.

The meteorite specialists are attempting to clinch the fossil evidence of life in stones from other parts of interstellar space.

And the planetary scientists are striving to detect the first true signs of nonearth life on the planets of our own solar system.

We will take up this last category in the next chapter, for it may furnish us the first thrilling proof that life can spring up — in whatever fashion — on another world than our own.

3

Planetary Clues

First of all, let us mention that the classical concept of our solar system with eight other dead planets and thirty-odd lifeless moons surrounding the living Earth has rapidly changed in the past decade. Scientists are no longer willing to state categorically that there is no life at all on the other planets, even on the coldest and most remote ones.

Jupiter, for instance. This most gigantic of planets, 88,770 miles in equatorial diameter and 484 million miles from the sun, was always thought to be abysmally frigid, somewhere around minus 202°F. But studies with ultraviolet and infrared instruments that could penetrate clouds showed that this low-temperature reading was at a high altitude above the surface, just as Earth's upper air is fantastically cold.

Down below, according to some data, the temperature of Jupiter could be as high as 70°F. In short, like a balmy summer

37

day on Earth. Under such thermal conditions, and with a known "reducing" atmosphere much like that of primeval Earth, there was little reason why life should not have sprung up there too.

In fact, Dr. Carl Sagan, the expert on planets at Cornell, had even postulated the possibility of teeming life there, whose variety of forms and sheer quantity would be hundreds of times greater than on Earth.

With an assist by Pioneer-10's data, Sagan's daring hypothesis may well turn out true. The Pioneer-10 space probe made a flyby of Jupiter on December 3, 1973. Its many sophisticated sensors discovered surprising new phenomena. One of them was that Jupiter's thick atmosphere thins out considerably at lower altitudes because it is boiling *hot*. In fact, the surface temperature may hit as high as 800°F., as hot as Venus.[1] If the giant planet has any lofty peaks where temperature would drop to reasonable levels, then indeed Jupiter may fairly crawl with life all over its vast surface.

Saturn, too, has gone through such a revision as to its temperature and whether or not it could support life. In 1972, several colleagues of Carl Sagan at Cornell University used the gigantic radio-telescope at Arecibo, Puerto Rico, to probe beneath the huge planet's cloudy atmosphere and pick up long radio wavelengths indicating that "Saturn, like Jupiter, is not entirely the frozen wasteland it was once thought to be."[2] And, furthermore, that "there are areas in Saturn's atmosphere much warmer and possible more conducive to life than scientists have previously thought likely."

The very latest is that solar-system scientists are now considering whether even remote Uranus, and perhaps such big moons as Titan (Saturn) and Ganymede or Calisto (Jupiter) might not be warm enough to harbor some kind of life, even if primeval.

We must make a point here. *If any kind of life, even the lowly lichen, algae, or some other one-celled micro-organism, is detected or found anywhere out in space away from Earth, it will instantly make tenable all speculations that the universe is filled with living worlds. And that will make intelligent life of such high probability that it will amount to dead certainty.*

Exobiology will then no longer be a set of theories seeking a science.

In passing, we might mention that Venus is not yet to be marked down as so super-hot that no life as we know it can possibly exist there. Even though scientists using radar techniques, and our close-approach space probes (Russian and American), have measured temperatures anywhere from 540°F. to above 800°F., they have been careful not to claim that this makes life impossible there.

Some probings have indicated much cooler temperatures in the polar-zones of Venus, where life might still lurk. Or it may be that living creatures, unable to evolve on the furnace-hot surface, instead made their debut in the cool regions of the upper atmosphere. With an estimated atmosphere at least ninety times more dense than Earth's, huge gelatinous creatures could *float* comfortably in the aerial reaches without ever touching the hell-hot surface.

And so, the exobiology race may be won (if the Russian space-signal claim proves invalid) by evidence of extraterrestrial life right in our own backyard, among the sun's family of planets.

Now we come to the "great white hope" — or red hope — of exobiology, the planet Mars.

As one science writer puts it, "Discovery of living organisms in other places [than Earth] would vastly expand the biologists' perspective. The immediate target in the search for extraterrestrial life is the planet Mars."[3]

In laboratory experiments with gases simulating Earth's ancient atmosphere, scientists have bombarded the gaseous mixture with high-energy radiation and have found that organic molecules were formed, including amino acids, the building blocks of vital protein.

A similar experiment was recently performed for Mars, with one difference — the gaseous mixture represented the Martian atmosphere *today.*[4] When bathed in ultraviolet radiation, the gases combined into organic molecules.

If nothing else, this proves the Martian atmosphere is not unfavorable to life there, if life exists at all.

By far the great majority of scientists of all disciplines believes someday word will come that life exists on Mars. Primitive life is the consensus, perhaps only rudimentary plant life and no animal life whatsoever, although some scientists more cautiously cover their bets and allow even simple animal species to be included — worms, slugs, insects, and the like.

One of the main reasons Mars has fascinated scientists, and given rise to speculations of indigenous life there, is because the planet's disk in any good-sized telescope has regularly displayed a spreading of greenish-gray colors *during the spring* in either hemisphere, plus a withering away of such *plant colors* during the winter season.

Large portions of the ocher-red areas on Mars are thought to be deserts (and give Mars its reddish hue as a star), but these are invaded regularly each Martian spring by the creeping green-gray mystery.

If there is plant life on Mars, what kind of vegetation is it? Is it utterly alien, or is it something akin to the Earth's greenery?

Recent spectroscopic examinations of the green areas of Mars show that the observed spectrum resembles the spectrum of lichen as observed here on Earth more than any other Earthly vegetation.[5]

In 1956, a new green area about the size of Texas was observed. It was located in an area that had shown only reddish desert hues before.

It is not surprising that, when a U.S. scientist undertook to grow lichen, it was in a partial vacuum that simulated, as nearly as possible, the conditions and gases that are understood to exist on Mars. The lichen grew and prospered.

The astounding conditions under which this lichen grew should be examined.[6] The temperature ranged from approximately minus 100°F. to plus 80°F., and the pressure was approximately 0.75 pounds per square inch. (The pressure on Earth's surface is about 14.7 pounds per square inch.) The only moisture was vapor in the form of dew. The oxygen was very low — so low that Man would die in it.

Yet this lichen grew and seemed to thrive.

There is a most happy agreement between the spectroscopic observations that indicate there are lichen-like plant growths in the green areas of Mars, and the astounding ability of Earth lichen to grow in a simulated Martian atmosphere.

Now, how does this information apply to the Earth-colony theory? In this way: It might well be that when the starmen first came to the solar system, ages ago, Mars had more atmosphere and water, thus offering them a liveable colony-world.

Or Mars may simply have been used as a convenient base of operations for the starmen in making visits to nearby Earth during their grand experiment in creating Hybrid Man. Either possibility is valid.

If Mars was their base in the past, it still may be that today. This would account for the *continued* phenomenon of probable green-lichen crops sprouting each year and spreading widely over the planet, and particularly for the surprising *new* areas that suddenly turn green for the first time.

It is unlikely that natural vegetation would so successfully encroach into territory that had apparently been arid and lifeless before. It is far easier to think of starmen agriculturists using advanced techniques to prepare the soil, furnish irrigation, and increase their edible acreage as needed.

We might also mention briefly, just for the record, that there seems to be a correlation between the oppositions of Mars to Earth (nearest approach) every twenty-six months, and the increased numbers of UFOs sighted around the world.

Second, strange radio-signals seem to be periodically picked up from Mars, according to claims that are unsubstantiated or, at least, rejected by scientists. Still, such famous electrical wizards as Tesla and Marconi firmly believed they had tuned in alien radio-messages from Mars.

And still today, stubborn reports come in from ham-radio operators of inexplicable shortwave signals from the same source.

Can they *all* be wrong?

It is hardly likely that the starmen at their presumed Martian camp are trying to communicate with Earth; but it might be that the signals picked up are simply "leaks" in their own communications links on Mars or from Mars to Earth — if they are acting in modern times as watchdogs on their Earth colony.

Again, we will not pursue the above nebulous speculations but will point out that if the Earth-colony/Hybrid Man theory is correct, all those points someday might well turn out to be close to the truth.

At any rate, we may soon find out if the spreading green-gray mystery of Mars represents plant life or not. In 1976, U.S. Martian-landers, aboard Viking spacecraft borne there by rockets, investigated the surface at first hand (perhaps preceded unfortunately by Soviet landers who will steal the glory).

Both Russian and American lander vehicles (unmanned, of course) will be equipped with one or more life-detection systems, ingenious, if tiny, "chemical labs" that will draw in Martian soil or air and analyze it for key life-ingredients. If something like nucleic acid is detected, or DNA, RNA, phosphates — there are a dozen similar key organic substances — that will do it!

Biologists will instantly announce that there is something *alive* on Mars, even if they haven't the slightest idea what *form* of life, whether primitive plant or protozoan representative of animal life.

But nothing more will be necessary to establish the fact that there *is* extraterrestrial life, from which will come a thundering series of "therefores."

Therefore, there can and must be life on staggering millions of other planets of other solar systems.

Therefore, by certain overwhelming statistical data, there must be evolved life on countless worlds, including intelligent beings.

We will add one special "therefore" of our own.

Therefore, the concept of starmen visiting Earth long ago to start a colony, and creating Hybrid Man, should take a strong position as the most likely theory as to the origin of mankind on Earth.

Yes, the discovery of life on Mars, or intelligent signals picked up by radio-telescopes, or the observation of organic space-clouds forming protein, or the presence of fossil protein molecules in meteorites, or perhaps the unexpected arrival of a spaceship itself — any one of these can infuse tremendous vitality into our theory of colony Earth and Hybrid Man.

And one of these signposts to universal life can come to fruition *any day*, or may have occurred before this book is published. (In fact, if the Russian claim of picking up alien outer-space signals in October 1973 has been verified, then the radio-astronomy people have won this "exobiology race.")

A word should also be said about the so-called *canals* of Mars, a controversial feature of the red Planet for almost a century, since Schiaparelli in 1877 first announced the intricate pattern of lines he saw on the face of Mars through his telescope.

The pros and cons over whether the canals were real or optical illusions raged for over half a century, with the negative forces slowly gaining ground. They have seemed fully vindicated through the U.S. Martian Mariners, the flyby and orbiting space vehicles that, since 1967 have taken many thousands of pictures and TV scannings of the planet's surface. The photos first of all turned up the rather jolting surprise (except to Immanuel Velikovsky, who *predicted* them in 1950) that the Martian surface was pitted with craters much like the Earth's moon.

But nary a canal showed up, except very vague streaks that could be some shadowy distortion or other geological formation.

That is, all *black-and-white* photos and TV transmissions (the only kind there are so far) show no canals.

Yet the authors wish to state firmly that we believe the canal controversy cannot be resolved until *color* pictures are transmitted from Mars-orbiting vehicles for a period of at least two years.

Why two years? Because the Martian year is almost twice as long as Earth's. Therefore, it takes two Earth years for Mars to go through one complete cycle of the four seasons: spring, summer, autumn, and winter.

And only by photographing from space this complete cycle in full color, to bring out the advance and retreat of the gray-green areas, can we then get a glimpse of the still-possible canals. For the green color will be most "alive" and thriving along any waterways that are filled, in the spring, with melting polar ice.

Earth's biggest telescopes could never photograph the canals that the human eye apparently detected on Mars. Neither can black-and-white cameras aboard orbiting vehicles detect them, for they are probably very narrow channels. Only by capturing the intense new green pathways of plants invigorated by fresh water can the implied presence of canals be registered — in color. The canals may be far too shallow to cast any shadows or give any direct hint of their presence.

There are certain clues to that possibility. For one thing, many observers through the years, independently of one another and without knowledge of the others' work, drew sketches of the canals they believed they saw.

And some of those canals were in precisely the *same places* in various drawings. Furthermore, certain photos that showed vague canal-like markings, when superimposed over the hand-drawn sketches also fitted in a way that seems beyond coincidence.

Still, why are those canals, if really there, not visible to the sharp lenses of space probes orbiting nearby?

There is one possible explanation. As is now established, Mars is not a "quiet, dead world" as once thought but is in a dynamic phase of constant "storms" and geographical changes. Among its most spectacular and regular weather features are huge dust storms of such a violent nature that they cover half the globe at a time.

The 1971 Martian probes met this kind of storm of yellowish dust, which obliterated the surface for months before the atmosphere finally cleared.

Dust? Yes, dust. And what does dust do when it is blown around over a planet's surface with many pits, craters and cracks in it? *It fills or partially fills them*, as proved by various Mariner photos.

Therefore, it is not at all unreasonable to suspect that those dust storms, operating for almost a century since Schiaparelli first saw his sensational lines across Mars, have *filled in* the canals. And just as high-altitude space satellites above Earth's surface have detected the outlines of subsea formations and, on land, of various kinds of terrain unseen in any other way, it may be that only from the distant vantage point of Earth can the dust-clogged canals of Mars stand out. It may even be that Martian orbiting probes with *color* cameras will in the future also trace out those buried canals, whose existence is so far denied.

Let us put it that the last word has not yet been said on whether the canals of Mars are myth or reality.

Canals aside, the Martian pictures that came back from the orbiters in 1971 and 1972 showed other gross features that stood out with sharp clarity. If the pictures did not show canals as such, they *did* show many signs of abundance of water on Mars in ages past, and other clues that indicate water may still exist on Mars today in free form, in greater quantities than expected.

Erosion, for instance The photos clearly show faults, ridges, and sand dunes, all definite signs of erosion by *water*, nothing else.[7] And such erosion signs could not all freeze into eternal surface features lasting for millions of years. Some of them must be recent erosion effects, in line with the current dynamic model of Martian meteorology.

Volcanic structures on Mars, and striated sediment layers, also proclaim the past or present action of water in considerable quantities — enough, in fact, to discard the old bone-dry Mars theory (as we discarded the dust-covered-moon theory after our astronauts landed there).

That Mars once had extensive water-resources is high-lighted by a report from the U.S. Geological Survey after their experts pored over the Mariner photos from Mars.[8]

"All along the northern edge of the high plateau," says [Harold] Masursky, "one can see stream channels that vary in size from very small to a kilometer in width and thousands of kilometers in length. They are highly braided tributaries. These sinuous channels [sic!] could be the result of 'ubiquitous water, or a fantastic series of volcanic channels that we do not understand.' "

Another great puzzle in Martian topography is the "canyonlands" bordering the Nix Olympica region in the planet's east.[9] "The canyonlands are a real puzzler," reports Masursky. "They seem to be a series of innumerable fissures, some of which may represent cracking of the crust by itself." But, he goes on, "Something else has gone on there. What that something is, is the biggest mystery at the moment."

The report goes on to give another hypothesis, that the precession cycle of the Martian poles might mean that alternately, every 50,000 years, one pole gains a greater ice cap than the other. "In between these periods, weather on Mars would be unstable, producing lots of rain."[10]

Interesting, indeed, for a planet supposedly as arid as a desert! Furthermore, "water may be trapped and frozen in the form of permafrost and released episodically into the atmosphere."

A space scientist who has thoroughly studied the Mars-Mariner photos also states he believes that water-ice (as distinguished from frozen carbon dioxide) is present as tiny crystals in two other areas — in the clouds that appear in the afternoon, and in two higher layers of haze (thin clouds) over the planet.[11]

Each report seems to find more evidence of water or ice or water vapor on the Red Planet.

Scientists are also baffled by the enormous system of rills (cracks) existing elsewhere on Mars. They are parallel fissures (many drawings of Martian canals show them as *two parallels*!) extending more than 1,800 kilometers and up to 1.6 kilometers wide. These too could be evidence of long-enduring action by one-time bodies of water in the ancient past of Mars.

Thus, even if our camera-eye space vehicles saw no canals, they did even *better* and showed that Mars was once well-watered and even today may exhibit actual small streams as the polar ice-caps melt — when more and better photos are obtained. And the possibility of life on Mars has thus been enhanced a hundredfold, canals or no canals.

Scientists who disbelieved in Martian life have become very quiet.

4

Fossil Clues

As some wit in anthropology has said — down from the trees but not out of the woods, bipedal mankind must go back to his prehistoric ancestors for knowledge about his origins.

Anthropology is the study of mankind from ancient, extinct species into the present day, and much of it is based on fossil finds of early men, overlapping somewhat with paleontology, the search for fossilized bones of any and all creatures. In fact *paleoanthropology* is the combination of the two that deals with manlike fossils.

Anthropology is one of the most fascinating fields into which the human mind is today making inquiries. Some of the finest contemporary work is being performed within this science discipline, and some of the most talented men available to science are attracted to the field. No one reading through the great number of excellent publications in this field can help but admire the ingenious means by which these researchers have managed to wrest information from the silent and buried records of the past.

If, in the following pages, we seem to be severely critical and sometimes outspoken against orthodox views, it is not the anthropologists personally we are jumping on, but their *theories.* And then only if the theory *deserves* castigation for being speculative, misleading, or downright unscientific.

This means no lack of respect for the fossil-hunters themselves, nor for their hard and often dedicated work; but we reserve the right to analyze and, if necessary, reject or even tear apart any concept or theory that is patently untenable. There will probably be a few hardnoses with arrogance and inflexibly orthodox attitudes, who will react only with scorn and even rage at our criticisms of so-called established facts in the field.

But the "facts" of one generation often, in the light of new knowledge, are the discards of the next.

And who can set himself up as a *guarantor* of such facts, which are often tentative and short-lived?

Let us remind the anthropologists in general that their greatest authorities for some forty years proclaimed the Piltdown Man's fossil bones as being unquestionably authentic before the blatant hoax was exposed. Anybody can be wrong — anybody. There are few absolutes in anthropology, and all is subject to change, review, reinterpretation.

Perhaps it might be considered impertinent for laymen like the authors to cast doubt on the theories and testimonies of the experts and authorities, but we do so only with honest intent to point out fallacies, inconsistencies, and below-par postulates, insofar as they can be reinterpreted as supporting a totally new theory — namely, the one we champion in this book.

And if we are "amateurs," we must reiterate that Darwin himself was a "rank amateur."

If the gentlemen of anthropology will be unbiased and examine our suggestions on merit alone, without prejudgment or partiality or condemnation out of hand, we feel that perhaps a whole new avenue of research into Man's origin can be revealed, to their own eventual benefit. We ask only for a fair hearing.

We, the authors, are not anthropological "authorities," but we do quote and present the comments of very authoritative experts whenever possible. We submit that even the amateur can have sufficient discrimination and common intelligence to point out errors and misdirections that crop up in any area of scientific endeavor. The important thing is for the authorities not to isolate themselves haughtily as unassailable, thereby protecting false premises and sterile concepts as well as the body of valid material.

Although anthropologists on the whole probably cannot readily accept the quite radical theory proposed in this book, it will undoubtedly have some impact on the field in ways unforeseen as yet. We do not claim *all* our ideas are correct, any more than all presently accepted anthropological data are correct, but only that *some* ideas may hit the truth and thereby earn some respect for our new theory.

Certainly, we do not expect and cannot accept a blanket denial or wholesale rejection of our entire work.

We feel that the same respect we have toward the anthropological experts should in all fairness be reciprocated and extended to the two nonexperts who have compiled this book and its — admittedly — blockbuster theory.

One thing we would like to emphasize should give pause to any reader, authority or not, before our theory is "laughed off" the stage.

If Man, *unknown to himself,* is a colony of hybrids of men from the stars, then it naturally follows that the anthropologists (who are part of the same colony) would be just as *unaware of this fact as anyone else.* No special or divine knowledge of theirs allows them to state categorically that no such colonization of Earth has happened.

They will have to examine all the anomalies we have listed, which do not fit the general anthropological milieu and, indeed, throw it out of kilter, and prove that those anomalies do not exist. It would be quite unscientific of them, and crassly arbitrary, to try to ignore all the unexplained and baffling mysteries of Man's origin, in order to hang onto their pet theories and consign ours to the scrap heap.

That is our measured and respectful challenge, in the interests of truth.

Now, if Earth is *unknowingly a* colony of starmen, there may have been acts committed in the dim and distant past expressly designed to *prevent* our present-day anthropologists from guessing the truth.

To be more precise, these acts were presumably done to prevent Man from proving, or knowing, that he is a hybrid, for reasons we will discuss in the last chapter.

If Man's ancestral race from the stars ever spent any great length of time on Earth, members of the expedition could have perished here from natural causes. Their remains may have been carefully carried off to their home planet for burial, to prevent future discovery of the bones by Earth scientists.

A contemporary anthropologist would be staggered to find an ultramodern skeleton with a 3,000 cubic centimeter brain-case, twice the human capacity and more. It would create havoc to try to fit this creature into what is known about Neanderthal Man, Cro-Magnon Man, and all early submen. This would be especially true if the remains of this superman were found in earth strata of an era prior to the earliest advent of Hominids on the earth scene.

A modern anthropologist would be in dire straits if he attempted to integrate such a find into the presently held picture of Man's pattern of Evolution. One thing stands out. When Cro-Magnon Man appeared upon the scene, Neanderthal Man was a cave tenant of long tenure but already dying out.

Cro-Magnon Man appeared with mysteriously improved skeletal characteristics and with a cranial capacity that is amazingly in excess by 100 cubic centimeters of that of modern Man.

We will briefly digress here to point out that there are various estimates of those cranial capacities that are different from the figures we are using. For example, in one anthropological work, brain sizes are given as 1,500 cubic centimeters for modern humans, about 1,590 cubic centimeters for Cro-Magnon Man, and from 1,400 cubic centimeters to 1,600 cubic centimeters for Neanderthal Man.[1] The latter had a variable brain size because his skull changed noticeably during an evolutionary period of 75,000 years of existence on Earth.

Whether we use one set of figures or the other, the main point is they both show that brain sizes were definitely larger in two species of prehistoric men than in present-day humans, surprising as that fact is. For simplicity, we will use the first set of figures — about 1,400 cubic centimeters for Neanderthal and Cro-Magnon, and 1,300 cubic centimeters for Homo sapiens of today.

Regardless of those different ratios of brain size, it is necessary to question where the oversized prehistoric skulls came from, and whether the concept of natural mutations by Evolution only can explain the mystery. A similarly large degree of brain expansion occurred in absolutely no other species on Earth in all the ages of the past, nor has any genus shown evidence of brain mutation of a comparable magnitude since antiquity.

If the above surmise about the starmen's "secrecy code" is true, however, then such a Starman skull of 3,000 cubic centimeters may never be found. Since all evidence may have been removed to maintain deliberate ignorance among humans, the anthropologists cannot help but assume that Cro-Magnon Man arose from *unexplained* sources rather than being a cross between starmen and dawn men.

But the Hybrid Man theory does encourage speculation on the difference of Cro-Magnon's 1,400 cubic-centimeter skull capacity and modern Man's lesser 1,300 cubic-centimeters. It could explain why no intermediate skeletal remains were found in the Neanderthal to Cro-Magnon time period that trace any gradual cranial Evolution of one species into the other, which did *not* happen, according to authorities.

This is only one example of how our Hybrid Man theory can be used to explain a mystery of anthropology. There are many other areas in the field to which it can be applied, and they are treated elsewhere in this book.

It is important to stress here that the modern anthropologist should carefully follow imminent discoveries in space exploration. His interest should exceed that of the simply intelligent citizen, for fossil-hunters most likely will find that they have a deep professional interest in the results of space pioneering on other planets.

The presence of intelligence on Mars in either past or present, whether indigenous or not, may soon be confirmed. This would instantly put pressure on anthropologists to determine, as a matter of intellectual duty, whether among the myriad artifacts and skeletal remains here on Earth, some evidence may be found of past visits by outer-space creatures.[2]

If one specimen or a series of strange specimens (in spite of our previous "secrecy" surmise) were found among femurs and tibias that could not be fitted into the accepted evolutionary picture, the discovery might represent a stage of mankind we have not yet reached. These would be the bones of the starmen.

Such dusty and forgotten specimens may already be resting on museum shelves.

The trained eye may have passed them off long ago as being "unexplained mysteries" or "freak" anomalies not to be taken seriously. Some researcher may already have catalogued them as they cropped up over the years throughout the world. This would be fortunate, for it might save a great deal of time if we find bona fide evidence of outer-space intelligence in the future.

Some of the most important characteristics of Man — the ones that truly separate him from the apes — are virtually impossible for anthropologists to discover in skeletal remains. For instance, the vocal cords of skeletons are almost beyond detection or even conjecture. Their presence or absence must be deduced through patient detective work of a type that constitutes a none-too-certain method of discovery.

For all its good work, anthropology has failed to penetrate one major mystery in the fossil records. *Why is there a 12-million-year gap between the earliest man-ape fossils and the fossils of the more recent Hominids?*

Hominids is the term for primate species that authorities admit to the pre-human family, as distinguished from the *Pongids,* or pure ape genera.

To continue basic definitions of terms that will appear frequently through the book, we will include here the system of classification of all fauna (animal life) and flora (plant life).

A *species* is an individual group of the same kind of creatures who can interbreed only among themselves (with some few exceptions) and have common characteristics.

Species that are similar to, yet distinctive from one another, and incapable of crossbreeding, are grouped together in a *genus.*

The genera (plural of genus) are again lumped together into *families,* a broad conglomerate of animals that follow a basic pattern of some sort.

The families, in turn, are filed in a still larger grouping called an *order,* and may by now include thousands of species and genera.

Orders of animals join a more generalized and wide-ranging fraternity called a *class.*

Finally, the classes with a few common denominators but widely divergent individual species, are indexed under a *phylum.*

All the *phyla* (plural of phylum) together make up the animal kingdom as distinguished from the vegetable kingdom.

Another set of definitions is less important but perhaps edifying, to help the reader understand the relative importance of various ideas and statements made by scientists.

A *postulate* is an assumption of what might be possible, in any field of science, but without any positive proof. Sometimes, if it is axiomatic, it is taken for granted. The *hypothesis* is one rank below a theory, usually offered as a tentative new idea requiring investigation before it can be accepted or rejected. It is meant as a possible stepping-stone to a theory, if all goes well.

Finally, the *theory* itself may be born out of one or more hypotheses that graduated into the big time, so to speak. Though it cannot be accepted as established fact, a theory carries considerable weight by way of a good deal of firm evidence and some empirical (experimental) proof. Yet a theory is always subject to modification and change, and sometimes final rejection if too many adverse facts against it come up.

Note that Evolution is a *theory* only, not an established body of factual data, with few of its "laws" of natural selection being accepted universally among the authorities in the field. It is, and has been, in a definite state of flux since its inception over a century ago.

Armed with these clarifying definitions, we can end our digression and return to our topic — the fossils of Man's extinct predecessors.

A book combining the views of the latest and greatest authorities on anthropology states quite frankly: "Considering the number and variety of primate fossils recovered in recent years from the late Miocene and early Pliocene, we should [expect to] be able to look confidently ahead to finding even more illuminating ones to fill the gap between this time and the beginning of the Pleistocene." [3]

Our italics follow: "*Astonishingly and maddeningly, we find nothing.* Almost the entire Pliocene is a *total blank* as far as human ancestors are concerned. That exasperating and cryptic epoch lasted for some 12 million years."

Some authorities will challenge this conclusion, but, for what they are worth, we will give the basic factors involved.

The earliest Hominid fossil known is that of Ramapithecus of 14 million years ago, who teetered between ape and human attributes, being neither one nor the other.

The next oldest accepted fossil specimen of a Hominid species is that of Zinjanthropus (nut-cracker man), found by the late Dr. Louis Leakey at the Olduvai Gorge in Tanzania.[4] Some anthropologists insist this specimen does not belong to the Australopithecus line but represents a new family, which they have named Paranthropus.

Under either name, this subhuman fossil has been dated as of 1.75 million years ago. There is a claim that the African Hominids go back 2 million and possibly as much as 2.6 million years, based on a fragment of an armbone found in northern Kenya [5] and also, recently, on a skull in Tanzania.

But even if this latter figure is admitted into the Hominid-fossil parade, it lops off less than a million years from that "maddening" blank of 12 million years in the human story. Even 11 million years without a valid humanoid fossil unearthed is still an enormous gap in the anthropological record, one that gravely weakens the Theory of Evolution as applied to mankind. True, that gap may be further closed by other finds of Hominid fossils, but it is unlikely that they will form an unbroken line back to *Ramapithecus.*

That gap, large or smaller, is what the anthropologists have long been trying to fill with the notorious "missing link."

Or perhaps the missing link goes still further back, as certain anthropologists feel, anywhere from 15 to 50 million years ago (which indicates how varied the views of the experts are in this uncertain field). What they are all looking for is some common ancestor of both apes and men, from which the two branches of anthropoids and Hominids split off.

For this purpose, *proconsul* was invented as a purely theoretical creature without any fossil pieces of him being known. When Leakey found some bones of an odd creature 20 million years old, older than Ramapithecus, he named it Kenyapithecus and believed it might be the very first ancient Hominid.[6] Or the "mythical" proconsul.

Few other authorities go along with him. This is the fate of many special theories or concepts in anthropology. As one writer in the field expresses it — "Paleoanthropology has been the most argumentative of sciences since its beginning. Experts who agree are rare."[7]

Professor Sherwood L. Washburn, University of California at Berkeley, says it in another way that might bring scowls from his colleagues — "The study of human Evolution is a game rather than a science in the usual sense."[8]

As for any authority thinking he has the correct solution to the mystery of the Hominids and the missing link, F. Clark Howell, who has dug up many puzzling fossils says — "Anyone who feels that we already have the problem [of Man's origin] solved is surely deluding himself."[9]

With this clear mandate to us to take none of the claims of anthropologists as established fact, we can go on with the confused picture of how and when Man's progenitors appeared in earthly history.

The whole controversy centers around the Australopithecines, the general name *(Australo* meaning southern hemisphere) for several different kinds of Hominid fossils, some found in Asia but most in southeast Africa. Various authorities recognize (or deny) various Hominids, such as *Africanus Boiset, A. Robustus, A. Africanus, Paranthropus,* and *A. Habilis.*

The last one has led to the most controversy, and one school of fossil hunters claims it is the first ancient *Homo* species, as distinguished from the Hominid ape-men.

Homo habilis would thus be the proto-man, first of his kind, and would presumably have evolved into the well-known *Homo erectus.* This would put the origin of Man's direct ancestors back to about 2 million years ago.

Still, this does not solve the mystery of the missing link, for there is no fossil lineage for Habilis (Hominid or Homo) that stretches back through that big 12-million-year gap between Ramapithecus and the Australopithecines.

Thus, the reward for finding that "missing person" of dim antiquity is still uncollected and unclaimed by any anthropologist.

Perhaps the answer is easier than they suspect.

We suggest, as mentioned before, that starmen are the real "missing link." That they came along 12 million years ago, when Ramapithecus roamed his apelike knuckle-walking way, and began experimenting with methods to improve him.

In short, *artificial Evolution,* by incredible biogenetic "magic."

The result, some 12 million years later, was a manlike creature of the Australopithecus genus. Or *A. Habilis.* And the "missing" fossils in between?

There might not have been any.

The starmen, for instance, rapidly developed small numbers of mutants in their biolabs, too few to leave fossil remains, or even took them away to be *Homogenized* on another world and replanted on Earth later. At any rate, their grand experiment took 12 million years to jump from primitive Ramapithecus to much more advanced Australopithecus.

Whether the above admitted speculations are anywhere near the truth is not relevant, only the undeniable fact that there is no record via fossils to show Man's turnabout from apehood to manhood via Evolution.

And there is no evolutionary record because the laws of natural selection and survival of the fittest did not operate in the classic manner.

The laws of *biogenetic selection* by the starmen could much more logically have operated in perhaps some fantastic way inconceivable to our less-advanced science.

We will find in another chapter that this concept of biogenetic hybridization of Hominids is bolstered considerably when it comes to explaining Man's great brain.

One more example of how anthropologists deal with palpably misfit aspects of Evolution, by hazarding explanations that can only be called "wild," is as follows. It is known that, contrary to the "smooth" transitions demanded by evolutionary theory, there were, at certain periods in the past, very sudden and wholesale changes of species.

Immanuel Velikovsky, who is considered a maverick by other scientists, has given his own theory for those gross changes in species — his "cataclysmic" theory of Earth periodically undergoing major geological catastrophes that wipe out most existing species, requiring a whole new line of species to appear through "emergency" mutations. Though we do not necessarily agree with Velikovsky's explanation for how the new species arise (we suspect Starman intervention), we do agree that the abrupt and worldwide changes in species, at certain times, is not explained by classic Evolution.

"The boundaries between eras, periods and epochs," reads one study of this phenomenon, "on the geological time scale generally denote sudden and significant changes in the character of fossil remains. For example, the boundary between the Triassic and Jurassic periods of the Mesozoic era [about 180 million years ago) was supposedly marked by spontaneous appearance of [many] new species."[10]

Even they admit that —"Researchers have sometimes come up with drastic explanations for these changes, such as an increase in mutation rates due to cosmic rays."

Then, offering a more "reasonable" explanation, a German authority denies that there are "sudden" changes of species, only sudden *diversification* of established species.[11] He claims that is "normal" Evolution and offers a sweeping change in worldwide ecology as the spark causing "diversification."

Somehow, that explanation seems less acceptable than even cosmic rays! It's simply juggling words semantically.

Yet, the cosmic-ray angle itself simply does not hold up, for it would mean that periodically the cosmic-ray bombardment of Earth shows sudden and enormous increases. But there is not one shred of proof that such cosmic-ray "bursts" occur at all, at least of sufficient strength and duration to affect the genes and cause mutations of living things all over the Earth.

The experts are definitely straining, and sacrificing credibility, when they offer suggestions like that out of left field.

The true answer? It comes out in a more credible way, we believe, from our Hybrid theory. The starmen, in order to increase the mutation rate of their widely flung Pongid and Hominid guinea pigs, showered down their own "cosmic radiation" by deforming the Van Allen belts from a spaceship, for instance.[12] The radiation inevitably struck other forms of life under this "shotgun" method and resulted in wholesale changes in species.

Since cosmic rays do *not* come in significant "bunches" at random times by natural means, certainly our guess as to *deliberate* radiation showers does not similarly violate any science facts or laws.

Nevertheless, still standing out like a sore thumb is that 12-million-year gap in the fossil record of prehuman species, with the elusive missing link still missing — and perhaps nonexistent.

5

Hominid Clues

Let us go back on the trail of Hominid and Pongid fossils and see what other snags the Theory of Evolution has run into that seriously undermine its whole application to the mystery of Man.

Even the picture of the Pongid apes, long before the Hominids appeared on the stage, is murky indeed from the fossil record. For instance, as a noted zoologist states in a famed best-seller, "What happened to the early apes?"[1]

He points out that about 30 million years ago, the ape family spread through a wide, forested area from western Africa to southeastern Asia. Then, about 15 million years ago, they began to vanish here and there until today they are in very restricted areas and are reduced to a total of 192 living species of monkeys and apes.

These great apes include the orangutan, gorilla, chimpanzee, gibbon, and baboon. Since 15 million years ago there were no big-game hunters and no commercial trapping for furs, we must look to another reason for the decline of the great apes.

This mystery may or may not be related to the Hybrid Man story, but it indicates again that Evolution can only give weak explanations for such ancient events.

If the apes were class-A specimens from the school of natural selection, why should they decline as if unable to compete with other animal species?

Now, the primate line in general, apes as well as man-apes and true men, displays one characteristic vastly superior to all other creatures on Earth — brainpower. Therefore, it is not out of line with our theory, even if lacking any firm proof, to suggest that, not inconceivably, the primate line was *imported* to Earth by the starmen. The primates would be their basic starting point for creating an eventual species of intelligent human.

We must keep stressing the point that the age-old civilization of original Man or Starman on a far-off homeworld would not be dismayed at a long-range biological project spanning millions and millions of years.

And that biological project was tested and tried previously on uncounted other worlds. The goal was sublimely worthwhile — populating the universe with humankind so that the glorious gift of intelligence would never die out.

We have several clues to the possible importation of extraterrestrial forms of life on Earth, fitting our basic theory.

One is the mystery of the complete lack of fossil remains of the present living desert flora and fauna.[2] No one knows at the present time why it is that, while countless fossil specimens of grasses, trees, ferns, and shrubs of tropical and semitropical climates can be found in many geological strata, not one single desert plant has left its fossil traceries in places where it can be found today. The desert palm tree is the one exception.

Another point difficult to understand is the rather astonishing basic difference in structure that exists between desert plants and most other Earth plants.

But these odd mysteries can be solved, if we assume that many hybridizing visits to Earth by our outer-space ancestors were required in order to infuse the proper mixtures into Hominids to create modern Man. It is not unreasonable to assume further that, on one of these fairly recent visits (geologically speaking), our outer-space sires brought desert forms of plants to Earth.

These desert types may have, all too often, been the only plant forms they knew. For, as was shown earlier, some of our outer-space ancestors might have spent the major part of their lives and times on waning planets that were not nearly as green as our lush planet Earth. Because of incessant population pressures, they would have had to dwell on planets that were drier, older, and dustier than we care to think about.

Consequently, desert-plant species that we see only in our dry regions are forms that may have been familiar to the starmen for perhaps millions of years. When our deserts developed, our starmen relatives may have seen an opportunity to bring some seeds from their dry and dusty homes elsewhere to plant in the new Earth world.

Our outer-space ancestors knew all too well that in a few million years or so, the desert areas on Earth would grow and grow. In time, earthmen would be thankful for the starmen's foresight in planting imported desert-plant species so soon, so well, and in such profusion.

There is another clue, among animal species, that the starmen may have planted certain creatures from other worlds on Earth. We refer to the puzzling "living fossils," or species that have existed through hundreds of millions of years practically unchanged and seemingly extinction-proof. Yet, by far the vast majority of species that go back that far have completely vanished except for their bones.

Among the "living fossils" are included the following:

The queer duckbilled platypus, which — most any reasoning biologist would say — because of its "mixed up" characteristics of being a mammal that lays eggs and has a duckbill, had the least staying power through the ages. Yet there it is today, flourishing as if eons of time had not gone by since its kind first appeared on Earth.

The oyster is another long-lived specimen of early life; also the opossum, the Australian lungfish, the horseshoe crab, the coelacanth fish, and, to include a botanical item, the ginkgo tree.

How much of a riddle they represent can be seen from the following review of what evolutionists think about these "time anomalies."[3] The so-called living fossils puzzle and annoy the evolutionists, who feel obligated to explain why, in a world of change, these forms continue in their old placid way without either changing or becoming extinct. In hundreds of million of years [since they originated] there must have been changes in climate, changes in the environment, new enemies, new parasites, new diseases. Yet these creatures, without showing any special virtues or abilities, continue unchanged.

Then the redoubtable G. G. Simpson of Harvard is quoted as saying that these unchanging and persistent species "are a standing challenge to the hypothesis of ceaseless flux and have defied the explanatory efforts of many famous biologists."[4]

We think the explanation might be profoundly simple: that they were imported to Earth by the starmen, for reasons not to be guessed at, unless it was as a test of the earthly environment, important for later Hybrid Man experiments.

Perhaps those time-lasting species came from some harsh world, so that earthly conditions, even though fluctuating wildly, seem like soft living to them, thus giving them their amazing durability.

Since other worlds can have an Evolution quite parallel to Earth's, those species might be closely related to similar but extinct species here and thus, to the paleontologist, would not seem grossly "alien" or out of line.

But now to return to our main theme in this chapter — early mankind.

In the so-called Evolution of humans there are two major steps to be accounted for. One is the use of crudely shaped tools by early Man, an attribute shared by no other creature, not even the apes. This subject will be taken up in detail in the next chapter.

The second question we will take up here: When did ape-men come down from the trees to become prehumans walking on two feet?

Again, a source book of anthropological authority presents that mystery in a nutshell: "From squatting in a tree to strolling upright in a meadow is an enormous leap. Any explanation of the change can be only speculative. But the speculations, even though there are no fossils to back them up, have an uncanny way of hanging together."[5]

The key phrase is "even though there are *no fossils* to back them up." Again the "stones and bones" men (archeologists plus anthropologists) must admit their fossil method of piecing together mankind's origin has the annoying habit of leaving gaps marring their pet theories. The 12-million-year gap between man-apes and submen again hides this major transition from tree-swinging apes to ground-walking men, and from knuckle-walking (when apes did occasionally descend to the ground) to full-time ground locomotion on two legs as practiced by humans.

Another authoritative work on early Man also has trouble bridging the gap between tree-dwellers and ground-walkers:

When Man's apelike ancestors descended from the trees, they must have been exposed to attacks from predators and, like male baboons, macaques and goril-

las, the male Hominids almost certainly possessed
[one would think] long canines which they used to
defend themselves, their females, and their young.
Had they not done so, the Hominids would surely
have been wiped out.[6]

Then comes the damaging admission: "Yet, the Australopithecine fossils show these little apelike men possessed
canines no longer or sharper than modern Man."

All of which is pithily highlighted by another quote:
"This problem [how Man got from the trees to the ground]
has puzzled experts for a long time and many imaginative
theories have been put forward."[7]
"Imaginative" is the word!
Which is the trap the authorities fall into, trying to explain
that disturbing anomaly, when they fish up this one — that the
Australopithecines of about 2 million years ago were not the
earliest representatives of the ground-walking Hominids.
But, as we saw before, the great Hominid fossil gap intrudes
by furnishing no pre-Australopithecus species for a long age,
thus giving them not the slightest evidence that their theory is
valid. It is not very scientific to predicate a hypothesis on what
should be, when the fossil proof is totally lacking. That is little
better than unscientific guessing.
Can our theory do any better? We believe so.
First of all, it is part of our concept that whenever Hominid
species in the past made inexplicable leaps ahead, in any area,
those leaps had one common cause — the *biomanipulations of
the starmen.* We, too, must resort to pure speculation (which at
least places us on an equal footing with the anthropologists) and
imagine that, as part of their plan to bring out the step-by-step
creation of Hybrid Man, our star-sires somehow got early Man
down to the ground on two feet.
But how? Here is where we will make another daring
proposal — it was done by *genetic control. By* the deliberate

introduction of specialized genes into the systems of the early Hominids.

As we now dimly realize in modern biology, the genes are a complex "ladder" of chromosome trails within each cell that control some memory-pattern or instinct or biochemical process for the whole body. Thus, if the starmen simply incorporated dominant new genes for walking upright, while turning the old tree-swinging genes into recessive traits, early Man would, in a few generations, abruptly switch from being an arboreal acrobat into a walking plainsman.

This was vitally necessary, for one cannot build civilization in the tops of trees. The starmen had to get the dawn men down on the ground before their magnificent earth colony could come to fruition.

Read any anthropological work that tries to explain just how the early men did exchange their tree life for prairie life, and you will see a tortuous interweaving of how the need for game, use of tools, seeing further when standing up, and other somewhat irrelevant or farfetched ideas are thrown together, begging the question entirely.

Which came first, the chicken or the egg?

It forms the forlorn basis for every tautological attempt, under evolutionary theory, to get early mankind out of the trees and down to solid ground.

And the theorizers only leave themselves higher in the air than Man was in the treetops.

If the forests did not decline but grew more lushly as time passed, why in the world should a tree-dwelling species of animal desert his original habitat? It is questions like these that tongue-tie the anthropologists.

We do not mean to denigrate them, but their "authority" on such ancient mysteries, when not backed up by *any fossils* — *their* basic tool — is certainly far from authoritative.

It is another big "hole" in Evolution, as applied to Man, that neither Darwin nor Wallace could ever cover in the first place.

Where did the *Homo* family of species come in, according to Evolution? *Homo*, meaning human or the true men as distinguished from the ape-men Hominids.

Homo erectus is the first such specimen following the long chain of Australopithecine ape-men (although Leakey, as we have seen before, sees Habilis as a *Homo* going back almost 2 million years).

Back in the 1890s, the famed Java Man's fossil was found, but it was first thought to be a *non-Homo* type and labeled Pithecanthropus erectus, meaning an ape-man who walked upright. But careful study revealed that he was much more manlike than apelike. A new genus was started under the *Homo* tag, and the Java Man became *Homo erectus.* He lived from 300,000 to 600,000 years ago (perhaps, according to some authorities, up to a million years ago).

Subsequently, many Erectus specimens were found, including the Peking Man and others around the World. Two major riddles arose.

1. How did Erectus, without vehicles or transportation of any kind, spread around much of the world?

2. Why did Erectus disappear completely about 300,000 years ago?

Classical Evolution cannot permit any single species of any animal to appear simultaneously at several different points around the Earth. A new species arises in one certain place under propitious conditions and then, if it is vigorous and prolific, it gradually spreads out. But for primitive Erectus to start from Africa, his presumed place of genesis, and eventually spread into Europe and Asia (but not into the New World), makes him an extraordinary globe-trotter.

Since the world of half a million years ago was still filled with fierce predators, and Erectus had no weapons beyond crude sticks and sharp flintstones held in the hand, his bold invasion of far-distant domains is entirely incongruous. There are many other controversial aspects of this "world conquest" by Erectus, too numerous to go into, that make it a deep mystery.

Again, as smoothly as gears locking into place, we can use our new Hybrid Man theory and simply propose that the starmen moved members of the Erectus species around the Earth.

Why? Because Erectus was a culmination of their strenuous hybridization program, representing the breakthrough, so to speak, from ape-man specimens to manlike specimens who could in time lead to true Man.

Such a hybridization program is perfectly plausible, even in terms of the budding science of biogenetics on Earth today. The spokesman for one team of Harvard biologists said that a well-financed crash program (à la the Manhattan Project) could make genetic engineering on human beings a reality within a few years. By that, he meant manipulating the genes of people to "make them over" in any way desired. If our kindergarten biogenetics know-how is already that close to the goal of "engineering" humans in miraculous ways, then surely the college techniques of the aliens could easily accomplish their programmed plans in changing around the subhuman species of prehistoric times.

As for Erectus then melting away into oblivion 300,000 years ago, this too may have been planned by the starmen when the next-higher type of Homo was bred. Not that Erectus was ruthlessly exterminated by them but was perhaps simply left to shift for himself. Prey to carnivores and to a hostile environment, and without the brain development to survive against such odds, Erectus huddled helplessly to be sent to the limbo for extinct species.

Erectus had to go because Neanderthal Man showed up, a far more advanced type of prehistoric human being with a much larger brain. Which leads to another "gap" that severely damages the case for Darwinian Evolution.

As our previously quoted book of anthropological authority puts it:

"The Auchelian [toolmaking] industry, introduced by *Homo erectus*, lasted from about 500,000 to 75,000 years ago, but *Homo erectus* [himself] did not. The last we know of him [via fossils] is more than 300,000 years ago, which means that there is a stretch of nearly 200,000 years from which no definite Homo erectus fossils are known, and at the end of which an entirely different type of man appears on the scene — Neanderthal man."[8]

An entirely different type of man! Is that part of the smooth, uninterrupted process of Evolution in which species gradually change in many transitions, with each step traced in fossils?

Hardly!

Borrowing a physics term, it is a quantum jump of a whole magnitude, from one species of early Man to one totally different and far more advanced.

It almost seems unnecessary to point out that such an abrupt leap forward in subhuman species is not only covered by the Hybrid Man theory but is *essential* to it. It almost shouts aloud that some *outside* factor manipulated the development of the human species, not in slow steps by natural selection but in giant steps, by means of "unnatural selection" or planned hybridization techniques.

From the evolutionary viewpoint, 200,000 years are *unaccounted* for. But, in the Hybrid Man theory, these are 200,000 years in which the starmen found the way to create Neanderthal Man from the basic stock of *Homo erectus*.

Of course, the anthropologists and evolutionists will always say confidently (or in wishful thinking?) that more and more digging in the ground will eventually reveal the "missing" fossils that will fill this gap and also will fill the 12-million-year gap between the earliest and latest Hominids.

In fact, Richard E. Leakey, following in his great father's footsteps, has recently announced new fossil-finds at Lake Rudolph in northern Kenya, including "what is almost certainly the oldest complete skull of early Man."[9]

He means a species of genus *homo,* not a Hominid of the Australopithecine type. This would antedate *Homo erectus* by far and put true Man's ancestry, back to *2.5* million years ago. However, these finds are too new yet to be fully evaluated and accepted, and Leakey's opinion must be called tentative. He first of all makes the startling suggestion that the *Homo* genus was contemporary with the Australopithecines, and that they both came from a common ancestral line (another unfound missing link), from which *Homo* broke off about 4 million years ago. This is highly speculative, it must be said, and will have to await much more close study by others than Leakey himself.

Obviously, Leakey is striving to fill that 12-million-year gap between the early and late Hominids, and he puts his faith in further fossil finds to bridge the chasm. But this easy way out — of thinking more fossils *will* conveniently be found — is sternly denied by Ernst Mayr of Harvard, leading authority in evolutionary matters.[10] He refers to the Sewall Wright Effect which postulates that missing fossils are those of a species of such low population, or of such short duration in the geological scale, that there was little chance of a highly accidental event like fossilizing to occur. In short, an extinct species of numerous members existing for millions of years will, by the law of averages, leave a few of its fossilized skeletal parts around, whereas species of low numbers and brief tenure may leave none.

It sounds very logical — except for the fact that fossils of the second type *have* been found many times, notably Steinheim and Swanscombe Man. The rarity of the species is no guide to whether it will show up or not. And the finds of the bone-digging anthropologists cannot depend purely on *geographical* luck. They most often dig in the most *likely* places for any particular type of fossil, hence putting the odds strongly in favor of finding even the rarer species.

At any rate, Mayr chided his fellow evolutionists on this score, saying that bringing up the Sewall Wright Effect as an "explanation" for gaps in the fossil record is very "farfetched" — a "cover-up" that may soothe the mind of the harassed anthropologist with the thought of missing fossils, but hardly scientific when it is a wholly "manufactured" excuse.

True, new finds like those of Leakey in Tanzania are great "bonanzas" that help fill the fossil gap for recent Hominids, but to blithely believe that "the more digging, the more fill-in fossils" is tantamount to believing in the pot of gold at the end of the rainbow.

Some fossil gaps will *never* be filled out, simply because there *are* no such "progressive" fossils. That is a false hope based on one great *fallacy* of Evolution — that an endless chain of microchanges in any certain species eventually results in a macrochange. This is disputed by the majority of evolutionists today.

In fact, Evolution Theory today no longer follows classical Darwinism, except for a stubbornly faithful group. Not that the remaining majority of evolutionists have agreed on any single concept or principle to replace Darwinism.

They have instead fragmented it into three separate "modes."[11]

1. *Speciation:* The formation of new subspecies and species by means of "point mutations," a complex viewpoint that is sponsored mainly by geneticists.

2. *Phyletic Evolution:* Paleontologists work at this phase, sorting out large groups of fossils into phylogenies, or "family trees."

3. *Macro-Evolution:* The concept that major changes in a species result from a long series of *micro-changes.*

But a fourth group has arisen that denies any evidence of micro-Evolution being necessary for macro-Evolution. Instead, they believe in *Quantum Evolution,* wherein species, for some unaccountable reason, make a sudden jump into a major change.

In the case of the origin of Man, this form of Quantum Evolution is plain to see and is the only possible concept that fits the facts.

And the cause of these "mysterious" quantum jumps would not baffle the experts if they accepted this book's proposal of wholesale biomanipulations by the starmen who created Hybrid Man and "jumped" from Homo erectus to Neanderthal Man to Cro-Magnon Man (the human race) in "macro" style.

The authors believe that, by the end of this book, they will have presented *overwhelming evidence* that this can be the *only* answer to Man's origin.

6

Homo Clues

We are now done with the pre-human Hominids and will deal with the various genus *Homo* species, or the "true" men, who have hardly any simian characteristics. The time period advances to about 600,000 years ago, the final days of Australopithecine Hominids. As we saw in the previous chapter, the first *Homo* species came in at that time — Homo erectus.

When *Homo erectus* rather mysteriously died out 300,000 years ago, we suggested that this might very well have been an extinction planned by the starmen to make room for newer and better *Homo* species.

The picture is not at all clear, from the fossil records, as to just what happened next. Anthropologists only know that *homo neandethalensis sapiens* appeared 110,000 years ago, after that fossil gap of almost 200,000 years. Neanderthal Man was a great leap forward in the Evolution of Man, for his brain was much larger than primitive Erectus — 1,400-1,500 cubic centimeters and about 975 cubic centimeters, respectively.

There are two fossils that form the only possible link between Erectus and Neanderthal, but they both appear "out of place" in the time scale and hence are among those baffling anomalies that give anthropologists sleepless nights.

One is Swanscombe Man, of perhaps 250,000 years ago, who amazingly has a skull shaped almost like modern Man's, plus a brain capacity close to ours. As one paleoanthropological writer puts it when talking about the Swanscombe skull bones found: "Their size, their proportions and particularly their curves are much the same as modern Man's; they are definitely not those of *Homo erectus.* This is absolutely astonishing. What on earth was a modern-looking skull like that doing way back there?"[1] A verbatim quote! From an apparently stupefied anthropologist.

He goes on to say that the Swanscombe skull "seems to indicate a kind of precocious modern Man sneaking into the picture along with, or even before, Neanderthal Man."

The reason he and his colleagues are "absolutely astonished" should be apparent. If a more modern skull and brain (Swanscombe) shows up *ahead* of a less modern skull and brain (Neanderthal), then Evolution is working *backward.* This almost undermines Darwin's theory in itself (in the case of mankind only), for the whole concept of natural selection is that Evolution always goes *forward* to better and better species.

Yet how easily Swanscombe can be accepted in the Hybrid Man theory!

He would simply be the result of an abortive genetic experiment by the starmen, an attempted "improvement" on Erectus, say, one that didn't work out. Perhaps, in spite of his "modern" skull, his brain was inferior because of a low blood-supply, or a paucity of nerve paths, or some other cerebral blemish that made him an inferior specimen of *Homo.* Only three bone-parts of one Swanscombe skull have ever been found, and we can assume this rarity means his stock was not allowed to perpetuate itself. The starmen superbiologists did not want this "freak" with faults to continue as a species.

One other skull, that of Steinheim Man, comes from that 200,000-year gap, and is also too "advanced" for its time. Unlike anthropologists to whom this threatens the very foundations of Evolution, our Hybrid theory can again accept it without fear — in fact, welcome it — as another abort in the great biogenetic program of the starmen.

We want to repeat this point: that out-of-place skulls and misfit *Homo* specimens *bolster* the Hybrid Theory, strongly indicating that a Man-controlled kind of "Evolution" was being practiced, with certain setbacks coming up during the experimentation.

But the evolutionists can only wish that those two missing links (Swanscombe and Steinheim) were missing in the fossil record.

Exit Swanscombe and Steinheim. Enter Neanderthal. *But he, too, was apparently an abort,* for he also vanished from the scene by 35,000 B.C.

This again is astonishing, because Neanderthal lasted some 75,000 long years altogether and spread widely over the Old World, with very heavy concentrations in Europe and the Middle East. His population might have been in the multiple thousands or even millions at its peak. And his brain-case of 1,400 cubic centimeters was *larger* than a modern Man's (average, 1,300 cubic centimeters).

Then why should this seemingly successful Homo species die out to the last man?

To this day, anthropologists have no positive answer, though many vague theories have been presented, none of which holds water. One example is that three Ice Ages that occurred in its time wiped the species out—but the Ice Ages never reached the Middle East, where Neanderthal was firmly entrenched.

This seems to fairly shout that the true answer, again, must lie with the starmen. Something was "wrong" with Neanderthal, which finally became apparent after his "trial" period on Earth of 75,000 years. What that "wrong" factor was can only be guesswork. A big brain but small mental capacity? A muscle-bound body? — Neanderthal was a mass of muscle. Some defect in his hands that made him clumsy with tools?

Nobody knows—except the starmen.

When the sad truth faced them, we can picture how the starmen sighed and again consigned an experimental Hybrid human to the list of extinct creatures. In what manner, we cannot fathom. But that it was humane seems unquestionable, for superintelligent colonizing aliens like that must have long ago bred all cruelty out of their systems and their society.

However, Neanderthal may not have been totally wiped out. One school of anthropology sees distinct traces of the Neanderthal physique in certain members of the human race, those who are extremely bulky in build, with low, beetling foreheads and hairy bodies. If true, this means that, though Neanderthal as a species vanished from the scene, he had managed to intermarry with Cro-Magnon to some extent and thus left his mark in *Homo sapiens* to come. (Again, other anthropologists believe that Neanderthal and Cro-Magnon, being two distinct species, could not interbreed at all.)

But whether or not Neanderthal disappeared without a trace or left something of himself in the human gene-pool, this prehistoric *Homo* once again adds *support* to the Hybrid theory. Every great anomaly in the chain of subhuman species is a bad blow to classic Evolution but a big boost for the Hybrid concept.

And the greatest riddle of all now comes up —*where did Cro-Magnon Man, the first of our own* Homo sapiens *species, come from 35,000 years ago?*

Not from Erectus, too great a jump. Not from Swanscombe or Steinheim, offshoots showing no cranial relationship. Not from Neanderthal, a quite different species.

Then, from *where? From the starmen.*

And that, quite simply, would solve another enormous anthropological mystery if our premise is right. Starmen at last made earthmen, in their worldwide "biolaboratory," in their own image. Or something similar.

The disappearance of Neanderthal Man and the advent of

Cro-Magnon Man at approximately the same time is one of the truly big stumbling blocks to the Evolution theory, for they are non sequitur species. Neanderthal most decidedly could not be the direct ancestor of Cro-Magnon, for they were two distinctly different types of human, physically and even skeletally.

Neanderthal was a squat, heavily muscled, beetlebrowed kind of Man whose culture, from the numerous relics collected with his fossil bones, was at the most primitive level. He was the traditional "caveman."

Cro-Magnon was taller, slimmer, with finer bones in his skull and face. His culture was a great magnitude above Neanderthal, as evidenced alone by the exquisite cave paintings he left depicting people and game animals. Cro-Magnon was classified as *Homo sapiens sapiens,* or the same species as modern Man.

Oddly enough, the early Cro-Magnons of 35,000 B.C. had a larger average brain-case than we do today (1,400 cubic centimeters compared to 1,300 cubic centimeters). Cro-Magnon is called our direct "ancestor," meaning that by gradual and subtle transitions, he became modern Man.

Since Neanderthal vanished around 35,000 B.C., and Cro-Magnon came on stage at the same time, one theory is that the latter killed off the former as an inferior competing species. But anthropological consensus now holds this as very doubtful and believes that the two species never really met except in sporadic encounters.

The abrupt disappearance of Neanderthal remains one of the greatest "whodunit" mysteries of mankind.

Neanderthal gave rise to another anomaly that again deals Evolution a low blow. As reported from the book quoted before:

Neanderthal Man endured both cold and mild cycles with apparently equal success. He continued to exist in western Europe right up to about 35,000 years ago, and then he abruptly disappeared. The evolutionary tendencies that he exhibited during this period are extremely puzzling. For he seems to have gotten more "primitive," not less so. The last fossils we have from western Europe are even squatter, bulkier and more beetle-browed than their predecessors.[2]

Further on: "In addition to stopping abruptly, the classic Neanderthaler is replaced with equal abruptness by people like ourselves [Cro-Magnons]. There is no blending, no gradual shading from one type to the other. It is as if modern men came storming in and dispossessed the Neanderthalers."

Classical Evolution theory simply cannot account for these two events. First, the *abrupt* disappearance of a whole well-entrenched species, plus the *abrupt* debut of a better species. Second, the fact that the Neanderthal species *retrogressed* and became more primitive as time went on. Natural selection and survival-of-the-fittest are square pegs that cannot be hammered into those round holes, whereas the Hybrid Theory *easily* accounts for them.

Who else but bio-overseers of a grand Man-creating program brought about the abrupt disappearance of Neanderthal, and then suddenly ushered in Cro-Magnon? Those events almost cry aloud that someone behind the scenes was manipulating early men as they would characters in a play.

Moreover, the *de*-evolution of Neanderthal even more loudly proclaims that the starmen perhaps *introduced retrogressive genes* into the race in order to wipe them out humanely over a period of time. Any species that becomes progressively more primitive is sure to lose out in the great worldwide struggle for survival, where competition is so keen.

Again, if Cro-Magnon was not, by any stretch of imagination, a descendant of Neanderthal nor from Swanscombe and Steinheim Man, where *did* he come from, with such a grand sweep he could take over the whole world, unchallenged, from 35,000 B.C. to date?

The fossil record, on which the anthropologists depend so heavily, leaves them out on a limb. But the Hybrid Theory forthrightly fits the Cro-Magnon enigma into its mold as the final great climax of the starmen's project in molding Man out of his primate breeding stock. The "abruptness" of his appearance is then no longer a riddle but simply the *expected* culmination after the starmen built up an original nucleus of humans and then sent them out to "inherit the earth." And it may well prove that the Bible is mainly a *history* of the starmen and their colonizing project.

For example, we have it from both the Bible and fossil finds that mankind seems to have had limited focal points from which he spread out, in six movements. Three such focal points are Africa, Asia, and the Mediterranean. But by far the greater focal point is in the Holy Land, from which three huge, spreading movements spoked out.

Could nature devise such a perfect system for spreading mankind over all Earth? Or was it a Starman-made plan, in which groups of *Homo sapiens* were separately "raised" in those focal areas and then sent to migrate around the planet?

Even among evolutionists, there is a suspicion that there may be an unknown guiding force behind the workings of natural selection. It is called the "Watchmaker," an allusion to a master craftsman who alone can put the tiny and intricate parts of a fine watch together. So, too, there is hypothesized a Watchmaker who is "putting together" the parts in the mysterious "plan" of Evolution.

Norman Macbeth, in his critical book on Darwinism, finds that many evolutionists write as if influenced by anthropomorphism.[3] That is, they forget natural selection is an *impersonal* force, working at random and not a *planning* force.

Darwin himself, he points out, said that "natural selection is daily and hourly *scrutinizing* ... every variation [in the species], even the slightest; *rejecting* that which is bad, *preserving* and adding up all that is good; silently and insensibly *working* ... at the improvement of each organic being."[4] (Italics added.)

The words we have italicized certainly are anthropomorphic, as if natural selection is a *sentient* force. Darwin did not mean it that way, but perhaps subconsciously he wondered if *someone* or *something* — *a* third party — had a guiding hand in Evolution.

And, of course, the someone or something would be the starmen, even though Darwin apparently had no inkling of them.

Again, a sober and well-known botanist repeatedly speaks of natural selection as a "guiding" or "directive" force, at one point likening it to a sculptor creating a statue by removing chips (species that become extinct) from a block of marble.[5]

That book's author remarks on his own that natural selection is supposed to be a *random* force that replaces all Watchmakers or other guiding powers, so that Evolution can be explained without calling in any external agency. Then he quotes another eminent evolutionist who speaks of the "opportunism" of Evolution, yet tries to deny any anthropomorphic implications.[6]

But if natural selection is *opportunistic,* that means it does things that are not due to blind chance.

If something does not work solely by blind chance, who is *tipping the scales?*

As an example of natural selection working in inexplicable ways, G. G. Simpson quite frankly admits that he cannot explain (by the rules of Evolution) why the average stature in the United States has increased since 1900.[7] There is simply no *reason* for it, if the rest of the human race does not also increase its average height.

We, too, will frankly admit that if the starmen biologists are behind that oddity, neither do we know *why.* Our theory cannot answer everything, naturally. Still, that anomaly further undermines the foundations of natural selection, which in turn bolsters the theory of an Earth colony guided by Watchmakers from the stars.

Again and again, top-notch biologists, anthropologists, and all-round evolutionists speak of certain "marvels" and "wonders" in the evolutionary history of various species that seem beyond the workings of natural selection.

Simpson, in 1969, made an extraordinary statement that is really food for thought. He said that natural selection "is usually and most strongly a stabilizing, normalizing influence preventing or slowing down and not hastening evolutionary change."[8]

Stabilizing and *slowing down* evolutionary change!

Then natural selection certainly did not make mankind spring forth and develop a great brain in a few million years. It would have *slowed down* that process. That practically eliminates Evolution as the factor behind the origin of Man and leaves it wide open for our theory — that the starmen biogeneticists *speeded up* mankind's debut, circumventing the slowdown tendencies of natural selection.

Just as the California Board of Education stipulated that the biblical Creation theory must be given equal status with Darwin's Theory, some scholars in the evolutionary field have voiced similar thoughts, apparently disillusioned with the shortcomings of the concept of natural selection.

Dr. Robert Broom, noted paleontologist, came out with a pronouncement that probably staggered all his colleagues, saying it was clear to him that Evolution was accomplished not by natural selection or mutations, but by *spiritual beings of various grades and various kinds of intelligence.*[9]

How much closer can you get to the starmen colonizers in our Hybrid Man theory?

Sir Julian Huxley, champion of Evolution, also admitted that only if you can rule out the hypothesis of "special creation" does the principle of natural selection and adaptation become valid. [10]

Some biologists candidly maintain that they believe the phrase "natural selection" to be a *metaphor,* or only an analogy of the true forces behind evolutionary change.[11] And if you once rule out natural selection as the primary cause of changing species, there is nothing left but special creation.

Yet they shy away from accepting the biblical version of creation, wanting something less "superstitious" and less mystical. Since they are looking for something logical and acceptable to their scientific minds, besides either natural selection or special creation, we wonder if they would not gladly *embrace* our theory of starmen who are superbiologists?

There is their "special creation," with all religious dogma stripped away and shining forth as a quite believable and scientific explanation.

Norman Macbeth himself says, "The vitalists and other persons who see a Watchmaker or the hand of God behind the marvels of nature should not be reckoned fools. They *feel* this presence, and the Darwinian arguments are not persuasive enough to overcome their feeling."[12]

It is such a simple step from religion or belief-by-faith-only to the Hybrid Man theory with all its immense scientific logic — if only scientists will accept it as a theory.

Macbeth adds that, ironically, after careful scrutiny of literature on the Darwin Theory, he suspects its staunchest supporters of treating Evolution as *their* religion. There is the same unquestioning "faith" and lack of critical attitude as in the church worshiper.

But faith cannot deny the many failings of the evolutionary theory. Too many of the "explanations" of anomalies are tautological — in other words, repetition of the same thing without really explaining anything.[13]

Now in this book you are reading, we are not enlisting the side of the many critics mentioned above, and we are not quarreling with natural selection — whether right or wrong — as it applies to *other creatures.*

But we do state unequivocally that Darwinian Evolution and natural selection *do not apply to mankind at all.* However, we think the thin ice upon which evolutionary theory skates in the case of nonhuman species makes it far more *probable* that our theory of Hybrid Man created by the starmen as an Earth colony is correct, or at least pointing in the right direction.

Perhaps all the bickering, confused, groping dissenters from classical Evolution can rally to a common cause, if they will open their minds and accept our theory for *intensive investigation.*

That is all we ask — a fair trial and further research. If they can't accept either natural selection or biblical Creation, what have they got to lose in trying our theory?

To resume our review of specific anomalies in the Evolution Theory as regards *Man*, it is intriguing to find the ethnologists and anthropologists stumped over another high hurdle in the "impersonal" workings of natural selection.

Namely — why is the human race so greatly variegated as to shape, size, skull structure, facial characteristics, and many other anatomical features?

Why particularly are there men of varicolored skin — white, red, yellow, brown, and black?

Think of the enormous variety of breeds of dogs, from the Pekingese to the Great Dane, so entirely different from one another that a Martian might deny that they could be of the same species.

And how did the dog species become so variegated — *only by manipulated breeding.*

So, too, how could mankind come in so many different kind of "breeds" unless somebody *made* them different? For one fact is undeniable, that this is unique with Man and does not occur with any other undomesticated creature on Earth. Each animal species is comparatively uniform in nature. All living gorillas are essentially the same, with very little differentiation among individuals.

In the source book frequently quoted,[14] we find that there are remarkable skeletal differences between the indigenous people of Europe, Asia, and Africa, "just as there are different skin colors, different hair textures, and different facial features, though no one knows for sure where they came from or when they appeared."

The scholars of Man's origin are baffled, but we think we know where those differences came from — via the biomanipulations of the starmen, who knew that the more variations a species had, the more chance it had of surviving and thriving. Weakness of one human variety would not appear in the other, and so on.

This utterly unique quality of the human race comprising

many "breeds," like dogs or other domesticated animals, we consider to be one of the more significant points proving, or strongly indicating, that the Hybrid Man theory is correct.

When it comes to skin coloring, we meet a peculiar situation that may be coincidental — or may not.

Generally speaking, Man is divided into three main categories throughout the world: Caucasian, Mongoloid, and Negro.[15] It is interesting to note that the great apes are also broadly divided into three main groups: the gorilla, the chimpanzee, and the orangutan.

Can there be any relationship in this strange coincidence that there are three main divisions of Man and three main divisions of anthropoid apes?

Oddly enough, both the Negro and the gorilla have skin that is black in color. The chimp, in turn, has a whitish skin, while the orangutan has a greyish-red color.

Now these three parallel divisions of men and apes certainly cannot mean that the three main races of humans descended directly from the trio of ape races. That is totally invalid, both in Darwin's theory and ours.

The only vague thought we have is that it all goes back to *before* both Hominids and Pongids were clearly defined species, and that perhaps the starmen experimented with the black/white/yellow-skinned anthropoids as "controls" for their greater Man-creating project, just as biologists today use monkeys and apes as controls for testing out drugs and therapies before using them with humans.

If this viewpoint is anywhere near the truth, it must go too far back in the starmen's biogenetic juggling for us to ferret it out. We will drop the matter as leading nowhere.

Still, somewhere in these mazes of controversial information, one can sense dimly seen pattern or order. That the concept of Man being a Hybrid fits solidly into this puzzle as part of a grand pattern seems to us as certain and sure and dependable as the swing of the planets through the heavens and the slow beat of the pulse in our veins.

"There is an order in the universe," as Einstein has said, and

Man — Hybrid Man — we believe is inevitably a part of this grand universal order.

Now we come to the great and still more tangled subject of tools as related to Man.

No other animals on earth use tools — not *shaped* tools. Apes or monkeys will sometimes pick up a stone and throw it, or use it to smash open a clamshell, but it is a totally haphazard act, usually initiated by an individual, and never becomes a racial trait. An anthropoid may also, on rare occasions, use a stick to knock down some luscious hanging fruit, but again it is a random, nonracial act. And they never "make" or fashion rock or sticks into *permanent* tools.

Man was the first and only creature to discover and invent tools, to manufacture them in quantity, and to use them consistently.

And now comes the great controversy — which came first, tools or brains?

Did Man's superior brain cause him to invent tools? Or did the increasing use of primitive tools help his brain grow through the ages? Anthropologists have argued the pros and cons endlessly, without coming to any unanimous conclusion.

We have a far simpler answer. The starmen gave both tools and a superior brain to mankind.

That is, the starmen taught primitive Man to make the first stone axes, flintstone knives, and crude clubs. More than likely, the starmen introduced fire also, then later the wheel. But we won't go into the last item, for that involves the whole rise of civilization. We are still back in primitive times.

As a corollary to the tool/brain problem, there is the angle that when mankind descended from the trees to walk upright, his hands were left free for other uses, leading in due time to the handling of primitive tools. But as we have seen, the transition from tree-dwelling to ground-walking is itself a bog of conflictions. It can hardly be a clear-cut clue to how Man began using and developing tools.

Our oft-quoted source book admits: "There is no separating

the tangled triple influence of bipedalism, brain development, and tool using. They are hopelessly interlocked, each depending on and stimulating the others."[16] That is a weird contradiction.

If tool-making *depended* on ground-walking, then how could it also *stimulate* that trait? If brain development depended on ground-walking and tool-making, then how could the latter two turn around and become the stimulants for the bigger brain?

Which came first—the chicken, the egg, or neither?

It makes no sense, really. Beyond such tongue-twisted vagaries must lie a much more direct and cogent answer — namely, starmen intervention. Suddenly, with this concise and simple answer, the confusion is over.

To illuminate the real confusion that this tool/brain/ bipedalism conundrum creates in anthropological ranks, note this quote:

> "In any event, if two-leggedness does depend on tool use, it stands to reason that Australopithecus [of 2 million years ago] who was two-legged, must have been a good tool user. It would be nice to be able to confirm this by finding some chipped-stone artifacts in the same strata that Dart's and Broom's [noted anthropologists] fossils came from."

> Now the sagging denouement: "But again we are stymied. Experts searched for tools to go with Australopithecus for years but did not find a single one."[17]

There goes another pet evolutionary hypothesis down the drain.

Louis Leakey, digging in the Olduvai Gorge in Tanzania, was particularly baffled. Whenever he found Australopithecus fossils, he found no tools.[18] And when he found tools there were no Hominid fossils! "But who had made them [the tools] was an utter mystery," the report concluded.

One cannot help but notice how many "utter mysteries" pop up in anthropological studies of the origin and development of mankind, far more than for any other species on Earth.

And those damning "gaps" in the fossil record occur over and over, too. In tools, also. "With all these advances in tool-making, it is hard not to visualize people who were also advancing. Here we encounter another of those frustrating blank pages in the history of early Man. The Auchelian industry [ancient flint tool techniques] introduced by *Homo erectus,* lasted from about 500,000 to 75,000 years ago."[19]

But then comes that 200,000 year gap without humanoid fossils, except the two strays, Swanscombe and Steinheim.

Who carried on the tool culture so that it survived for 200,000 years and came to Neanderthal Man?

Who else but the starmen? That is *our* answer, starkly and forcefully.

When inadequate *Homo erectus* died out (perforce?), the starmen waited until Neanderthal Man came out of their open-air genetic lab and then handed him toolmaking. Neanderthal improved considerably on the simple, crude Erectus tools, again under the direct tutelage, we suggest, of the starmen overseers.

However, we must be fair to the anthropologists who have spent much energy and time and thought on this problem, and their alternative suggestions are not to be ignored. There are two main ones.

First, that Ice Ages during those 200,000 years may have lowered sea-levels down by 300 to 400 feet, exposing attractive living sites to some portion of the remaining Erectus species — or perhaps some as yet undiscovered types of submen. Then, when the sea inevitably rose again with the melting of the ice, those sites would be buried so deeply that they have not yet been located to see if the tool-making technique was being carried on.

Second, with evidence of violent upheavals in that era, great volcanic outpourings may have buried those ancient, and therefore unknown, custodians of tool-making, creating the blank of 2,000 centuries in our fossil records of who acted as the "liaison" between Erectus and Neanderthal.

The weakness in both these theories, it seems to us, is the necessary presumption of *wholesale* destruction by ice ages or volcanic and geological upheavals — a principle of "catastrophism theory," championed by Immanuel Velikovsky but vitriolically rejected, oddly enough, by mainstream science.

Nevertheless, one might say that even if destruction was widespread among those tribes of early men, the law of averages would allow *some* survivors, at least 5% or 10%. There should not be such a *total* obliteration of signs of the in-between subhumans who theoretically filled the stretch of time between vanishing Erectus in 300,000 B.C. and Neanderthal in 110,000 B.C..

If the signs are missing, it seems the species must also be missing.

As for our Hybrid/Earth-colony explanation, we think there are fewer, if any, glaring objections to it. For one thing, there is good reason to believe, from almost universal ancient legends, that our outer-space sires dealt quite *directly* with these subhuman creatures, knowing they would never figure out who their benefactors were or where they came from — a secret that the starmen are careful to keep hidden from us even *today,* for reasons to be explored in the last chapter.

7

Hairy Clues

If Man is a Hybrid, the evidence should be all around us. Consider the human body: It is a virtual storehouse of information, though there are still many mysteries about its functions. These *physiological* mysteries, we believe, constitute some of the most *scientific proofs* that Man is not strictly an Earth product of Evolution.

Out of literally hundreds of examples, only the major aspects of Man's physical differences from other species of primates, and from all animals, will be discussed in relationship to the Hybrid theory, extending into several chapters ahead.

1. Man is the only truly hairless mammal.
2. Only Man cries copious emotional tears.
3. Man has delicate fingers and sensitive skin.
4. The human skin has a low healing rate.
5. Man lacks diastemata (tooth gaps).
6. Subcutaneous fat in humans only.
7. Man has extraordinary facial mobility.
8. Man has a unique speaking apparatus.
9. Man swallows slowly.
10. Man has incredible eyes and seeing ability.

Through these and other data, Man's uniqueness could easily be established today via computer analysis. This would prove beyond doubt that, because of Man's many points of difference from other earthly creatures, he simply cannot be claimed as the end product of classical Evolution.

He must therefore be the result of *another unknown factor.* Of course, even the computers could not be expected to name that unknown factor, but we can — the starmen biomasters who created us. But the analysis could at least send science searching for the "unknown factor."

And we wish here to state our willingness, in fact eagerness, to have this book's full data submitted to computer analysis.

The voluminous "fine points" we have gathered will lend themselves admirably to comparative computer studies. Just as the computers handling election-day figures can quickly cut through extraneous matter and strike at the core of what the results will be, so could computers weigh the many unique qualities of mankind and quickly give the answer, figuratively speaking: *Man is not solely a product of Earthly evolution.*

Therefore, to complete our open offer to science, computer start-ups on this vital analysis await only the attention of scientists who read this book. If computer analysis proves our basic theory *wrong,* we will bow to the verdict.

But we will *not* feel it necessary to bow to the verdict of scientists and their own opinions. Let the book have a fair trial by an electronic calculator — a disinterested and completely objective third party. We feel that no scientist in advance can prejudge whether our data — which are indeed revolutionary — hold the germ of a great new truth. Scientists are prone to be humanly biased, at times, in controversial matters. Computers do not become swayed by such human failures.

We earnestly make this appeal to the scientific world to subject the theory of Hybrid mankind to this kind of accurate, unprejudiced evaluation by computer, in the name of fair play and objectivity.

Aside from computer calculations, scientists throughout the past century have had many doubts about the stubborn human animal who refuses to fit into the evolutionary pattern. One such man was England's Sir Arthur Keith, the greatest medical anthropologist of his time, the early twentieth century. He made such outstanding contributions to the field that he was knighted in 1921. At the time Sir Arthur wrote the data we will present below, he was the most honored member of the Royal College of Surgeons in London.

The time is 1911 and Sir Arthur is writing for a distinguished English science publication: [1]

> From 1890 to 1900 I devoted myself to an investigation of the Higher Primates making complete dissections of more than eighty animals. ... An extensive analysis was made of the structural characters of each of these animal forms. ... Some characters are common to all the members of the Higher Primates (Man, gorilla, chimpanzee, orang, gibbon) ... and then a considerable number which are peculiar to each member, and may be regarded as acquisitions.

By "acquisitions" he meant separate traits acquired exclusively by one species. He comes to this emphatic conclusion: "Whatever theory is propounded [evidently *beyond* Darwin's theory!] for the origin of the several members of the Higher Primates must account for their structural and functional characters."

Sir Arthur made an analytical list of the anatomical characteristics peculiar to each species, calling them "generic characters," and he came out with this summary:

MAN	GORILLA	CHIMPANZEE	ORANGUTAN	GIBBON
312	75	109	113	116

In short, each of these animals can be set apart from the others by individualistic traits. And this table, prepared by one of the world's foremost anthropologists, is of *paramount importance* as scientific support for the Hybrid Man theory.

Out of it leaps this tremendous fact: Of the higher primates, Man has 312 physiological characteristics *peculiar to humans alone,* many more than any other species.

Does this sound as though Man were some "close relation" to the great apes? Not if Man has *three times as many differences* from his "fellow primates" as any of the other specimens.

This seems to us convincing evidence that significantly lifts our concept out of the hypothetical class into a bonafide theory. And into a theory with such immense supportive evidence that it can, in our opinion, seriously challenge the classic Theory of Evolution.

Or, to put it another way, let us advance our thinking one more enormous step.

Let us suppose that if we knew all the facts of Man's origin, each and every one of those unique peculiarities of humans could be perfectly *explained* by reason of those characteristics having evolved elsewhere than on Earth — namely, in Man's space-ancestors on some other planet.

That puts us in new country again, breathing the fresh air of pioneer thinking.

For now we can begin to sketch in the first faint outlines of what our outer-space sires looked like and how they acquired unique non-earth-evolutionary characteristics that exist in *their* bodies — and perforce in *our* bodies here on Earth.

Is this to be our first glimpse of people we will meet some day? A meeting of ancestors and Hybrid progeny?

First we will point out that beyond Sir Arthur Keith's purely physical and anatomical attributes setting mankind apart from the primates, there are almost as many *physiological* differences, as partly listed before.

We shall now take those up one by one and also try to explain each in turn. In this chapter we will take up a major human mystery — *why is Man the only truly hairless mammal on Earth?*

In an authoritative book quoted from before, we are told that out of some 4,237 species of mammals existing today, all are hairy or at least partly haired.[2] Some semi-hairless creatures can be eliminated for special environmental reasons—ground-burrowing moles who always remain warm underground, armored animals like the armadillo, the wings (only) of bats, and aquatic animals like the whale and dolphin where streamlining has dictated a paucity of hairiness.

But, the author concludes, "the naked ape [Man] stands alone, marked off by his nudity from all the thousands of hairy, shaggy, or furry land-dwelling mammalian species."

Then his "punch line," so to speak — "If the hair has to go [in any species' evolutionary development], then clearly there must be a powerful reason for abolishing it."

But how does an animal species devise of *its own doing* such a "powerful reason?"

According to Evolution, there is nothing unique in Man's *background* that could be classified as a "powerful reason." The sentence should really read, "then clearly there must be a powerful reason, *in the hybridization experimentation of the starmen*, for abolishing it."

Doesn't this statement suddenly make great sense? Now, just why would the starmen want Hybrid Man to be hairless, when a fur pelt is such good protection against cold and wounds and other hazards of daily living?

Explanation. It may have been an accidental gene-trait transmitted to mankind during mating experiments of the starmen with the early men, simply because the starmen themselves were already hairless.

Why hairless? Because an intelligent race that has existed for long ages would obviously have worn clothing all that time, long enough to cause their own evolutionary change to hairlessness.

An Arctic explorer's skin, in his single lifetime, will adapt and become "tough" to withstand bitter conditions (even though it is not a trait inheritable by his children). But if the opposite happens, and men are constantly protected from any adverse environment, then the skin will not toughen up and will, indeed, let its hairy pelt wither or thin out.

In time, that is. And remember, the starmen had tens of millions of years for such evolutionary processes to operate, to the point where the gene of hairlessness became universal in all their race. But they, in turn, speeded it up and changed Man on Earth from the hairy Homo erectus to hairless Homo sapiens in a mere 500,000 years.

Doesn't that one glaring fact admit of no other explanation than the Hybrid theory? Darwin and Wallace both, and most evolutionists to this day, find Man's naked skin the greatest stumbling block to claiming earthbound natural selection for being the sole origin of Man.

To recapitulate: A hundred years ago, Darwin himself asked why Man did not have fur (hairy pelt) and found no really satisfactory answer.[3] He knew that the Australian aborigine, who has never worn clothes, is as hair-shy as Western Man. The monkeys and apes had an equal amount of time in which to develop hairless skin, but they did not.

We are maintaining that only the concept of Man as a Hybrid explains this enigma fully, completely, and perfectly.

To reiterate for clarity's sake, Man's lack of a pelt could be a direct inheritance from his outer-space ancestors. It is probable that a race which has been evolving for many millions of years would have worn clothing for eons and thus lost the need for protective hair.

Then, when Man's outer-space ancestors came to Earth and crossbred with the highest ape forms, a similarly hairless manlike creature was produced. This hybrid creature developed not just as a median form of Man with a reduced amount of hair but as an advanced form with *no* coarse hair, like the American Indians, who have no facial hair and do not shave. There is, however, apparent among humans a retrogressive type that has a virtual coating of real fur or, at least, very heavy hair. These varieties have been seen at the beaches. We will show how they, too, fit our theory, in a later chapter about simultaneous regression.

It almost seems axiomatic to say that, if evolutionary forces were entirely and solely responsible for Man's relatively hairless condition, then monkeys, apes, and other primates should show various *gradations* of hairless and hairy skins, for they have had equal time in which to develop such a condition.

But all the primates are thickly endowed with hairy fur. Man's hairless skin, therefore, supports the concept that Man can only be a unique hybrid, setting him completely apart from every earthly beast known.

A whole book by a noted zoologist, under the title of *The Naked Ape*,[4] was devoted to this strange "anomaly."

We are not yet done with the question of hair.

Each earthman carries another mystery of Evolution with him at all times — in the mop of hair on the top of his head. For, although Man is classified as a primate, he has very long hair on the *top* of his head — a *characteristic possessed by none of the anthropoids.*

If it is thought that only the ape's arboreal life keeps him "bald" by means of branches constantly yanking out his head hair, zookeepers have observed that, when living in safe cages rather than trees, apes still do not grow hair on the head.

The female of our species also possesses *very long* hair on the head, which is again a characteristic that no other mammal displays. Where did this extraordinary topknot come from? What is its purpose, and why did Man evolve it though no other member of the primate family did? Then, too, how does the long-hair characteristic tie in with the Hybrid theory?[5]

Explanation.

We again go back to when Man (Starman) evolved on a distant planet many millions of years ago. The passage of time and the unfolding of normal social patterns would, in the due course of time, cause Starman to adopt clothing, as we have stipulated. [6]

But in time, extraterrestrial Man would also adopt the custom that still prevails in many sections of our world, of covering the head with some form of hat or cap. An unusual and disturbing discovery may have been made one day. It may have been recognized that the cultures that adopted and maintained head-coverings for use indoors and out become slightly and, in some cases even greatly, decadent. Culturally, scientifically, ethically, and in other ways, their progress began to stop. These conclusions may have been at an unconscious rather than a conscious level.

It is sufficient for this book's theory, to speculate that our outer-space ancestors concluded that those cultures that went *bareheaded* were the ones that evolved most rapidly toward the ultimate in civilization.

No, we are not violating the scientific procedure and fitting a fictional fact to our theory. There is a *real reason* for bareheadedness being conducive to mental progress, because during cold weather the unprotected head needs an *additional supply of blood* in order to maintain a normal temperature. This increased blood-supply is then accompanied by nourishment that produces an increase in mental and creative activity.[7]

And so, long long ago, Starman progressed, did research, and invented. He toiled toward ever more shining goals, and he did it all bareheaded, whether knowingly or not.

The hair may also have become lengthy because there was a long period of time on Starman's original home-world — perhaps a stretch, say, of a million years — in which the head was the only unclothed part of the body in fair weather or foul. Nature gradually evolved hair follicles on the head that would grow long, luxuriant hair.

Thus, we can see how our own earthly topknot of hair, possessed by no other primate, is no mystery at all if it came as a direct hand-me-down from our outer-space ancestors. It is one more physiological piece of evidence that we humans may indeed be hybrid creations of starmen by odds, perhaps, of, in our estimation, ten to one.

No hair over our bodies, unlike the primates, yet *flowing* hair atop our heads, again unlike the anthropoids. Evolution could never have pulled that double trick, which is totally against the principles of natural selection.

One more point, based on sound scientific fact, adds to the "hair clue" for Man's hybrid status.

In the womb, a human fetus is endowed with hair all over —
which is *lost* a month or two before birth. Dwell on that a
moment.

As is well known, the human fetus goes through all the
rudimentary stages of total Evolution, from a fishlike and
amphibian form to the mammalian, finally. But if all other
primates and animals produce fetuses that remain hairy at birth,
why should *Man alone come out naked?*

We are apes *only* up to the prenatal moment when we become
Man.

That magic moment, in the womb, brings forth a touch that
can perhaps be called divine, for the starmen too are the
creatures of God. At that magic moment when we lose our hair
as an unborn child, we are forever human . . . nonearthly . . .
exalted above all lesser animals. We are also consigned to being
alone on this planet, estranged and separated by a vast gulf from
our animal companions, who are at best distant half-cousins to
us. We are demigods among common creatures.

And this, you see, goes into the mystic reaches of religion
itself, an attribute of Man's mental and spiritual life unknown to
animals that very likely was also brought to us by the starmen.

And still we are not done with this "hairy" anthropological
problem of Man with his naked skin.

Note this quotation from a book referred to before:

> In order to clear up a strange feature of our [slight]
> body-hair tracts. Close examination reveals that on our
> backs the directions of our tiny remnant hairs differ
> strikingly from those of the apes. In us they point
> diagonally backwards and inwards toward the spine.
> This follows the direction of flow of water passing
> over a swimming body and indicates that, if the coat
> of hair was modified before it was lost, then it was
> modified in exactly the right way to reduce resistance
> when swimming.[8]

From this, the author mentions how certain anthropologists drew the daring thought that before he [Man] became a hunting ape, the original ground ape that had left the forests went through a long phase as an *aquatic ape* [italics mine].... He is envisaged as moving to the tropical sea-shores in search of food (and) during this process, it is argued, he will have lost his hair like other mammals that have returned to the sea [dolphin and whale, for instance].

This rather farfetched theory does seem to explain one thing — why humans are so agile in water while our closest living primate relative, the chimpanzee, is so helpless he quickly drowns.

However, the fossil evidence for Homo aquatis is absolutely nil (at least so far), and thus the above hypothesis perforce becomes null and void at the start.

Still, how can this "patterned hair" be accounted for, if not by earthly Evolution?

Explanation.

Again, we can fit it into our theory of Man's extraterrestrial-in-part origin, along with certain assumptions.

Let us assume that after the "space age" began for the starmen, they thereafter indulged in a tremendous amount of space travel. This would include perhaps *lifelong* trips to faraway colony worlds, or even *generations* of travel with periods of high-g acceleration and deceleration.

Now, as NASA has pointed out, the easiest way to survive high-g forces with aplomb is to be *immersed in water*. Most of the shock and strain of accelerative forces are canceled out by the cushioning liquid medium in which the crew is submerged.

If we postulate millions of years of space travel by the colonizing stem of the Starman race, we see that evolutionary forces would have time to work and *streamline* their body hair for swimming. For it would be deadly dull to merely float for years in a tub of water aboard the spaceship. A bit of ingenuity would devise huge tanks in which the crew members — including women and children on colonizing trips — would swim and enjoy aquatic sports.

Or we might make the alternative assumption that during their planet-hopping activities the starmen settled at times on "water worlds" consisting of vast oceans and little land. Quite logically, they might gradually switch to an underwater life; evolutionary and mutational strains might have been produced that became perfectly adapted to a "swimming life." In due time, this would genetically cause the hair on their backs to become streamlined for swimming, and this trait would be pooled into their racial genes.

Speculative as this may sound, it is no more speculative than the "missing *marine* link," whose fossils have never been, and perhaps never will be found on Earth at the seashores. And most disastrous of all to such a theory is the implication that our Hominid ancestors first lived on the land, then took to the sea for an age, and once again *returned* to the land. But why haven't the whale, dolphin, or seal likewise returned to the land from the sea? This triple switchabout never occurred with any other creature and becomes highly untenable when applied to humanity.

Evolution is here standing on sand — wet sand. If it has no better way for explaining mankind's patterned hair, displayed by no other earthly primate, then we think that this hair anomaly comes from the superadvanced "primates" of space who fashioned Hybrid Man.

8

Physiological Clues

We will now take up further key physiological clues that point to Man being a star-bred Hybrid and not a product of purely earthly Evolution. The points below are all human peculiarities that anthropologists, anatomists, and physiologists have been unable to fit into what Man should be, according to evolutionary rules.

We will then show how these arresting details of Man's makeup can only be successfully attributed to inheritance from nonearth beings.

1. *Man alone sheds copious and "special" tears.*

The shedding of tears—from dust in the eyes, an irritation, or when crying from emotion—is a commonplace we take for granted. But it becomes a truly singular ability when you suddenly realize that no other primate, or any animal, can shed tears as we do. [1]

Yes, many animals can shed tears too. But of a *limited* quantity, with a vast difference in both degree and kind.

The tear-making ability is obviously for the protection of the eye, mostly to "wash" it. But where it takes heavy dust, severe irritations, and painful injuries to make an animal's tear-ducts work, Man's eyes water at the wispiest kind of dust of the finest particles, and Man will even find his eyes watering in a strong wind or from the sting of coldness. Animals display no such sensitivity to outside conditions.

But one factor is not duplicated at all by animals — the fact that humans shed "psychic" tears. By that we do not mean anything connected with the paranormal, simply connected to his *psyche.*

For instance, no animal sheds tears of grief or joy, nor any other emotion, as does Man. No animal can match the feat of actors who can upon demand produce tears when so required by the role they are playing. And humans shed tears far more *copiously* than animals.

It is this "psychic" tear-making ability that sets Man apart from the lower creatures by a margin far too wide to be accounted for by natural selection. In that case, chimps and other primates should shed *emotional* tears but never do.

Another curious sidelight to this matter arises. It is possible that early men were like the animals and could only shed basic, nonpsychic tears. Unfortunately, skeletal remains cannot tell the anthropologist whether or not the specimen under consideration had the ability possessed by modern Man to shed emotional tears.[2]

It seems quite likely that, before the advent of *Homo sapiens* (Cro-Magnon Man) some 35,000 years ago, all prior species of submen lacked the necessary highly developed nervous system that allowed for tears of grief, joy, frustration, anger, and all the other powerful emotions to activate the tear ducts.

Homo erectus probably only watered his eyes when volcanic dust or the smoke of raging forest fires blew fiercely into his face, or when he was suffering from the agonies of a mortal wound. He looked upon the death of others stoically, without being moved to tears. We can assume that other, finer emotions were either absent or rudimentary.

At any rate, no adequate explanation for this singular ability of a modern human to shed tears copiously, not only for the eye's protection but from an overwhelming emotional bout within himself, has ever been advanced by the evolutionists. They leave the subject strictly alone.

In our considered opinion, it seems quite likely that on Earth, Man alone acquired the large-capacity tear ducts that could supply endless quantities of tears.

And the moment it is assumed that Man is a Hybrid, a possible explanation exists of *how* Man acquired the ability to shed tears. It could simply be an ability that came from Man's interstellar ancestors, who brought it with them across the vast cold of space, and that they, in turn, inherited from their forebears.

This, of course, does not explain why and how our *ancestors* acquired this peculiar ability. An interesting line of reasoning can be used, however, to solve the mystery.

Explanation.

Previously, we have postulated that planet after planet was colonized, then discarded in due course of time as its atmosphere drifted away. It is well known that planets have a fairly well-defined life course: They grow green, they gradually decline, and they fade away.[3] This life cycle is intimately bound up with several variable factors, but it is sufficient to comment here that planets like Mars, Venus, and Earth probably have somewhat similar life cycles, and, of course, this would include countless worlds in outer space.

It is reasonable to suppose that once a colony was es-tablished on a planet, it tended to attempt to continue exercising tenure upon that planet. It would seem to follow that as moisture drifted away from a planet, as it has on Mars, the colony would try, perhaps by canal systems and other irrigation projects, to make up for the extremely dry conditions that were gradually overtaking the planet. Great dust storms would then be commonplace on those planets nearing the end of their human-habitable cycle.

Our ancestors have presumably lived through dozens of those terminal struggles for existence on dying worlds. It thus seems logical to suppose that over the millions of years of time, the planet-hopping starmen evolved a supersystem of washing away from their eyes the continuous irritating clouds of dust that were their lot.

In other words — tears and tear ducts were gained. Starman's ability to have tears available to wash out his all-important eyes is most likely a natural product of *his* Evolution. Not Evolution as we know it here on Earth, but Evolution that took place millions of years ago, on planets that are now old and cold and dead. Mars, today, would be an excellent place to have our tear-making capabilities, for it is known that great dust storms rage over that planet during certain times of the year.[4]

Along with this protective mechanism for the eye, we can assume a parallel development of Starman's emotions, finer and more complex all the time. His ever closer ties to his fellows, his growing sense of love, his keener and sharper empathy would cause him to shed tears for reasons other than physical protection of the eyeball.

He began to shed tears when his eyes somehow became the focal point or perhaps the outlet for powerful emotions at either end of the scale — grief or joy. For, after all, he could be hurt by more than a painful injury, such as the painful loss of a loved one. And he could display more than the slight glistening of basic "joy" in the eye of an animal coming upon delicious food. Starman's soulstirring emotional joys were triggered by far greater psychic rewards than mere food.

There we have it — Starman gaining another subtle and almost sublime means of expression, so vital in human relationships, of shedding emotional tears that told far more than words.

Therefore Man — the only earthly primate that sheds psychic tears, and very copiously — cries because he is a Hybrid of the crying starmen. If this is not the true explanation for human tears, then it still remains to be discovered by the evolutionists why Man evolved this ability when no other primate did. The other primates had the same conditions to combat as humans on Earth and the same length of time to evolve tears of emotion, but did not do so.

A telling point, we submit.

2. *Man's flexible hand and fingertips.*

Another bit of mystery about the human body that fits well into the concept of Man as a Hybrid is the mystery of the extraordinary sensitivity of the skin on the hands of Man as compared to similar areas on the lower animals.[5]

Not only does the ten-times-more-efficient brain of Man analyze and process information sent from his fingertips with far greater efficiency than that experienced by all lower animals, but far *more* information is sent to the human brain per second than is sent by the paws and digits of the lower animals.

Second, Man has an intricately boned hand that can grip strongly like a chimp, yet so finely organized in structure that he can wind a watch — which no ape can do. None of the anthropoids can use his thumb and index finger to pick up small things like BB-shot, nor can he type, nor hold a pencil with enough control to fill a page with fine writing.

Explanation.

There are, at present, approximately 4,300 species of mammals. There is no doubt whatsoever that nature would very much like to endow many of these creatures with a sense of touch equal to that of Man. But Mother Nature has been unable to do this for exactly the same reason, we may argue, as holds for the extraordinary neural capacity of Man's brain.

It is simply *that there has not been enough time,* here on Earth, for these most unusual human qualities to develop. They could only develop over many millions of years upon some far-off planet or planets.

Understandably, some people will argue that Man's use of tools through the last few hundred thousand years has caused this extraordinary skin sensitivity of the human hand. But, if this is so, why hasn't the kangaroo developed equal sensitivity? Kangaroos move around on their hind legs as we do and thus have their front paws free to use for a great many things. Maximum sensitivity in the skin of their "finger" pads would definitely give them advantages over other competing life-forms in their ecology.

Let's face it, considering that kangaroos have been around this old planet far longer than Man, the concept of Man as Hybrid — whose ancestors came from outer space — is the best available explanation for the supersensitive fingertips of humans.

3. *Human skin's low healing rate.*

Another factor that sets mankind apart from all other animals, including the anthropoids, is the appalling ineptitude of the human skin to heal itself quickly. Our skin has no self-healing capacity comparable to the animals, whose skin wounds heal relatively swiftly, almost like magic. No stitches are ever required, either — anytime, anywhere — with any animal.

Man alone, among all earthly creatures, requires stitches to close skin wounds over a certain "threshold" size, otherwise immobilization or disfigurement results.

Explanation.

The starmen, as a consequence of refined and completely safe living through great technology for eons of time, probably lost the power to self-heal skin wounds. It is a tenet of Evolution that if any natural endowment of the body is not used it will in time atrophy (our appendix is a racial example) in the species, just as the muscle tissue of an individual will become lax and useless if it is not exercised during long hospital-confinements in bed.

Strange, isn't it, how so many of Man's "alien" peculiarities, as contrasted to other animals, instantly make sense through the application of our premise of extraterrestrial hybridizing intervention, which gave us an inheritance of the traits of our galactic sires.

Traits that Evolution totally fails to account for by natural selection as it occurs here on Earth among all other animals — but not by Man.

4. *Man's lack of tooth gaps.*

This may seem to be a minor or even trivial point, but it is not. The shape, size, and jawbone setting of teeth in fossil skulls are a major means of determining whether extinct species are Pongid apes, Hominid ape-men, or *Homo* representatives.

And, has been mentioned, if our basic theory of the origin of Man is correct, there should be many odd peculiarities in the anatomical structure of Man that can be explained only through application of this theory. Happily, in the dental profession, one finds an odd fact that can be explained only by reference to the theory that Man may be a Hybrid.

In fact, nothing about human teeth is very mysterious except for one little item, and this goes by the uncommon word, "diastemata." Diastemata means "usable, appreciable space between the teeth."

In the dog, diastemata occurs in the very front part of the upper jaw, where the lower canine projects upward between the upper canine and the incisor. In order for this lower canine to be as long and as smoothly fitting as Evolution dictates, there is a definite space between the upper canine and its adjacent incisor tooth. This space is easily discernible and has a very useful function. It allows the important incisors to keep growing, as they are vital for hunting purposes. Thus, this trait will persist in the species for untold generations to come.

But consider Man, who has come so far up from the caves and into the Space Age Man, who is supposed to be only an Earth mammal, no different in kind, body, and brain, from any other animal who roams the Earth.

But this Man is different from all other animals; he is the only living creature *without diastemata.*[6]

Why is this so? Is it because, in part, his dentition comes from human-like species that have developed over long periods of time on some other planet?

Surely, this is a most attractive explanation. For it also explains certain minute tooth-structure characteristics that are exclusively peculiar to Man. Further, it explains how diastemata does appear in ancient human fossil skulls and then, as the brain-case becomes larger and larger in more recent specimens, the canines recede and diastemata concurrently disappears.

In our concept, the more Starman genes that were incorporated in the biological systems of the early men, the more such a characteristic as nondiastemata would show up and remain in the human stock thereafter.

It has been claimed by orthodox anthropology that Man's increase in brain capacity, plus a change in diet to one that was largely vegetarian among the early *Homos,* produced this strange anomaly of the nonexistent diastemata. However, cows and horses, who are purely vegetarians, *do* have diastemata.

Actually, we do not know of any remains of manlike bones that are associated with fossil evidence of any but an omnivorous diet. Thus, Man should *still* have diastemata. Gorillas, chimpanzees, and orangutans all have diastemata and they all had equal time, with Man, to eliminate it — and didn't.[7]

The Hybrid Theory alone seems to provide the one acceptable explanation for this odd freak of human dentition that also smoothly integrates with so many other anomalies peculiar to mankind alone.

Explanation.

To account for Starman not having teeth-spaces and transmitting that trait to us terrestrial humans, we can only make an educated surmise. Through the long development of his dental apparatus, and in order to prevent food particles from wedging between teeth and causing decay, Starman's evolutionary process closed up the tooth gaps.

That is the *whole basis of natural selection* — operating through long ages to *improve* the species in countless ways, large and small.[8]

For such a change as diastemata existing with our early Hominids, then vanishing with Homo species, to occur within 2 million years is quite unbelievable. Nature works too slowly for such radical departures from the normal pace of Evolution. Only Starman's genes and hybridization techniques could have bestowed gapless, and hence healthier, teeth on modern Man.

5. *Only humans possess a layer of subcutaneous fat.*

Subcutaneous means under the skin, of course. It does not refer, however, to layers of fat below the full derma, such as in hogs. This point of subcutaneous fat comes out of the "aquatic hominid" theory mentioned before, presumably bolstering it.

Other mammals who took to the sea, like the whale, dolphin, seal, and otter, for instance, have layers of fat or blubber under their outer skin, for purposes of keeping them warm in icy waters.

The fact that modern Man also has a layer of fat as part of the skin itself is supposedly evidence that he went through a phase of marine existence during his climb up the evolutionary ladder.

We don't believe this holds water (to make a pun) but the entrancing mystery is still there because no other land mammal has a subcutaneous swathing of thin but protective fat tissue. Why should humans alone be so endowed?

We can simply surmise that Man got it from Starman. But just where and how did Starman develop his underskin fat - layer?

Explanation

We can logically hypothesize that somewhere in Starman's long, long Evolution and colonization program, there *was* an aquatic *hominid* with whom he interbred. Why not, out of thousands of worlds he colonized? Why not a few dozen worlds covered mainly with oceans (as per previous chapter) so that the Starman colonists soon left their islands for the sea and eventually evolved into an aquatic form.

We must reiterate that Starman's enormous stretch of evolutionary development is far different in both degree and kind from our tick-of-the-clock appearance here on Earth. Anything is possible during multi-millions of years of natural selection operating in classical style, as it must have for the original Starman race.

And thus, as the colonists from aquatic worlds returned at times to the home world, to add their special traits to the gene pool of the entire race, Starman obtained a layer of fat — quite thin, mind you, not like the thick sheaths of whales — that henceforth became part of the inherited physiological characteristics he spread to other colonized planets — and to Earthman.

It bears repeating that all this is understandable in its true context only by realizing these processes began in Starman before even the simplest one-celled protozoan appeared on Earth some half a billion years ago. And the colonization of thousands upon thousands of diverse worlds then affected the gene pool of the home race, constantly modifying the original physical body of *homo universalis,* if we may coin a term.

6. *Man's extraordinary facial mobility.*

This exclusive quality of Mankind is best expressed in a previously quoted book:

> As a primate species we have the best developed and most complex facial musculature of the entire group. Indeed, we have the most subtle and complex facial expression system of all living animals. By making tiny movements of the flesh around the mouth, nose, eyes, eyebrows, and on the forehead, and by re-combining the movements in a wide variety of ways, we can convey a whole range of complex mood-changes.[9]

Further on:

> ". . .the lips of our species are a unique feature, not found elsewhere in the primates. Of course, all primates have lips, but not turned inside-out like ours. . . . [We] have permanently everted, rolled-back lips."

What all this means is that we can, and often do, as anyone knows, use facial dexterity as a form of nonverbal *communication.* Scowls, smirks, smiles, disgust, anger, bewilderment — all these can be openly read on a human face but are forever beyond the reach of the wooden-faced ape.

And only Man displays a true smile,[10] as no ape can, except in trained imitations that are meaningless and convey no type of "communication" to others of his tribe.

Finally, the book comes to its denouement over Man's remarkable "communications" ability to "talk" with his face quite expressively without using words — "Puzzling over the significance of our unique mucous [moist] lips, anatomists have stated that their Evolution 'is not as yet clearly understood.'"

A true understatement!

Then:

> . . .and have suggested that perhaps it has something to do with the increased amount of sucking that is required of the infant at the breast [through the human infant's long babyhood]. But the young chimpanzee also does a great deal of very efficient sucking and its more muscular and prehensile lips would seem, if anything, to be better equipped for the job.

Once more, the scientists are nonplussed for an evolutionary explanation that will stick to account for Man's mobile face and tremendously varied lip movements. Where, then, did this "puzzling" attribute come from but from our starmen sires?

One final small but not-to-be-slighted aspect of the human face might be introduced by Mark Twain's pithy statement: "Man is the only animal that blushes — and the only one that needs to."

Aside from Twain's typical wry humor, the statement is true. Man's smooth, bare facial skin with its fine texture is a sensitive barometer to his inner feelings — embarrassment, anger, fear, being flustered, and many more subtle variations that we are all familiar with.

All this comes about through *emotional* triggers that react on Man's internal glandular or circulatory system so as to control the flow of blood to the sensitive blood vessels in his face. Anger brings an increased flow of blood and a red face. Fear does the opposite, draining away blood and leaving the face pale.

But no primate or any animal ever blushes or indicates his internal emotional state to the eye. It is a special attribute again of Man's mobile face and is a sort of involuntary type of "communication," along with smiles, facial expressions, and the rest.

This blushing or flushing (or paling) trait of Man is not as unimportant as it might seem, for it clearly sets him apart from the lower animals, who *never* display embarrassment, for instance, in any shape, manner, or form. To even have any sense of embarrassment, one must have the mental equipment and all the finer attributes that go with it, particularly a huge repertory of emotions.

Animals may show fear, or anger, in other ways, but only in the context of a life-or-death situation, and then only instinctively. It is never part of the animal's daily living in peaceful situations. What animal could ever flush for "hurting the feelings" of another animal?

And that, again, separates Man, with his great emotional and empathetic nervous system, from all other "cold-blooded" creatures, even if they are warm-blooded mammals.

Explanation.

As to how and why our starmen ancestors developed this varied ability of facial "communication," we can simply suggest that through their megamillion years of Evolution, increasing intelligence and the need for more intimate relationships molded their facial muscles, blood vessels, and nervous systems into fine tools that could do the job.

Nature, or Evolution, comes through when something is *needed.*

9

Anatomical Clues

We have three last physiological traits of mankind to inspect, to see if they can be a product of earthly Evolution, or whether they point clearly to an extraterrestrial source. Anatomically, these three human attributes are exceedingly remarkable, as we shall see as we take them up in turn.

Man's ability to speak.

No one will deny that this is truly an ability of mankind that no other creature on Earth possesses. Dolphins may be trained in time to communicate with underwater whistles and hoots, but this communication will not even remotely resemble the intricate and highly complex system of speech used by humans.

And here we meet one of the most amazing of all revelations in anatomy. In an educational magazine, we find this report from research scientists: ". . . human speech did not develop 'out of' primate (ape) vocalization, but arose from new tissue."[1]

New tissue? Tissue not found in the throat of any other primate species!

From where?

Explanation.

Need we make the obvious statement that, quite like our facial mobility, the aforementioned new tissue came from the starmen, who probably had speech for geological ages before the first grunt came out of an ape-man on Earth.

Some gene injected into the *Homo* line on Earth, by interbreeding or biomanipulation, carried with it the "instructions" for special tissue to form in the Hominid throat to enable him to shape it as a versatile instrument for uttering an incredible variety of sounds. Sounds far beyond the howls of wolves, yowls of cats, barking of dogs, or the grunts and whines of apes.

The ape may have a primitive "language" with a vocabulary of perhaps a dozen or two "words" (different sounds). Man has twenty-six alphabet sounds making up 250,000 different words in the English language alone. And he has devised some 5,000 living and dead languages, each requiring special lip-and-throat sounds of its own.

Speech by itself makes Man stand out so starkly from all the other nontalking animals on this planet that it amounts to almost clear proof of our Starman origin.

And ponder this: True speech in the modern sense did not start with either Neanderthal or Cro-Magnon Man, though they had brain weights greater than ours. They may have had a primitive language, but systematic grammarian language was "invented" suddenly, completely, and wholly unexpectedly only some 10,000 years ago at the most.

Invented? It sounds very much like language was *handed* to us on a silver platter! The whole riddle of "instant civilization" that has baffled all archeologists would require a whole new book.

At any rate, speech is one of the most important signposts pointing to another human ability that was *imported* to Earth.

Man swallows slowly.

In connection with the above, and in the pursuit of *facts* that may be used as supportive data for the Hybrid theory, we come to another significantly odd one.

Man swallows very, very slowly in comparison to the other animals.

Man takes about six seconds to transport food from the mouth (after the act of swallowing) to the stomach.[2] All other animals have practically zero transit-time from mouth to stomach. Food in the dog's esophagus is actually shot into the stomach.[3]

Can this strange fact be interpreted as being strong support for the theory that Man is a Hybrid with outer-space ancestors? Yes, it is quite easy to do so.

Man has had the dog as his companion much of the time he has had the tranquility that supposedly would cause him to swallow slowly. But man takes six seconds and the dog takes perhaps a half or a quarter of a second. It seems that something other than tranquility of existence on Earth must be involved in causing Man to have such a phenomenally long transit time from mouth to stomach.

Explanation.

Of course, if we accept the theory that Man is a Hybrid, we see at once that many millions of years of peaceful existence on the planets of some other star or stars could produce this slow esophagal transit-time. And so, one more unusual fact is smoothly integrated into our basic theory.

By the way, to backtrack a bit, we should note that natural selection operates in such a way as to ensure that muscles will operate in the most *efficient* manner possible. Thus, if the muscles that erect each individual hair in cold weather were powerful enough to produce this stiffness in one-tenth of a second, they would have to be much larger than they are. But such speed is decidedly not necessary, so these muscles are tiny mechanisms that take up virtually no space at all in mammals' skin.

So it was with the esophagal contractual muscles of Starman, we may assume. He did not live in continuous "flight or fight" as the animals do. He could afford to swallow slowly with no fear of being interrupted or facing a fight to the death. Prior to this, undoubtedly, be had also begun to chew his food slowly, thus extracting every bit of taste pleasure out of it.

No animal can really "taste" or derive any sort of gourmet appreciation from its food when it is forced to cram that food from mouth to stomach in seconds or split seconds. That is why most omniverous animals, including the apes (who, occasionally do turn to fleshy foods out of necessity) are able to eat what humans consider "revolting" food — carrion and rotted meats, flesh with hair on it, small live animals still kicking, noisome creatures like toads and snakes, bloody intestines, and all other varieties of uncooked, uncleaned, uncut protoplasm.

It is only man who *enjoys* his food, savoring every subtle flavor and aroma as he eats in his nonhurried way. And it all goes back to Starman, lacking any threat to his life and having time to swallow leisurely. His esophagal contractural muscles became small, slow-acting affairs — which were then contributed into our earthly gene-pool by the starmen. It must, however, have taken millions and millions of years for gene and chromosome changes to reflect the change in the eating habits of Starman. And we know that truly manlike creatures have roamed the Earth for far shorter periods than the time necessary to effect these chromosome changes by Evolution.

Ergo: Slow swallowing in mankind, in sharp contrast to other earthly animals, is another physiological gift from the stars.

Man's extraordinary eyes and full-color vision.

We have saved this item, the most potent of all the physiological phenomena, for the last.

We can introduce this subject best by means of an authoritative quote, with our italics added:

> Scientists estimate that some 90% of all the information stored in the brain arrived there through the agency of the eyes. Not surprisingly, Man's eyes are attuned precisely to his needs. *For general seeing they are unsurpassed by any in the world.*

A hawk may see more sharply but cannot move its eyes easily and generally moves its head to follow its prey. A dragonfly can follow faster movement than a man but cannot focus a sharp image. A horse can see almost completely behind its head but has difficulty seeing objects straight ahead at close range.

Most important, among higher animals only Man and his nearest primate relatives have the special combination of *full stereoscopic and color vision.*

Man's eyes, placed at the front of his head rather than the sides, can focus together on an object so that it is perceived as a single three-dimensional image in the brain. Within this image his color vision enables him to pick out details by hue as well as by form and brightness.

Taken together, color and depth perception bring Man *enormous advantages over most other animals,* the majority of which are color-blind and have a relatively poor capacity to judge visual distances or focus in fine detail upon particular objects.[4]

And to top it all off, of course, Man's superb brain interprets the images he sees with much more precision and acumen than even the apes can muster with their second-class brains.

Therefore, Man's eyes with an assist from his brain are *unparalleled* instruments for viewing the outside world, head and shoulders above the chimp and other primates as well as above all other creatures alive.

The same book goes on to specify that the human visual system can distinguish among some 10 million gradations of color.[5] It can also adjust to the 10-billion-fold range between the dimmest thing it can discern (at night) and the brightest object (by day).

Now, along with Man's astounding brain, his eyes are the next most "impossible" bodily feature that natural selection could have produced. This has been plainly stated by some of the foremost experts on Evolution.

A critical book about Darwinism declares that "the Evolution of the eye in Man ... is a *major mystery;* and that, small as it is, the eye is an enormously complex structure of retina, cornea, rods and cones, visual purple, muscles, nerves, and fluids. *Supporters of natural selection tend to play down this complexity,* while opponents emphasize it." (Italics added.)[6]

Why do they tend to play it down? Because it makes hash out of the laws of natural selection. There is no way to trace the development of the eye from the most primitive forms of life all the way to the fantastically sharp seeing organ of Man.

But don't take our word for it. Here is what the authorities say.

Dr. William Paley, Archdeacon of Carlisle, demands to know how chance alone — by the workings of "blind" natural selection — can possibly produce such elaborate designs of organs as displayed by both the human eye and brain.[7]

Richard B. Goldschmidt, first-class geneticist of the University of California, calls it the "famous old problem of the eye."[8] He says the development of the human eye depends on one basic premise — photosensitivity. But when you try to explain how one certain portion of human protoplasm should become selectively adapted to seeing by photosensitivity, he says, you bog down when confronted with the great number of biological details of the eye. He concludes by stating his opinion that it is "impossible" to explain the human eye and its workings via the Theory of Evolution, no matter how cleverly you mix up natural selection, mutations, and adaptations.

But the clincher comes from Professor Hardin, University of California, who stated:

> *"That damned eye* [his italics] ... the human eye... which Darwin freely conceded to constitute a severe strain on his Theory of Evolution. Is so simple a prin- ciple as natural selection equal to explaining so complex a structure as the image-producing eye? Can the step-by-step process of Darwinian Evolution carry adaptation so far?"[9]

Our *italics* follow in his final words: *"Competent opinion* [among evolutionists and biologists] *has wavered on this point."*

And as the book's author points out, competent opinion has never to this day come up with an acceptable explanation for the human eye.

To cap it all off, let us hear from the master himself, who quite honestly wrote in his original book on Evolution: "To suppose that the eye with all its inimitable contrivances ... could have been formed by natural selection, seems, I freely confess, absurd in the highest degree."[10] And he never did come up with any attempt to cover that major black mark against his theory.

We think we can safely say that next to the human brain (see chapters ahead) the human pair of eyes is another strike-three count against classical Evolution. Its followers cannot explain the phenomenal eyesight of the human race, because it didn't arise on Earth at all.

Yet, if it came from our starmen sires, just how did *they* obtain this tremendous visual gift?

Explanation.

Actually, since it seems entirely out of range of natural selection on this or any world, we cannot resort to saying that superlong stretches of Evolution produced Starman's eye on his home-world.

The answer in that case must be *genetic control and deliberate improvement of the eye on their part.*

And why not? If they long ago realized, after their evolutionary climb to humanhood, that the eye furnished 90 percent of all outside stimuli to feed data to the brain, then why would they not set about to use advanced biotechniques to develop their eyesight themselves? Geneticists on Earth, who are probably one-thousandth as skilled as the starmen, are already talking excitedly of "improving" the human race by genetic means. Assuming they can isolate the genes that control the formation of the eyes and learn to manipulate them in new ways, even earthly scientists could then proudly display a man with 100-100 (percent) vision.

But by the time the starmen came to Earth to speed up Evolution for mankind, it was past history how they had endowed themselves with super-eyes. And those super-eyes, or some factor of them, were then inherited by the human race during hybridization procedures.

Super-eyes, which plagued Darwin from the start and are still plaguing evolutionists today, a century later.

Our theory of Hybrid Man being a created product of the starmen almost presupposes that their biogenetic doings are, to our limited minds, superscientific "Magic," nothing less. Hence, our theory does not have to strain to make the assumption that Starman, on his own world, *speeded up his own Evolution artificially.*

Along with Hybrid Man on Earth, Starman "created" himself in his new image, vastly superior to anything the blind-chance syndrome of natural selection could ever accomplish for him. If you take the "blind chance" out of Evolution, you can save millions of years and reach your goal without false starts and aborted biological changes consuming ages of time.

So why not take over the reins from natural Evolution and improve their own breed? The marvelous human eye, the superb brain, and all the other special attributes of man may actually have been achieved by "auto-evolution." Self-evolution as master geneticists took over the task of changing the human body and its organs into a new and superior kind of "animal species" that nature itself could never produce.

In that case, Darwinian Evolution and natural selection had no part at all in the ultimate product of the starmen, and never could have. This would account particularly for the human brain, that incredible organ that was an "overendowment" created by Starman himself, step by step, as he learned how the wondrous DNA chain of genes was the key to constant improvement of the breed.

A startling thought. A shocking thought. We will not pursue it here except to offer it as an alternative explanation to Evolution, which even in its snail-slow march might *never* have created the powerful brain of thinking humans.

Incidentally, classical Evolution depends heavily on natural "mutations," members of species in whom genes randomly produce a "better" animal. By interbreeding, these mutations supposedly multiply and eventually replace the older species that is "inferior."

Modern genetics give a resounding "no way!" to that. First of all, science has yet to discover where any species of any creature, from small to large, is *presently* in the stage of mutating into another type of species. And this happens to be *essential* to the theory of Evolution, that new species should be constantly arising as they did in the past.

Furthermore, when mutations are found in nature, they are predominantly abnormalities that are inferior to the main species, not superior. In fact, the evidence of modern experiments in producing even artificial mutants indicates that, by far, they are deleterious to the species. No useful mutations have appeared in the lab, and none are expected. The consensus is that over 99 percent of all mutated genes are harmful.

In research with humans, geneticists (who are indeed a thorn in the side of evolutionists) believe that a good gene that can reproduce and become effective is a rare event. It occurs only once in a million animals, or once in the lifetime of a million human beings. Mutations are so far apart that it happens only once in 100,000 generations.

The knock-out blow is that researchers estimate any single human gene may remain stable for 2.5 million years. Evolution's dependence on the mutational straw it grasps is a lost cause.

On that basis, it would seem only the *deliberate* production of new and worthwhile genes by the starmen could reasonably have created themselves into a unique form of superbrained species that would never exist under the rules of the far-short strivings of evolution.

Reviewing all the remarkable physiological anomalies of humanity, we might point out that Man is actually a *walking museum of anatomical curios from another planet,* if scientists would but take note and bury their prejudices against new ideas.

It is rather ironic to think of researchers laboring in biolabs day and night, archeologists digging industriously around the world, and anthropologists painstakingly patching fossil bones together, in the attempt to solve the mystery of Man — *when all it would take is to examine Man himself.*

One man who recognized this is Professor John Tyler Bonner of Harvard, who deplored the lack of answers we had as to the mysteries of Evolution.[11] He then said, "The answers may come with further study, but they must be discovered by physiological experiments, not by complacent speculation."

Physiological experiments! Sage words, and exactly what we are recommending in this chapter as an untapped gold mine of information about ourselves.

We might say that Man is the "hardware" (material proof) that pins down his extraterrestrial origin, and the germ of his species was really the *first* thing brought in from space (by the starmen), not the moon rocks of the Apollo expeditions!

If the biologists would only look, what fantastic "records" are locked up in our genes and chromosomes that ordered our transformation into a thinking, talking, inventing creature? That elevated us to a majesty and destiny beyond the power of blind evolutionary forces to mold?

The Bible constantly reiterates that "divine" intervention lifted stumbling mankind into the light. Can it be (is it heresy to seek the truth?) that starmen have been the "angels" and emissaries of God, in an indirect way, with the mission of creating sentient life on Earth? Are we the "Sons of God" by virtue of colonization by a people so highly advanced in morals, ethics, intelligence, and spiritual wisdom that it is part of a Greater Plan than we know?

10

Sexuality Clues

If Man is distinctly different from the apes and all animals in physiological ways, there is a still greater gulf between them in Man's sexual habits and his reproductive cycle. Sexually, the human animal's activities are vastly removed from any resemblance to animal sexuality.

This is put forth succinctly by an authority who says:

How does our sexual behavior compare with that of the other living primates? Straightaway we can see that there is much more intense sexual activity in our own species than in any other primates, including our closest relations. . . . The precopulatory patterns in apes are brief and usually consist of no more than a few facial expressions and simple vocalizations.

Copulation itself is also very brief. In baboons, for instance, the time taken from mounting to ejaculation is no more than seven or eight seconds, with a total of no more than 15 pelvic thrusts, often fewer. The female does not appear to experience any kind of orgasm.[1]

Pointing out that sex foreplay occupies a much longer time between human couples, that the actual joining takes minutes rather than seconds, and that both the female and male often enjoy mutual orgasm, the author concludes:

"Clearly, the naked ape [Man] is the sexiest primate alive."

We hardly need proof, looking around at the 4 billion or more human beings living on Earth today, outnumbering all animals by species except perhaps a few prolific rodents. It is nothing less than superfecundity. (And that, incidentally, is also a hallmark of the breeding vigor of any hybrid—another clue to our basic theme's soundness.)

Why is Man, far above and beyond any other animal, such a sexually active creature? The human female, first and foremost, has no counterpart in the animal kingdom, for she alone:

1. Enjoys orgasm during sex intercourse.
2. Is almost always "in heat."
3. Has a vaginal angle conducive to either front or back mating.
4. Possesses voluptuous breasts and buttocks that are spurs to male desire.
5. Possesses a hymen during virginity.

Taking these traits in turn, the author above states, "If there is anything that could be called an orgasm [in female apes] it is a trivial response when compared with that of the female of our own species."[2]

The orgasms experienced by human females are hardly a "trivial response," as most males on Earth well know. It is part and parcel of the sex act among us, usually expected and often taken for granted. The passion and body response of the female during coitus make her an *equal* partner to the always-eager male, a situation that is obtained with no other animal on Earth, apes included.

They do not "enjoy" sex in the sense that humans do. It is more a "reproductive duty" instilled instinctively in them to ensure the survival of the species.

Again it is pointed out that:

> If the human male continues to copulate for a longer period of time (than the briefest time required), the female also eventually reaches a consummatory moment, an explosive orgasmic experience, as violent and tension-releasing as the male's . . . Some females may reach this point very quickly (and enjoy repetitions) . . . But on the average it is attained between ten and twenty minutes after the start of copulation.[3]

And that also is a vast departure from copulating male animals, all of whom reach their ejaculatory climax in seconds. Human males take minutes and can often extend the sex act longer than a half-hour in order to give the female maximum orgasmic delight and also to increase the degree of his own climactic rapture when he reaches his orgasmic paroxysm.

Only in Man, and Woman, is there "sex for sex's sake," or embraces outside of the want or need for offspring, purely for the sensory ecstasies involved. In fact, what with birth-control methods and social acceptance of sex "fun" as normal, there is far more indulgence in sex for pure pleasure than for conceiving children.

There is more than just a hedonistic pleasure-seeking syndrome in this. Man's essential drive for sex contacts and gratification thereof is definitely linked with his *intelligence,* incredible as this may seem. Also much of culture, ethics, indeed the fabric of civilization itself, is a more-or-less direct offshoot of Man's great preoccupation with sex gratification, for it all involves the very hormones and brain stimulants that suffuse the human body, and also sublimation of the sex-drive into creative channels.

But let us return to the basic factors, which are established scientific fact, that make men and women the sexiest animals alive.

Point number two — human females are always in heat. The previous oft-quoted authority says:

> "The period of sexual receptivity of the female monkey or ape is more restricted [than in humans]. It usually lasts for about a week, or a little more, of their monthly cycle. Even this is an advance on the lower mammals, where it is limited more severely to the actual time of ovulation, but in our own species the primate trend toward longer receptivity has been pushed to the very limit, so that the [human] female is receptive at virtually all times."[4]

That means day and night, and winter, spring, fall, and summer. There is no "closed" season.

He points out another thing completely unknown among the primates or lower animals:

> "Once a female monkey or ape becomes pregnant, or is nursing a baby, she ceases to be sexually active. Again, our [human) species has spread its sexual activities into those periods, so that there is only a brief time just before and just after parturition [birth] when mating is seriously limited."

One might paraphrase an old saying: Time, death, taxes, and *sex* go on forever.

It is also well known and accepted in modern society, as extolled in numerous "sex manuals," that a person's sex life need not stop (and never really has stopped) when his or her procreative years are over. People are urged, one might say, to continue enjoying sexual delights far beyond the time of menopause in women or the onset of senior years in men. We constantly read in our news media of couples remarrying in their sixties and, in many cases, not just for platonic "companionship."

Man, the sexy animal, spreads mating delights throughout his life, almost to the hour of natural death.

And we might note this strange difference between other animals and Man, even though it does not deal with what nature bestows. In other animals, the male is endowed by nature far more attractively than the female, whereas with humans the female adorns herself with cosmetics, jewelry, perfume, and employs many other skilled ways to attract the male.

A woman hardly "dresses well" for other women, nor for herself. Let's face it, it is to create interest and incipient sex desire in males. Much of our modern advertising, too, features the physical charms of voluptuous women, which is both an appeal and stimulant to the male's sexual drives.

All this lifts human sex relations entirely out of the realm of animal sex under evolutionary rules. Where did all these "oversexed" aspects of mankind come from?

If we accept the assumption that mankind's true ancestors came from space, we can also assume that the starmen, the original humans, lived for virtual eons of time on their home-planet. And there the basic laws of survival operated for those eons of time, far longer than on Earth.

If so, wouldn't the woman who enjoyed sex the most, adorned herself to be the most ravishing beauty, and thus attracted the most desirable men into her embrace, win out in that particular "battle of the fittest," while her weaker and less appealing sisters would fall by the wayside? If, then, random mutations eventually produced a woman (among the starmen race) who could enjoy orgasm as fully as the male, she would obviously become the choicest sex partner.

In short, she would be the sexiest and count the most males among her conquests.

And there is reason to believe, because it is the rule in the animal kingdom, that it is the human female who "invites" the male rather than the male "pursuing" the female. Social custom may twist this around but it does not conceal the basic facts.

Furthermore, this alters the popular concept that it is only the male who is promiscuous and wants to impregnate every possible female who is willing, as part of nature's "tricks" to make the race increase. Many students of human nature in relation to the sex-drive believe that it is women who have the urge to quite naturally, if secretly, seek a wide variety of sex partners for the instinctive drive to have offspring.

And it is the human male who, through his wishes for possession of any given female, has set up moral codes and monogamous marriages, not to restrict his own promiscuousness but to confine that of the female. A sorry example is the medieval chastity belt.

This is not an attempt to call all women "wantons" by nature, but simply a review of the inescapable fundamentals of our sexual natures, in order to get the picture straight.

It is far too long and intricate a subject to go into, but quite possibly Earthman himself did not institute strict morality and marriage to limit too much sexual freedom — but that these sexual "laws," too, came from the starmen.

Back to the human female on Earth. The breasts and buttocks of women are a universal stimulant to men's sex urges. Yet why do our anthropoid female cousins display no such natural enticements or "feminine charms"?

Female apes have hardly noticeable breasts, mostly hidden by hair, and their buttocks protrude very slightly. The erotic effect of prominent and well-shaped breasts, and their tactile enjoyment by men (and by the women themselves) is definitely a spur to sexual union. Also the well-rounded buttocks lending a woman her seductive "curves" are a sex magnet to male eyes and gonads.

Since we cannot see how Evolution excluded all other primates to give only human females such extra sex-gifts, we again must conclude that they come from the genes of the starmen — who must have been even sexier than Earthpeople!

And we can immediately make another suggestion as to *why* the starpeople should have naturally (or deliberately) promoted sexual intercourse by these body developments — in order to *populate the universe*. To carry on a vast colonization program involving thousands of other worlds, they had to produce offspring by the millions, billions, indeed trillions.

Only great sex activity could accomplish that goal. And that sex drive came down to us. At least this is a logical attempt to explain humanity's super sex-drives, whereas Evolution is dumb for an answer.

The vaginal angle of the human female is another great departure from the primates. As the above author puts it:

"Finally, there is the basic anatomy of the female vaginal passage, the angle of which has swung forward to a marked degree, when compared with other species of the primates. It has moved forward more than would be expected simply as a passive result of the process of becoming a vertical species [walking upright]."[5]

Now comes a direct criticism of Evolution: "Undoubtedly, if it had been important for the female of our species to present her genitals to the male for rear mounting, natural selection would soon have favored that trend and the females would by now have a more posteriorly directed vaginal tract."

But natural selection did *not* follow the "favored trend" and instead "it seems plausible to consider that face-to-face copulation is basic to our species, and in America, investigators have estimated that in their culture 70 percent of the population employs this position."

But *why?* If it cannot be the expected result of natural selection, how did this anti-evolutionary trend ever come about?

The zoologist author has no answer himself, but we have. Namely, another sex innovation fostered through starmen's long evolutionary climb to make mating more desirable, because in the face-to-face position the partners can kiss as well as copulate. Surely that is no small addition to the act of physical love, as no doubt most men and women reading this will agree, excluding prudes and the "sex-is-sin" contingent (if any today).

What more intimate and endearing way to make love with the acme of sensual titillations can there be than for a man and woman to embrace frontally, with both lips and genitals joined? If this produces the greatest orgasms and most copious ejaculations in men, would that not be exactly what the starmen would promote in their prolific drive to put human-like progeny on multithousands of worlds in the galaxy?

It all comes down to the ingenious utilization of the basic function of sex — to bring male sperm in contact with the female ovum in the surest and most decisive way by means of both oft-repeated sex acts and high-powered performances.

All this may seem "lascivious" in tone, but many psychologists can state the reasons why the sexual aspects of our lives are highly important by having improved our intellectual capacities and promoted the advent of invention, science, and all civilization.

Another sex "stimulant" displayed by both males and females is that our lower earlobes hang loose and fleshy — again an anatomical feature denied to any other primate. Pulling at the partner's earlobes, or even nibbling them, is a well-known practice in sex foreplay among Homo sapiens.

We can readily surmise that through ages of time, pulling at the earlobes gradually elongated them for the star-people, to blossom out eventually as a physical aphrodisiac. The starmen certainly did not miss a bet in perfecting the fine art of sexual lovemaking. And nature (Evolution) wholeheartedly cooperated, since she *did* have an axe to grind — namely, preservation of the race.

Starman extended it to the preservation of pleasure as well as race.

He aimed for maximum proliferation in order to spread his kind throughout space in all directions and to every habitable world. It was a "mission," we can safely surmise, that was fulfilled with enthusiasm.

Last, among the sexual and reproductive aspects of the human female, we come to one more special factor shared by no other primate or animal. The female hymen.

"Another related feature," says the zoologist we've quoted extensively, "and one that appears to be unique to our species, is the retention of the hymen or maidenhead in the female.... Its persistence means that the first copulation will meet with some difficulty."[6]

Why the hymen should exist cannot be explained by that author, and even our explanation in this case must be rather tentative.

We can only assume that it is a *protective* device for the young female, to prevent dust or grime or harmful substances from inadvertently entering the vagina. (It certainly doesn't and isn't meant to deter a determined penis, however.)

Taking the racial point of view, the human female's vagina is *very precious.* It is the life-giving receptacle that must be available to the male semen. Thus, it must be given extra protection, which no other animal receives in the same manner. Life is cheap under nature's tooth-and-claw setup, but was far from cheap to the colonizing starmen, who could not afford to lose lives unnecessarily.

Once the young girl is ready and her first copulation breaks the hymen, it can be assumed that from then on there is no further need for vaginal protection during maturity.

This nature-grown sheath for the immature human female's vagina can again be attributed to natural selection in the starpeople's Evolution. Young females without the hymen would tend to develop diseases or injuries that killed them off or rendered them infertile. Natural selection would favor those who gradually developed that vaginal guard to the sex aperture, until, in time, the entire feminine portion of the race was so equipped.

Now we come to the human male and whatever special qualities he displays that relate to his sexual equipment. In his case there is only one focal point — his penis.

The peculiarity that follows is quite astounding in any and all terms — biological, anatomical, physiological, and sexual.

It seems that Man is the only primate without a penis bone. [7]

Not only that, in a broader degree he may be the only land-roving mammal without a penis bone. How can this be? How can our supposedly infallible laws of natural selection endow and maintain penis bones in the large primates and in the largest mammal families and then, in one fell swoop, give Man and only Man the largest primate brain *as well* as no penis bone?

Both factors are completely out of phase with Evolution. Do we have here, in this incredible inconsistency, another beautiful example of how Man must be a Hybrid? And how his extraordinary characteristics, if correctly interpreted, lead invariably to the conclusion that Man's ancestry, in large part, came from outer space?

To see how this fits into our Hybrid theory, let us consider other animals. Deer, cows, dogs, cats, horses, and other animals are known to have penis bones,[8] and, amazingly so do whales.[9] The incomplete but already significant evidence indicates that Man is the sole land-roving mammal without such a bone.

The penis bone is recessed ordinarily but when the animal is sexually excited, the bone thrusts upward into the flesh of the penis to give it rigidity as it extends out from beneath the belly.

This situation of leaving out human males is virtually without parallel, for where nature endows one animal preferentially, she usually shows at least partial endowment of this same characteristic to related species. Astoundingly, this has not happened to Man. The other large primates all have penis bones. And why, may we ask?

There are several good reasons why animals require the penis bone, which makes their sex organ very rigid. Wild animals often have to mate rapidly out in the open and are helpless at the time and open prey for predators. So the less time taken for the sex act, the better. Also the male, in many cases, must force his attentions on the female (or at least consummate their union rapidly so she does not dash off at some sudden fright or out of impatience).

Perhaps most pertinent is the fact that the male, in almost all species, has to battle rival males to win the female in heat at the moment. By the time the fierce struggle is over, the male may be so weary and exhausted, even wounded, that if he did not have a penis bone to achieve a firm erection, the sex act might never be consummated and the species would die out.

But Man needs no penis bone. Why?

With little effort, we can trace this anomaly back to the starmen. In their case, the lack of the above mating hazards for long eons plus the human female's ready willingness and cooperation during the sex act, would inevitably through evolutionary laws eliminate the need for a stiffening penis bone. Instead, more blood is allowed to flow into the penis at pressures sufficient to erect it to almost bonelike rigidity. This, in turn, increases the pleasure response of the penis with no space taken up by a bone that has no sensitivity and does not contribute to orgasm.

Hence, when Starman, without a penis bone, mated with early *Hominid* or *Homo* females on Earth, he genetically transmitted this same attribute to the hybrid human race that was to follow.

But much more amazing is the second endowment featured by the human male — the largeness of his penis.

It is well known to all anatomists and sexologists that the human male's penis in erection is larger, thicker, and longer than that of any other primate. And by far.

As our authoritative zoologist puts it, the human organ "is not only long when fully erect but also very thick when compared with the penises of other species [of primates]. The chimpanzee's is a mere spike by comparison."[10]

There is a clue here to the great heights of orgasm attained by a woman during coitus, for, he continues:

> This broadening of the penis results in the female's external genitals being subjected to much more pushing and pulling during the performance of pelvic thrusts [by the male]. With each inward thrust of the penis, the clitoral region is pulled downward, and then, with each withdrawal, it moves up again. Add to this the rhythmic pressure being exerted on the clitoral region by the pubic region of the frontally copulating male, and you have a repeated massaging of the clitoris that — were she a male — would virtually be masturbatory.

In short, the male's large penis in action not only performs the basic function of ejaculating its semen, but in the interim also "masturbates" the female and excites her sensitive clitoris so powerfully that she experiences tremendous surges of orgasmic pleasure. No wonder she "comes back for more," so that this feature, too, enhanced the needed proliferation of the starmen, who aimed to fill the universe with their kind.

The same author has another rather wry comment on what should be Man's most admired possession:

> "He [Man] is proud that he has the biggest brain of all the primates but attempts to conceal the fact [publicly, at any rate] that he also has the biggest penis, preferring to accord that honor falsely to the mighty gorilla."[11]

That huge beast, however, has a penis only *half as long* as a human male's during erection. Since the average for men is about six inches, that leaves the gorilla with a paltry three inches.

This is immediately astonishing, for the male gorilla can stretch to ten feet in length and weigh nearly 500 pounds. One would automatically think such a giant creature would have proportionately larger genital organs than puny men.

Since it is likely that all earthly Hominids and Homos (with no way for anthropologists to actually check via fossils) had small penises, this again is a telling point, indicating that the modern male's sexual apparatus was not acquired from any earthly "missing link" but from our absentee link among the stars — the starmen.

As to why the starmen should have developed such a large sex organ, there is an interesting but complex explanation involving the relationship between the spacemen and their women in general. Only the starpeople, it seems, developed a pleasure-for-pleasure's-sake attitude toward sex, aside from its reproductive function.

This could only come from a superior brain that could reason and think and feel beyond the here-and-now and follow new lines of total body/intellect integration into areas of sensuality forever beyond animals.

And by improving the relationship between Starman and wife — and later Man and wife — via heightened sexual enjoyment, the family-unit or stable-coupling concept greatly advanced civilization in ways too subtle to follow in this book.

Man being proud of his brain but not (except in private, perhaps) his penis — that phrase may be the real keynote of it all in another way.

If we assume that the starmen have brain-cases of 3,000 cubic centimeters or more (1,300 cubic centimeters for Earthmen), the heads of their babies would be inordinately large and require women, by Evolution, to develop larger vaginas.

This would in turn spur the male to develop a larger penis. Certainly a small penis in an enlarged vagina would reduce the frictional factor during coitus and thus deprive the male, not to mention the female, of full orgasmic ecstasy. Therefore, it is overwhelmingly logical to surmise that natural selection among starmen favored men with larger and larger penises as vaginas enlarged. Through this, he would gain the favors of more women and have more children, among whom the male offspring would by inheritance also have larger sex organs, and so on.

At any rate, this incongruous anatomical riddle of the 160-pound human male having a penis twice as big as the 500-pound gorilla, if it cannot be explained by the physiologists or evolutionists, could well be explained by Earthmen being Hybrids resulting from the union of starmen with oversized, and Hominids with undersized, sex organs.

11

Reproductive Clues

One other key anomaly in human women relates to the aftermath of sex intercourse — the reproductive cycle. In the conceiving of the human embryo, a really startling fact has baffled the physiologists.

Among all animals on Earth, only the fertilized ovum of the human female burrows into the wall of the uterus, to remain securely anchored so that the budding embryo will not be dislodged and perhaps swept away as a discharge. This is a physiological procedure that no other primate follows.[1]

Another reference[2] points this up by saying, "It would appear that the smaller human ovum enters earlier and, unlike the monkey [and ape] ovum, soon becomes completely buried in the endometrium [outer wall of the uterus]." Further on, "Indeed, the [human] ovum behaves like an invading parasite." Another work described it as a "savage invasion" of the uterus wall.

All this is to emphasize that the implantation of the fertilized ovum in the human female's uterus is a much more rapid and penetrative process than in other primates. Man is again unique on Earth by his female producing an ovum that tenaciously burrows into the wall of the womb and remains far more firmly fixed than with any other animal known.

No prevailing scientific explanation is available for this distinct reproductive peculiarity of mankind. But on the assumption that Man is a Hybrid, it would be comparatively easy to explain this strange aspect of the human reproductive system as coming from our star-sires.

We can even surmise why and how our outer-space ancestors acquired this characteristic, for an answer can be postulated that is quite compatible with what is known about Evolution and the reproductive system of man. Exploring a little of the latter will contribute to an understanding of the hybrid theory.

Competent authorities have noted that Man's reproductive system is *superior* in a very real sense to that of the gorilla, chimpanzee, and other apes. This superiority results from the fewer spontaneous abortions or accidental miscarriages that human females have, on the average, over other members of the primate family. This is due to the fact previously noted: The "savage" burrowing of the human ovum into the wall of the uterus, where it cannot be easily jarred loose by violent physical exertion or by a sudden jolt, such as a fall or minor automobile collision.

This is not true of the other primates. A fall to the ground, a fight, a life-or-death flight through the trees will often bring on miscarriage. Poof — another heir or heiress is lost forever to the family.

Man stands out distinctly on this score from other primates. It permits a very reasonable explanation. We will assume that it was on some distant planet or planets where the valuable characteristic that all human females — earthly and otherwise — now possess was first evolved. The fertilized ovum came to use great speed and force to burrow into and to become a literal part of the wall of the womb, where it remained safe and sound.

Now for our prime point.

The self-attaching, tenacious ovum probably came about *after starmen achieved space travel.* It was either a natural adaptation that occurred through many thousands of years and many space trips for the race, or it was a *deliberate* gene-induced trait because of its importance.

Why important? The well-protected ovum was then undisturbed by space flight with high-g take-off and landing due to jolting acceleration and deceleration.

In order to planet-hop, according to our basic picture of the starmen, our pregnant women forebears had to develop the superefficient ovum-burrowing technique so that they would not lose their babies when journeying to some other planet. It is conceivable that, through the millions of years Starman's forebears could "leisurely" develop and evolve, it was those families in which this ovum-burrowing ability was most advanced that were also the most prolific, because of fewer miscarriages. Such a physical development was necessary for their constant and somewhat rough space-travel technique.

Yes, this theory would follow "classic Evolution" in the case of the starmen. We do not deny that its principles might have applied for our space ancestors, even if not for Earthmen.

The key factor is that for them Evolution had *time* to operate for many millions of years.

What we are saying is that mankind on *Earth* could not have evolved in so short a time as the anthropologists suppose, and that this time distortion badly undermines Darwin's theory.

We think it is self-evident that any remarkable trait like the burrowing-ovum, if not shared by the other primates, means that such a trait had no time to develop in the great apes — nor *in Man on Earth.*

Man only obtained this inherited blessing by the grace of his star sires.

We take up another matter now, going back to the peculiar linkage between the large human penis and the large human brain, which leads quite naturally into the subject of human babies, with heads at birth that are *huge* compared to any other primate. They have to be huge to contain the bulky human brain, literally gigantic in comparison to all other species.

Medical men claim that the greatest single problem when the modern female is in childbirth is that of successfully passing the enormous head of the infant through the birth canal.[3]

At the time of birth, the human brain comprises about 15 percent of the infant's weight, whereas in the adult the brain is only about 2.2 percent of the total body weight. The limiting factor in the increase in Man's cranial capacity is the ability of the human female to give birth successfully to larger-and larger-headed infants.

The limit in size that can occur through birth restrictions had, quite possibly, been reached among Earth people, and ample evidence is available to support this contention. The principal proof is Aurignacian (Cro-Magnon) Man's brain-case being larger than modern man's by about 100 cubic centimeters or more.[4] Many primitive women must have died in childbirth while attempting to give birth to extraordinarily large-headed children.

Today, when there is any question about the mother's ability to deliver a child successfully, the doctor simply orders a Caesarian section. This surgical practice opens the way for the evolutionary development of people on Earth who have larger and larger heads, with comparable intellects.

In connection with the above, why should human women only, never animals, have birth pains? Is it because something is out of line and the baby brain is just too large for the birth canal? But Evolution would certainly not *handicap* any species this way, requiring the use of Caesarian section never known to nature.

Isn't the answer boomingly clear here?

That our big-brained star sires, by injecting their cranial genes into the Hominids on Earth, thereby caused big-headed babies to be born, even though the Earth female's reproductive apparatus had not "caught up"? If not, what other answer is there for this anatomical discrepancy, which evolutionary laws would decisively say cannot exist?

The experts have this to say:

> It was these twin needs [intellectual capacity and childhood learning] that together were responsible for perhaps the most extraordinary of all the changes which have marked man's evolutionary history. A little reflection will show that, as the human brain grew larger, human females were faced with a peculiarly difficult situation. An infant's skull had to be big enough to house the enlarged human brain. At the same time, it also had to be small enough to emerge through the mother's birth canal. The obvious solution, one might suppose, would have been for females to acquire a larger birth canal. But they couldn't.[5]

Why not? Why couldn't Evolution match those two conditions?

The experts give a significant answer: "The characteristics needed for bipedal walking made the enlargement of the birth canal a physical impossibility beyond a certain limit."

Why is that an impossibility? They really should have explained further. The authors have never yet heard a good explanation for this claim (and would deeply appreciate, as a matter of fact, hearing from any authority who can decisively clear up the point).

As an engineer, one of the authors, Max H. Flindt, can conjecture as to why the female pelvis cannot accommodate a larger birth canal for our too-large-headed babies. Going purely by mechanistic principles, he surmises that as the pelvis would widen, the underneath leg support would be inadequate. But the human female's legs could not become sturdy enough without a radical change in bone structure. The only alternative for nature would be to add pelvic support in the form of internal "padding" or "webbing." But this would simply defeat its purpose by again restricting the enlargement of the birth canal.

Hence, in pure engineering terms, it seems that natural selection simply could not produce a female with a larger birth canal without practically changing her into a horse in build. But that would change the species too much in the "wrong" direction and natural selection would call a halt.

This probably means, then, that even the starmen's females have always had birth canals too small for big-headed babies, which strongly suggests the possibility that they *deliberately* used gene techniques to increase brain size, at the same time accepting the penalty of the inadequate birth canal that nothing could correct.

All such rarefied speculation aside, the too-small birth canal of human women remains as a complete puzzle to biologists, gynecologists, anatomists, and all others concerned — especially the evolutionists.

Any tentative explanations we have seen are purely argumentative, obfuscating the issue. We feel it is much less in the nature of obfuscation for us to intimate that this out-of-phase aspect of the big-headed child and too-small birth canal is the result of *tampering* with normal Evolution.

Tampering with a purpose, done by the starmen.

And in their vast, complex, and difficult program to introduce super-Evolution and produce big-brained humans in record time, they were unable to take care of all contingent factors, particularly enlargement of the female birth canal.

No other animal has this big-headed birth problem. Only Man. Evolution, which is supposed to be "fair" and "impartial" with all species, must obviously be zeroed out as an explanation in relation to this badly askew birth anomaly among humans.

After birth comes the growing child. And again we come up against something that sets Man's offspring entirely apart from those of apes or any lower animal. For the human child goes through an extraordinarily long childhood unmatched by any anthropoid youngling.

First of all, the human baby is utterly helpless at birth and must depend solely on its mother or its parent to survive. A newborn monkey or ape, on the other hand, can cling to its mother's fur from birth onward, already gaining a degree of independent action.[6]

The human child continues to remain comparatively helpless much longer than any primate offspring. Human babies don't learn to walk until they are about fifteen months of age (average), while primate young are able to scamper around within a month.

Primates are all "adults" at the age of one to three years and become independent of their mothers.[7] Humans are still adolescent into the teen years before they become relatively self-sufficient.

In fact, for one-fourth or one-fifth of our lives we are "growing up," physically and mentally.

In the mental arena, this does not mean a slower rate of learning than primates but an immensely greater *amount* of learning to be absorbed. Where the anthropoid's learning processes stop with the simple fundamentals of life and survival, human learning goes on into motor skills, speech, writing, schooling, and thought-development, all of these forever beyond the reach of apes.

One completely unbridgeable chasm separates ape children from human children — the ability to learn to speak. All progress in the ape stops short of this tremendous new step. For the human child, it is the mere *beginning* of his fully rounded mental capabilities.

But now comes the enigma — just when and why did the human ape turn from brief child-rearing to the lengthy upbringing allowing great mental growth?

Again there is a jump here, a gap, that the Theory of Evolution cannot bridge except by very shaky premises. Human behavior in the child-rearing area is far too different from all other earthly species, primate or otherwise, to be simply a process of "natural selection."

Natural selection of *what?*

Because it cannot be named or defined, it blocks every attempt at evolutionary explanation. Man's long childhood simply could not have "followed" in orderly progression from the rapid ape-childhood that ends so soon, not when the two are in the fantastic ratio of five to one.

We must postulate again that only the nonearthly portion of our ancestry seems to fill out the *true* picture.

In their own life on their home-world (or worlds) the star-people had long evolutionary periods in which to slowly develop longer and longer periods of childhood, instead of it all being incredibly telescoped into a short million or two years, as on Earth.

There is another possible angle to this — that our outerspace ancestors had lives spanning hundreds of years (perhaps achieved through very advanced medical research). Then their children would quite naturally require a long childhood-development, and we inherited that trait, though our lifespans on Earth are only three score and ten.

Our children at eighteen would seem like "infants" to a race living lives 300 or 500 years long.

This ties in with the rather strange records of the Bible, in which people of B.C. times apparently lived long Methuselah-lives measured in centuries. Did mankind then somehow lose his longevity? And is Starman patiently preparing to renew that factor in human lives when the time is ripe?

For we must not lose sight of the possibility that the starmen, working behind the scenes, are still *today* improving the human race, biologically. This double subject, of longevity and current bio-experiments going on now, will be explored more fully in the final chapter.

At any rate, we can return to our original point and infer that the starmen, in their crossbreeding or genetic program on Earth, imparted to us the physiological and/or cultural heritage of a long and rich childhood in keeping with a great new brain that needed such a lengthy period to achieve its full powers.

For this quantum leap from the fast-growing ape-child to the "slow-motion" growth and development of the human child to occur by hit-or-miss Evolution in a short million years or so, is sheer belief in magic or miracles. Scientifically, it must be rejected as not being a valid explanation.

The slow sweep of natural Evolution, which will take 50 or 100 million years to develop a new species or genus, could not have produced mankind with all his nonape peculiarities in a single million-year tick of the evolutionary clock. That would jar loose all the time consuming laws of natural selection.

The book that "retries Darwin" quotes T. H. Huxley, the famed biologist, as saying that "Large changes [in species] occur over tens of millions of years, while really major ones [macro-changes] take a hundred million or so." [8]

Sewall Wright, another big name in biology and evolutionary theory, is also quoted — "nature did not make leaps *(Natura non facit saltum)*" — meaning that natural selection did not and could not make a gigantic leap ahead with any species on an "overnight" basis. The inexorable time element required that all changes or series of "adaptations" could only occur through multimillions of years, never in "short" spurts.

If we look at ourselves in this light we are, in a sense, the humanity of the *future* in earthly terms, a stage of development we might not have reached — without the star-men's biological intervention — for another 10 or 20 million years.

And it was a humanoid race on another world, which *did* evolve naturally, that came to Earth and "colonized" it, first speeding up Evolution through interbreeding and/or highly advanced bio-techniques, in order to create a rational creature long before its time.

To them, Earth was a huge biological "laboratory," with a thousand and one experiments to conduct to achieve their great and really noble aim.

Once again, we feel that the Hybrid Man theory has scored decisively.

12

Brain Clues

Even more than physiological clues, even more than sexuality clues, even more than fossil clues or any clues previously given, we now come to the *greatest single clue* to Man's nonearthly origin. Only in keeping with the concept that Man is a hybrid can his possession of a fantastically advanced mental apparatus be explained.

In short, we mean Man's masterful, awesome, overwhelming brain. This problem harries the evolutionists most of all, as witness the following statements.

"The road from A to M [ape to Man] is rough and rocky [for anthropologists]. It includes the development of language, the achievement of an upright posture, and all the other differences of kind or degree between ape and Man."[1]   This speaker goes on to say that two Jesuit priests queried professional biologists about how this great "transition" occurred. The conclusion: "They had enough material to dispel any feeling that the transition had been explained."

In short, biologists could not see where Evolution and natural selection had any explanation for why Man the primate rose far above the primate apes, especially in *mental powers.*

In an imaginary conversation between scientists, the same writer has a skeptic ask Darwin: "But Mr. Darwin, how can a blind and automatic sifting process like [natural] selection, operating on a blind and undirected process like mutation, produce organs like the eye or the brain, with their almost incredible complexity and delicacy of adjustment?"[2]

Darwin's halting (if fictitious) answer: "Natural selection is a mechanism for generating an exceedingly high degree of improbability."

Improbability?

Yes, this was the studied conclusion (not fictional) of an authoritative professor after he had minutely examined the supposed progression of fossils from a primitive to an advanced form. On the basis of the scientific principle of causality, he could only declare that the results were not impossible — but highly unlikely.

The most devastating blow came from none other than Alfred Russell Wallace, codiscoverer of Evolution with Darwin but later one of its most outspoken critics. Perceiving that the gap between the brain of the ape and that of the lowest savage was too big, Wallace unloaded this gasping heresy: "An instrument [the human brain] has been developed in advance of the needs of its possessor."[3]

This, of course, violated the law against overendowment in any species.

Wallace acted like a bull in a china shop by expressing himself even more forthrightly. "He challenged the whole Darwinian position," says the author, "by insisting that artistic, mathematical, and musical abilities could not be explained on the basis of natural selection and the struggle for existence [among species]. Something else, he contended . . . must have been at work in the elaboration of the human brain."[4]

Wallace named that factor as "some unknown *spiritual element.*" (Italics added.)

Or was it the starmen?

Punching home his point, Wallace went on to state that "Natural selection could only have endowed the savages with a brain a *little* superior to that of the ape [our italics], whereas he actually possesses one very little inferior to that of the average member of our learned societies."

Darwin was so distressed at Wallace's speech that he wrote him in anguish, "I hope you have not murdered too completely your own and my child."

Darwin himself fully realized that the tremendously advanced brain of mankind had no place at all in the scale of Evolution. It was an insurmountable obstacle that to this day makes all biologists and anthropologists hastily change the subject if you bring it up.

Darwin must have been ready to toss out his theory of natural selection at times. In his *Origin Of Species* in 1859, he let his hair down. "Long before the reader has arrived at this part of my work, a crowd of difficulties will have occurred to him. Some of them are so serious that to this day I can hardly reflect on them without being in some degree staggered."

A British scientist of the time analyzed Darwin's book with an eagle eye and said, "It has been estimated [by me] that no fewer than 800 phrases in the subjunctive mood — such as 'Let us assume,' or 'We may well suppose,' etc. — are to be found between the covers."[5]

Eight hundred *assumptions* by Darwin, none of them a fact but mere conjecture on his part! We doubt if our book has that many pure assumptions. At least it shows that the Theory of Evolution is not an unassailable monolith of hard fact, but is more like a leaning tower with falsities constantly undermining its already shaky foundations.

It would seem as if the authors of this book have a more ironclad answer to most of Darwin's assumptions, in the theory of Hybrid Man and the starmen.

Getting back to the brain, it is apparent that if Man's celestial ancestors evolved on distant planets through a long period of millions of years (or if they used "autoevolution"), their brains would indubitably have developed beyond anything known on Earth (a relatively young planet).

Very probably, these same planet-hopping ancestors we have postulated (who came to Earth, where they successfully bred with the highest forms of Earth life — the apemen or Hominids — by virtue of their highly advanced medical knowledge) brought the "radar-TV-screen mind." It was this supermind that transformed this Earth, in a few short millennia, from the abode of slaves of nature to the masters of nature.

One superlatively strong argument in favor of our concept is the time factor for the human brain's development. Roughly, the length of the age of the dinosaurs is known — 150 million years — during which time they developed and flowered before final decline.

Each major revolutionary step in Evolution has taken many *millions* of years to complete.

But this is paradoxically not so in the case of Man's brain, which is an organ far more complex in itself than all the total brains of the dinosaurs. We are confident that we can show why the human brain is *impossible* under evolutionary laws and processes in the earthly time-span.

Assume that the great apes of Earth represented the best that nature could do to develop a high-grade brain. Now, the following claim is based upon the fact that a particularly successful line of evolutionary development always shows up in many different species.

For instance, there is the condition of four legs, which came into being when ancient amphibian species first climbed onto land from the sea and launched all the diverse creatures using four legs. But what about an efficient brain? Only two land mammals developed such a brain — apes and men (and possibly, in the sea domain, the dolphin). This is evidence that nature found a superefficient brain to be a most *difficult* construction project, so to speak. Except for Man, the best that nature could do was to develop the brains of the three great-ape families.

This means that it took nature 500 million years (from the earliest Cambrian life forms) *to develop the 1 billion neurons* that make up an anthropoid's brain. At this rate, one neuron (brain cell) was developed every six months —two neurons a year. That was the *fastest* rate nature could achieve—with all the land animals to play with.

Man is the bombshell exception.

For Man, with his *10 billion neurons,* should have taken *ten times as long* as the great apes in order to develop his incomparable brain. By simple arithmetic, ten times 500 million years is *5 billion years.*

But Earth has not been habitable for 5 billion years. It was barely formed then out of primordial matter. Since a *little* time has to be allowed for the Earth to cool down, it's easy to see that something is very, very wrong somewhere. Thus, about 4 billion years ago, when Man *should* have had 2 billion neurons, this old Earth did not even have one single drop of liquid water on it, nor one speck of life. It was all steam.

Would you have liked to live on Earth then? Probably not — everyone likes to be warm, but not at molten lava temperatures. Man's outer-space ancestors very likely felt that way, too. They stayed away for many ages and waited until this steaming orb cooled down to a point where some semblance of life could exist in the seas, and the first vestiges of land began to show dimly through the mists of the oceans. That was about 500-600 million B.C.

That the mind of Man could not have developed on this Earth will seem even more incontrovertible in a moment. That brainpower must have developed elsewhere, upon a series of planets, and it took literally billions of years to reach its peak from the earliest life forms. Let us envision how this incredible development may have taken place in the dim and distant past on other worlds.

Somewhere and sometime — no one knows how far back in time this may have happened — extraterrestrial Man evolved on some distant planet, as we must reiterate to keep the record clear. But, and this is the main point, before his planet became old, cold, and worn out, Man had time to develop sufficient intelligence to enable him to conquer space and begin planet-hopping. (He may, of course, have used "auto-evolution" to speed it all up: That alternative is always there.)

When Starman had successfully planet-hopped many times and had become established on other planets that were new, fresh, young, and ready to support him for further eons, he continued to develop mentally.

This process had proceeded at a tumultuous pace on his former home-planet — it was the process of developing his science, his social orders, his ethics, and all that goes with the mental level of life. It probably required more time than could be lived on one planet to develop that magnificent brain possessed by Man's outer-space ancestors. Who can say for certain? So many factors enter into this speculation that there can be no hard and fast conclusions.

Perhaps the moves to dozens of planets — different homes — were needed to bring the marvelous brain of our forebears to fruition. Perhaps many more were required, maybe in the hundreds.

At any rate, it is certain that tremendous progress did occur and that incredible lengths of time were required. Only the concept of a planet-hopping, *ever-evolving* race that traveled through space for millions of years fits the surmise of an ancestral race as well developed as we — the resulting Hybrids — give testimony to.

But to return to the main point: that Man *must* be a Hybrid, because there has not been *enough time* on Earth to permit his marvelous mind to develop.

To illustrate this point, imagine taking a baby ape or chimpanzee into our homes (as many researchers have attempted to do) to "humanize" the primate by bringing it up in a home atmosphere. If Evolution is correct and we are not hybrids but have evolved from *common stock* along with the ape, it naturally follows that baby apes would show, when raised in a human family, a real and measurable increase in IQ, or at least learning ability.

But this does *not* happen! The ape's IQ remains the same.

Something is obviously wrong. Somehow, the notion that Man evolved from common stock with the apes (the famed "missing link") has error in it. Otherwise, apes would respond and would show real improvements in their ability to cope with their environment. They would climb a rung or two up the evolutionary ladder when they are raised in one of our homes, for they would then possess *learning* brains like ours.

Thus the IQ gap between apes and men is far too great to be covered by any miracle of "quickie" evolution that produced the human mind.

This fallacy has been condemned over and over by others. In another book reviewing evolution, the author puts it that Man would have to be a "special case of a highly improbable acceleration of evolution."[6] The human brain, he goes on, could have reached its present peak only if "given enough time." Further on: "The accepted idea of an evolution that dragged along for half a million years [with Hominids] and then suddenly spurted forward [for mankind] rests on countless 'justifications' that are totally outdated." It is all likened to the many cunning Ptolemic "proofs" that the sun revolved about the Earth, prior to Copernicus.

There is yet another point perhaps of even greater importance than the above item. What we have learned of the human brain leads us to believe that it is so much more highly developed, so much more complex, involved and complicated than an ape's brain, that not only great stretches of time but also *quality* separate the two types of brain — anthropoid and humanoid.

By rough analogy, we can assume that the average ape's brain is comparable to a radio set in complexity while the average human brain is like a television set. Actually, the example is not too strained, for: "The chimpanzee cannot retain an image long enough to reflect upon it." Thus, comparing an ape's brain to a radio is more appropriate.

Now consider Man's brain. He is able to project a picture

—any picture he wishes — on his mental screen. At last we begin to see why the human brain is so comparatively great, so awesome in its complexity and sheer power to create, to reason, and to visualize, as contrasted to any ape brain.

In electronic terms, the marvelous television set that is our brain must also have the functions of a radar screen and a tape-recorder, and a switching facility so complex that it truly staggers the imagination.

To illustrate: Recall or remember, with a picture in your mind, the last walk you took just before sitting down to read this page. Even the process of remembering or imagining any short walk is very complicated. If an attempt were made to construct an electrical device or computer that could reproduce the functions of the human brain, it would take all the workingmen in industry *all over the world* one year to wire up the circuits. Neurologists estimate that some single brain-cells are connected to 11,000 other cells, creating a network of electroneural contacts that the electronics industry could never duplicate.

This gives us some idea of the fantastic intricacy of the human brain. It is by far supreme on Earth in thinking capacity, even if not in size or bulk, among the tenth-rate brains of all other earthly creatures.

Other mammals with larger brains than Man do not show anywhere near the intelligence that Man possesses with his three-pound brain. There are three such animals — dolphin, elephant, and whale. The elephant, which has a brain weight of about 5,000 grams (11 pounds), and the whale, with a weight of about 10,000 grams (22 pounds), were subjected to intensive investigation by many competent investigators.

So far, no one has claimed that the intelligence of either animal is equal to Man's. The thinking power of these animals was tested in every way, with the aim of possibly discovering some specific area in which their intelligence was greater than that of Man.

These experiments have not been successful. In no way did

the big-brained but small-IQ animals come close to humans.

The dolphin is a slightly different case. This animal's gross brain-weight is somewhat greater than the human's, averaging almost four pounds in the various species. And its brain comprises a good 1.2 percent of its body weight, comparing favorably with Man's 2 percent. Scientific tests have proved it is perhaps the most intelligent of all animals on Earth, next to Man. This playful and amiable aquatic creature is well known for its antics before crowds.

But further than that, scientists have conducted extensive tests in which the dolphin was taught many acts to perform and also to understand "messages." These messages were delivered in the dolphin's own underwater "language" of whistles, hoots, and various grunts, painstakingly pieced together by researchers so they could reproduce the "talking" with mechanical instruments.

One major project, not yet concluded, is the reverse —to teach the dolphins simplified human speech. First to understand it, then to even "speak" it with vocal sounds as close to human speech as possible. If this fully succeeds (there has been some progress), it will give the dolphin a *"genius"* rating far above the chimp or any other earthly animal.

But still — and let us get this clear — even the *least* intelligent of human beings (including idiots and morons) will be as *far above* the dolphin intellectually as the dolphin is above the chimp. The dolphin is not by any stretch of imagination equal in brainpower to humans, and represents the *best* that Evolution could do in evolving anything approaching a human-like brain.

In fact, the dolphin, representing the true scope of natural selection on Earth, is a clear sign of the *limitations* of Evolution in trying to achieve a first-class thinking organ like Man's.

Evolution could *never* produce the latter, only a very poor (in comparison) second-class dolphin brain.

Since none of the three creatures with brains physically larger and heavier than Man's (dolphin, elephant, whale) shows any degree of real intelligence of the human type, we are forced to develop a rather obvious conclusion to account for what we know about the relative brain-sizes in relationship to intelligence ratings of the various mammals, including Man.

Man's intelligence is obviously independent of his brain *size,* which indicates that something besides sheer weight or volume is involved. Supporting this latter contention is the knowledge that, in the historical past, some intellectual giants, such as Voltaire, had relatively small cranial capacities.

Indeed, it can now be proven without a doubt that, while Man's brain is only three times as large as the brain of our most intelligent ape, it is about *ten times as efficient.*

As mentioned before, a chimpanzee's brain contains about a billion nerve cells, while the brain of Man contains some 10 billion neurons. This tends to force the conclusion upon us that the human brain *must* be a more efficient brain than that possessed by any other animal. It is certainly more efficient than the elephant's or the whale's brain *despite* the theoretically equal length of time all mammals had on Earth to develop their intellectual capacities.

To repeat our point, something besides mere brain weight makes the difference — namely, *the number of neurons and their efficiency.*

The large-brained two — elephant and whale — have neurons, too, but *fewer in number* than the human brain, despite their greater size. Their brain cells (neurons) are comparatively big, so that the total number of neurons is below the human total, despite the animal's huge brain.

The dolphin is again an exception, with an equal number of brain cells to humans, but much of their brain is especially adapted to sonar analysis rather than "thinking" like men.

And therein lies the whole story. With his unmatched *quality* and *quantity* of 10 billion tinier neurons, Man's brain is far more powerful. Also it is more efficient because of the *rapidity* with which nerve impulses are handled by the central "control switchboard" of the brain.

Another factor is how many convolutions (folds) exist around the surface of the brain's cerebrum (80 percent of the total brain weight). In some obscure way, the number of convolutions in the cortex (outer envelope) of the human brain increases its thinking powers to formidable proportions, far above other animals with less-convoluted brains.

To indicate what a supremely superb thinking device our lump of "gray matter" is, neurologists point out that each single brain is more complex in "wiring" (nerve circuits) than all the worldwide networks of radio, television, telephone, telegraph, and orbiting relay-satellites combined. The association of ideas, thoughts generated, memories retained, and the vast storehouse of knowledge piled high in the average human brain is simply unbeatable by any mechanical or electronic system yet known.

In assuming that Man is a Hybrid, the very source of Man's more efficient brain — namely, the starmen — reveals why their more efficient brain was developed in the first place.

It seems evident that Starman, slowly and in good time, evolved the marvelous mental instrument of which our brain, which we all carry around with us, is a hereditary offshoot. Furthermore, that cerebral device of Starman was developed in times gone past to receive and retain much more knowledge than earthman has to deal with today, and thus we inherited *excess* brainpower. The lives and accomplishments of men like Einstein, Edison, Newton, and Darwin tend to prove this. They simply developed and used the mental abilities that we all latently possess to their *maximum* powers, or close to it.

No one has ever heard of an elephant doing calculus or of a whale devising a new theory of relativity, and they both have larger brains than Man — but not the immense mental power packed into Man's small skull, thanks to the starmen.

When mathematics is applied to this brain phenomenon, staggering results are obtained. The use of mathematical deduction on the data that was just presented brings the finding that Man is hundreds of times more *unique* than has heretofore been supposed. He is so incredibly "unearthlike," that only through hybridization by extraterrestrials could his uniqueness have been realized.

Consider the large animals that roam the world — animals that size for size could have developed a brain of similar weight and the intelligence of Man. Among these animals are the horse, cow, lion, camel, moose, rhinoceros, bear, and hippopotamus. If one assumes that these animals had *equal opportunity* to develop Man's brain and intelligence, then it is necessary to conclude that Man is nine times more unique than they are.

Taking special human characteristics, each one of these nine animals had *equal opportunity* to also develop, for example, the valuable characteristic of the burrowing ovum. Thus, on that scale, humans are eighty-one times more unique than any one of our sample animals.

None of these animals can talk either, as Man does, but they had equal time to develop this useful characteristic. So, nine times eighty-one equals seven hundred and twenty-nine.

This by no means exhausts Man's roster of unique qualities, but he is probably many thousand times more unique than these nine man-sized families. The concept of Man as no more than a half-earthly hybrid gives an explanation for the strange and mysterious differences that separate Man and *all* species of animals in the world, past or present.

Even more specific in the case of the "species race" to achieve intelligence is the popular notion among anthropologists that when Man left the trees and walked upright on the ground, this left his two upper limbs free, as arms and hands, to manipulate objects. This, presumably, then led to fingering many things out of curiosity and to making tools, thereby spurring his brain to grow with great rapidity.

Now let us see if there is a rebuttal to that specious idea.

Our argument is that long ago, in the age of dinosaurs, there appeared in North America a dinosaur of awesome proportions. Some specimens grew to be as long as forty-eight feet, stood twenty feet high, and had a head six feet long. This was the ferocious, carnivorous monster known as *Tyrannosaurus rex.*

Now we know from studies made of this incredible beast's skeleton that he walked upon his rear legs *exclusively* and used his front legs for everything *but* body support.[7]

Tyrannosaurus rex lived for 20 million years or more as a species. He was not the only one of his general type to roam the Earth, for in North America there existed along with him another similar species, while there were also several related species in Europe.

These reptiles all had one thing in common: *They did not use their front legs, or paws, for body support.* Consequently, this left their front limbs absolutely free to examine and handle things, just like Man, when he became a creature walking on two legs.

Well, this fearsome beast evolved quite in the opposite direction from Man. Yet, according to highly respected anthropologists, since bipedalism presumably accounts for Man's intelligence, *Tyrannosaurus rex* also had the necessary prerequisites for developing into a species of largebrained intellectuals — but *they did not so develop.* In fact, they have been described as "the largest creatures with the smallest brains ever to inhabit the Earth."[8]

Rex's singular failure to develop a huge brain, with a head almost six feet long, affording plenty of room, is shared by the age-old kangaroo genus and its species.

The kangaroo too does not need his forepaws at all for locomotion, since he moves by use of his powerful hind legs in a series of great hops. Thus, his "hands" were also free, for many millions of years — far longer than the Hominids —without becoming developed into tool-using dexterous appendages.

Why not? The forepaws of a kangaroo may look "ineffective" but are far from it, at least when it comes to delivering blows with them.

The big red kangaroo of a British circus-owner had a remarkable career. Sidney (the kangaroo) was trained to box and thereafter won bouts over dozens of human opponents. It was no fakery or publicity stunt, as Sidney bested both British and German heavyweight champions. In other words, the dexterity of his forepaws was even superior to that of humans, if he could deliver blows and feints and left hooks with boxing gloves to dazzle skilled ring champs.[9]

Then, if the various kangaroo species possessed these agile and well-coordinated forepaws an age ago, why did natural selection "choose" to *not* promote them into firstclass tool-making hands? Was it *natural* for natural selection to skip past the kangaroo and settle on Hominid ape-men as the ones to thereby develop a big brain?

If free hands leading to intelligence is a "rule" of Evolution, why are there more exceptions to the rule than otherwise? Certainly, such a far-from-airtight explanation for Man's mighty brain cannot be defended on that score. It clearly demonstrates that an *upright posture* does not and cannot on this earth, *by itself,* guarantee surpassing intelligence.

Darwin himself fell into this trap and innocently stated that "Man could not have attained his present dominant position in the world without the use of his hands. But the hands and arms could hardly have become perfect enough to have manufactured weapons — as long as they were used for locomotion."

Also ignoring the *T. rex* and kangaroo cases, Dobzhansky says: "The use of the arms for handling objects rather than for walking... has... stimulated further progress in intelligence."[10]

How can that bland statement be true? We can see that at least five extinct dinosaurs and one presently living kangaroo species have, or had, the physical characteristics (upright posture), which eminent anthropologists solemnly claim to be the main prerequisite for higher intelligence.

Yet, those bipedal creatures did not develop Man's intelligence in ten times the length of evolutionary time humans have had.

Why not? Apparently because having their hands free did not make the brains of Hominids suddenly grow abnormally large in a brief million years, or even 10 million years. That is not the answer to human intelligence, yet it is the only poor answer available under earthly conditions and evolutionary rules.

Since earthly conditions cannot apply, we once again put

forth our theme — that the big brain was an "import" brought by the starmen. Thus Man, and hybridized Man alone, has this incredible brain, this supreme machine of all organic machines, this ultimate jewel of all Earth nerve-systems that run living organisms.

It is a priceless gift like this from outer space that forever sets men apart from, and ultimately so far above his earthbound relatives — the lower animals.

Another favorite theory of the evolutionists is that the opposable thumb in Man's hand led to his superbrain, by virtue of allowing him to grasp and handle things with great dexterity, which, in turn, presumably led to the use of tools, which stimulated rapid brain growth. Aside from the previous confusion we noted over whether tool-using or upright walking or whatever led to intelligence, we might cite the following inconsistencies in relation to the opposable thumb.

As reported in a science-digest publication:

> Hypsilophodon, a small, two-legged herbivorous dinosaur, is generally thought to have been a tree dweller.... Its skeletal structure, say the proponents of this view, was ideally suited to life in the trees... The toes of the hind feet were long and flexible. The clincher, however, is that... the first digit appears to be opposable, like a thumb, so that the foot would be capable of grasping.[11]

Now, if the opposable thumb was an *important* factor in the development of Man's big brain, why didn't that small dinosaur — with a head start of perhaps 80 million years — gain intelligence?

Many early primates had an opposable thumb, or at least a thumb that allowed them to grasp things with a firm grip — which was something no other lower animal could do. As an authoritative work reveals, the tree shrew, loris, tarsier, marmoset, and macaque back in antiquity all had grasping hands much like the human hand.[12] The macaque ape and chimpanzee both go a big step beyond the other anthropoids with opposable thumbs, giving them the dexterity to pick up fairly small things, like a flintstone chip to use as a tool.

But — they never learned to pick up or use such tools except by sheer accident. And their opposable thumb did not launch them on the road to intelligence, as with Man.

As an escape from this opposable-thumb theory failing to account for intelligence, some experts say that it was a combination of ground-dwelling *and* a tool-grasping hand that sparked the growth of Man's big brain.

True, the other primates are tree-dwellers and were so in the past — except the baboon. That is, though living mainly in the treetops, baboon tribes will often forage for food on the ground. And they have learned the simple trick of using a handy stick as a sort of "tool" to pry up tasty roots and grubs.

Now, there we have the pregnant situation of another primate who spent much time on the ground and used his hand with the opposable thumb to wield at least a simple nonshaped "tool."

Just as early Man did.

Why didn't this ground life of baboons first of all lead to upright walking and, second, to intelligence? Baboon species existed up to 20 million years ago, before Ramapithecus, the earliest Hominid, and therefore had more than an even chance to develop an intelligent brain *ahead* of the Hominids.

It never happened.

According to Evolution and natural selection, it *should* have happened. That is, *if Man's brain in the first place is a result of natural selection.* Ergo, natural selection by earthly evolutionary rules and conditions did *not* produce the sapient brain of Man.

How many "exceptions" can the evolutionists expect to bring forth if humans *are* an exception to their rules? All the creatures who walked on hind legs and had their forepaws free; the creatures with opposable thumbs; the primates who became part-time ground-dwellers; the primates who were users of basic "tools" or pretools (including the chimp) — a couple of dozen species who, by rights, should have gone on the road to intelligence.

Yet they never did.

They are the "exceptions" to the rule that two-legged, thumb-handed, ground-dwelling, tool-using species "should" gain a big brain. Only Hominid man somehow "fortuitously" sprang ahead of the pack and developed his intelligent brain.

If Evolution works for one, why doesn't it work for all?

The zoologist quoted before typifies the expediency employed by experts in regard to the development of Man's brain.

"First," he says, in connection with early Hominids, "he had to hunt if he was to survive. Second, he had to have a better brain to make up for his poor hunting body. Third, he had to have a longer childhood to grow the bigger brain and to educate it. Fourth, the females had to stay put and mind the babies while the males went hunting. Fifth, the males had to cooperate with one another on the hunt. Sixth, they had to stand up straight and use the weapons for the hunt to succeed."[13]

He then modifies his "timetable" by saying, "I am not implying that these changes happened in that order; on the contrary they undoubtedly all developed gradually at the same time, each modification helping the others along."

It all sounds quite "logical," except for the plain fact that species do *not* change that readily, nor that rapidly — nor that radically — not in a short one or two million years. The opposum, for instance, has changed hardly at all for at least 75 million years. And Man has supposedly evolved from the apes (or a common ancestor) in a fiftieth of that time.

True, the opposum is not to be taken as a standard. To be fair and unbiased, we will quote another authority, who points out: "In the horse, a rather rapidly evolving type, average [time required] in change from one genus to another was... well over 5 million years."[14]

Now a change of *genus* is quite a change, whereas the appearance of a new *species* within a genus happens more often. A change of species occurred in the horse in only

500,000 years.

But the same authority then states "rates of evolutionary [change] ... vary enormously. ... *And the fastest of them seem very slow to human* [changes]." (Italics added.)

No matter how swiftly some animals evolve into new species and then into an entire new genus, Man's seven-league-boot-jumps up the evolutionary ladder are unrivaled. No animal can match it.

The horse is still a horse, not a thinking animal. His brain grew larger in jumps, but only because his body grew larger in jumps from tiny dog-sized Eohippus to the modern horse. Brain size merely kept up with increased body sizes and their more elaborate nervous systems, but the animal became no "smarter" than before.

Man's oversized brain, however, completely outgrew his body — which did *not* grow noticeably bigger. Thus, this brain riddle has utterly confounded anthropologists ever since the Theory of Evolution came in, and one could quote dozens of disturbed skeptics.

As an example, back in 1899 this statement was made:

"If we do not admit that latent capacities in the savage brain [of Hominids] were implanted for use at some time in the distant future [namely, today], we can only say that they are the result of a force which we do not know, and of a law we have not guessed."[15]

Implanted! ... force!... law!

Doesn't that sound exactly as if the speaker, too, suspected that some *outside agency,* not classical Evolution, accounted for the amazing growth of the Hominid-Homo brain in the past few million years?

Perhaps it is not quite clear to the reader how truly extraordinary Man's brain is as compared to other creatures. As mentioned before, the ratio of a given animal's brain weight to total body weight is the key factor. Man stands head and shoulders above any animal, extinct or living, in this respect (with the unimportant exception of the tiny hummingbird, in which the brain had reached the minimum size to function as any sort of central "nerve box" and hence remained relatively large).

The following table clearly shows how Man's brain represents a thinking organ of enormous proportions in relation to the body.[16]

SPECIES	WEIGHT OF BRAIN (grams)	RATIO TO BODY WEIGHT	COMPARATIVE VALUE
Man	1375	1:30	35.0
Chimp	400	1:75	5.2
Orangutan	400	1:124	3.0
Gorilla	425	1:231	2.0
Horse	520	1:534	0.97
Blue Whale	7000	1:15,000	0.47
Dog	102	1:250	0.37
Cat	32	1:128	0.025
Sparrow	0.84	1:29	0.029
Ostrich	29	1:1200	0.24

The significant figure is the last one, where the brain-weight to body-weight proportion has been "corrected." This means that certain other organs or portions of the body, of certain species, need to be unproportionately large for survival considerations and should not count in the gross body-weight.

For example, the blue whale carries an enormous extra weight in blubber, or fat, simply because his organism must be protected from icy waters in his daily life. When the blubber is "scaled down" to reasonable proportions, a more "average" body weight results, making for a more valid comparison with brain weight.

Anyway, we can see at a glance that Man far outstrips all other creatures in the *comparative* size of his brain, by a factor of 35. The chimp comes in a very poor second with a factor of 5.2. Thus, Man's brain is seven times as "large" as the chimp's, not in actual weight, but in proportion to its functions and abilities. This comes close to the other comparative figure we gave before, where Man has ten times as many neurons (brain cells) as the chimp: 10 billion to 1 billion.

From whatever angle the problem is examined, we are left with the stark truth that the human brain is a superanomaly that is hopeless for Evolution to explain.

Our superbrained starmen sires are the true answer.

13

I.Q. Clues

Let us start with a quote from a recent best seller by a noted researcher in archeology and anthropology: "Certainly the track of racial development from Hominids to *Homo sapiens* can be followed back clearly for millions of years."[1]

We, the authors of this book, are not so sure about *that!*

To continue his statement: "but we cannot make nearly so definite a statement about the *origin of intelligence.* ...So far I have not been fortunate to hear an explanation [from the anthropologists] of the origin of intelligence in Man that is even tolerably convincing."

He then later admits that even the *physical* development of Hominids is not as "clearly" traceable as he stated above, when he says, "Several million years passed before anthropoids came into being through natural mutations, but after that the dawn men [early ape-men] underwent a lightning-like development."

He then switches to mental development. "All of a sudden, tremendous advances appear about 40,000 years ago. The club was discovered as a weapon; the bow was invented for hunting; fire was used to serve Man's own ends; stone wedges [of advanced design] were used as tools, the first paintings appeared on the walls of caves [by Cro-Magnon Man]."

Then he, in turn, quotes Loren Eisley, professor of anthropology at the University of Pennsylvania, who stated that Man emerged from the animal world over a period of millions of years and only slowly assumed human features.

"But," Professor Eisley goes on, "there is one exception to this rule. To all appearances his [Man's] brain ultimately underwent a rapid development and it was only then that Man finally became distinguished from his other [primate] relatives."

The book's author makes his own evaluation, first saying that Man is a result of an *artificial* mutation (not through nature), then reenforcing that bold concept: "I voiced the suspicion that *Homo sapiens* became separated from the ape tribe by a *deliberately planned mutation.*" (Italics added.)[2]

He has been forced into this heretical (to science) conclusion because of the fantastic growth of the Hominid brain to its present human capacity. Let us examine this growth in more startling detail.

Going back to the true apes of 15 to 30 million years ago, their brains ranged from 325 cubic centimeters to 500 cubic centimeters in bulk or volume. The early chimp, for instance, rated at 400 cubic centimeters.

Now, the first-known Hominid, among the fossil finds of Dr. Louis Leakey in East Africa, was *A. africanus,* a very primitive Hominid of 2.7 million years ago who boasted of a 442 cubic centimeter brain — even less than the apes.

However, living concurrently with him was a more advanced Hominid, *A. robustus,* who jumps to 530 cubic centimeters and immediately goes a cut above the anthropoids. Man, and his big brain, were already on the way.

Australopithecus of a million years ago reached a brain capacity of 660 cubic centimeters, definitely above the apes.

But then there came an enormous jump, and by 600,000 B.C., *Homo erectus* sported a brain up to 1,000 cubic centimeters in size. He was, as we previously noted, the first true Man of the genus *Homo,* and had already left the ape-brain far, far, behind.

Now we come to one of the other major mysteries of the "descent of Man," as Darwin put it, which really turns out to be an "ascent" of a remarkable nature.

For after Erectus, the human brain not only reached its present-day peak but *beyond.* To quote an authority, "as we proceed backward in time the human brain increases rather than decreases in volume."[3]

Measurements of the capacity of Neanderthal Man's skull and brain-case, from many hundreds of specimens, indicates that, way back in 50,000 B.C., his brain was a whopping 1,400 to 1,600 cubic centimeters. Modern Man's is 1,300 cubic centimeters on the average!

Cro-Magnon, modern Man's immediate predecessor, had an even more astonishing mass of gray matter, for he averaged up to 1,500 cubic centimeters.[4]

This again is contra-evolutionary, as natural selection never endows a creature with a special trait and then lets it decline. The horse got bigger, the wolf family grew larger canines, the cat family became superbly muscled, the eland and kin became swifter runners. None of them fell off from those peaks of physical endowment.

Nor did the brain matter in their heads show the slightest reduction as time went on, but rather increased slowly and steadily.

So we have another anomaly confounding the evolutionists — why does Man's ancestry alone show a *decline* in brain size from about 50,000 B.C. to the present day?

What other answer can there be except an *outside* influence related neither to Evolution nor to Earth — namely, the starmen biologists.

Another quote indicates how anthropological authorities inadvertently supported our theory, without actually naming that outside influence. "Both sides [Man's physical and mental development] are expressions of a third element which in essense escapes our definitive powers."[5] A "third element" that, like an invisible ghost, constantly haunts the evolutionary halls and cannot be exorcised.

A similar uneasy feeling — uneasy with Evolution's quixotic attempts at explaining Man's miraculous intelligence — is expressed by another authority: "Unutterably alone, Man senses the great division between his mind and theirs [the other animals]. He has completed a fearful passage, but of the nature and causation even the modern biologist is still profoundly ignorant."[b]

"Fearful passage"? "Causation"? Was the author hinting at *space travel,* and a *causation by starmen?*

Understandably, even if he thought about extraterrestrials visiting Earth to cause the great "division" between the brains of Man and other creatures, he would not dare state this openly. He would be hooted out of the scientific fraternity and jeopardize his standing and career. Yet many such obscure quotes from honestly baffled scholars of human origins can be found scattered profusely throughout the literature of archeology, anthropology, and biology.

Everywhere and in each generation since Darwin, those cautious skeptics admit that the human brain is "out-of-this-world," and they thereby skirt on the very edges of proclaiming a nonearthly origin for this priceless gift.

Returning to Neanderthal and Cro-Magnon Man, we might add our own comment, that their mental endowment amounts to having had an extra big brain yet virtually nothing to think about. For along with that huge brain did *not,* immediately, come civilization nor any advanced culture. Why did they advance so slowly and painfully where intellectual progress was concerned?

This paradoxical situation reached its absurd peak when Cro-Magnon Man, who emerged on the world stage in 35,000 B.C., lived much like a primitive savage up to about 10,000 B.C. What accounts for that long empty gap of some 25,000 years in which his brain — just as big and sharp at the start as at the finish — did not in the least stir itself out of brutehood?

There's something rotten in Evolution, if not Denmark, to misquote Shakespeare.

Once more, of course, we step into the breach with our Hybrid Man theory. We can make the educated guess here that the Neanderthal/Cro-Magnon brains were not as "finished" as modern Man's. That the starmen super-biologists realized this and *improved* the brain neurally (involving nerve paths, synapses, reaction time to stimuli, and so on) and succeeded so well, they were able to *reduce* the volume of the follow-on brain of *Homo sapiens* of today.

Geneticists from another world, armed with great biological skills, could conceivably accomplish this brain-size reduction. Evolution never could, by its very definition. Evolution means *advancement* from a lower to a higher state.

It allows for no retrogressions or backslidings. Each new endowment granted by natural selection through better mutations sticks tenaciously in the species, since it helps the species to thrive and multiply and spread.

This brings us to another major point (briefly mentioned before) in the Theory of Evolution — natural selection never *overendows* a species.

That is, natural selection bestows upon creatures only as much of a new and better physical trend as is needed to keep the species in the running, as it were.

Since survival of the fittest is the rule, each creature is given only a slight edge over others in order to promote its survival. Mutations never became so all-powerful that they dominate and kill off all rival species.

As the authoritative anthropologists of today put it, "Animals only acquire new characteristics if they provide some immediate advantage. They are never acquired merely by accident, to be stored away, as it were, like money in the bank."[7]

But the Neanderthal-Cro-Magnon-sapiens brain, which already came forth 35,000 years ago, was never *fully used.* The human brain's power did not truly manifest itself for another 25,000 years.

Isn't that "money in the bank" that was stored away for future use?

Yet such a superior trait is "never acquired." So say the evolutionists, and they're stuck with it.

To repeat, all specimens of animal life are in a sort of neck-and-neck race for survival. Natural selection, being a blind force born of necessity, does not and cannot shove one species ahead too far to become the all-out winner. Each species makes a tiny jump ahead in some way, but they all remain more or less even in the great race for survival.

Except Man with his great brain.

The awesome thinking organ of Man, at least ten times as efficient and "powerful" as that of the nearest anthropoid, and dozens or hundreds of times beyond the capability of the lower animals, is entirely out of line with the workings of natural selection.

Yet it is one of the most basic of Evolution's "laws" that natural selection cannot overendow any species with more abilities than it *needs.*

Then isn't the mighty human brain, which has given us lordship over all other living creatures, the most *flagrant overendowment* possible?

Anthropologists have scrambled frantically but futilely to cover this glaring blemish in evolutionary theory.

One rather fancy brainstorm (the originator shall remain mercifully unnamed) is that somewhere the brain of early Man acquired "feedback," much like a computer. That is, his memory cells became so sharp that he was able to compare and weigh and evaluate things more accurately than animals, thus giving his brain a boost toward more complexity.

But if this happened with the first Hominids whose line led to modern Man, then why did it take some 2 million years or more for that great "feedback" brain to manifest itself to its true extent? Why did the first glimmerings of applied intelligence and the start of civilization (a true "feedback" mechanism of the brain) have to wait until 10,000 B.C. for its debut?

As in Carl Sagan's Sumerian legends before, there is more evidence that the *very* sudden process of mankind catapulting from brutehood to civilization on an overnight basis was also instigated by our starmen stagehands behind the scenes.

But right now, to continue our premise that the human brain represents an *over*endowment to Man that is totally unallowable by Evolution's rules.

Another statement by an authority gives a more definitive — and very significant — clue to this overendowment factor:

"The neocortex of the Hominids evolved in the last half-million years, from the middle Pleistocene onward, at an explosive speed, which so far as we know is unprecedented."[8]

Explosive speed . . . unprecedented. Two very revealing phrases. In short, beyond whatever changes or improvements in a given species that natural selection had ever accomplished before.

The title of the article is in itself startling: "Man — One of Evolution's Mistakes."

Anthropologist Loran C. Eisley said that the advent of the human brain "measured in geological terms, appears to have been surprisingly sudden." He speaks of this "huge mushroom of a brain which has arisen magically between night and morning." To make it plain he added, "When I said that the human brain *exploded*, I meant no less."

The cortex is the part of Man's brain that includes all his higher functions of thinking, calculating, abstract thought, and the intricate sorting out of sensory impressions. It includes the so-called forebrain (cerebrum), which furnishes Man with his gigantic intellectual abilities.[9]

Most other animals have no forebrain at all. The primates like the chimp have a very small one. But the forebrain and cortex as a whole in Man constitute no less than 70 percent to 80 percent of his brain, with the remaining portion devoted to the cerebellum — hindbrain and midbrain.

Together, these last two control all of Man's automatic bodily functions such as breathing, heartbeat, and the general autonomous workings of the body. The hindbrain, which controls Man's residue of "instinctive" drives — self-preservation, and so on — is the smallest part of the total brain mass, whereas in other animals it is by far the most dominant part.

Obviously, it is the cortex (cerebrum, particularly) that has given Man his enormous intelligence, and that part, according to the article, developed with "explosive speed," too explosively for the anthropologists to weakly explain away by mutations, stimulation by tool-making, or any other wholly inadequate factor.

The shadow of an *outside* influence again looms in the background, as the only possible way for the seat of Man's great intellect to develop in a mere 500,000 or a million years to its present huge size in the human skull.

Need we hint that this shadow is that of the starmen who hybridized mankind and genetically, or by crossbreeding, injected cortex-growth chromosomes into the human race's gene pool?

Anthropological authority highlights another peculiar aspect of this inexplicable brain-growth, when it says, "the inference must be that the evolutionary processes that led to the emergence of more modern individuals from *Homo erectus* [the basic stock] were working more swiftly on the back of the head than on the face." [10]

Note again the word "swiftly" with the implication that the entire brain grew rapidly, but the back of the head even *more* swiftly. And the back of the head (from the brow-ridges to neck) is where the cerebral portion of the brain bulges the most, giving Man his tremendous intelligence.

Let us get it more clear that natural selection absolutely "forbids" overendowment of any kind among any species, for this evolutionary fault is one of the sturdiest pillars by which our theory of Hybrid Man is supported.

Among animals, the horse is an example of how natural selection can produce "jumps" in brain-size, for this happened among the equine species several times in relatively short (500,000-year) time-periods.

But the end and final result is a bigger brain, for a bigger present-day species of horse, that is *not intelligent.* In other words, nature supplied the horse with successively bigger brains (to handle a bigger body) but stopped short of *overendowment.* The horse did not end up a brainy rival of mankind.

So it was with every other earthly class of animals. No matter how much individual species or genera developed bigger and better brains, none of them achieved anything remotely resembling the power of reasoning and intellect possessed by Man alone. This, of course, includes all the apes.

Our closest rival, the chimp, cannot produce mental images (imagination), cannot conjure up any extraneous thought (abstract thinking) beyond what is necessary for immediate daily life and survival. Comparing the mental abilities of Man and ape is like comparing a whale to a mouse and ignoring size to say, "See? they are both warm-blooded."

The gulf between the ape-brain's capability and that of Man's is quite as huge as the gulf between the body sizes of a whale and a mouse.

Now, up to the Australopithecine Hominids of some 1 to 2 million years ago, their brain-sizes and capacities were not much more than the requirements for survival, as with other creatures. But when we come to *Homo erectus* in 600,000 B.C., the first true manlike species, we have the jump to overendowment. If Australopithecines survived for 1.5 million years, their brains obviously were adequate for their general purposes of keeping alive.

Why, then, did nature go wild and double the brain between the Hominid phase and the Homo phase? *Why did early Man need a brain twice as big as he formerly had?*

Certainly not to make better flint tools and hunting weapons — Hominids had done nicely with their crude ones, thank you.

Certainly not to invent or discover fire, the wheel, and smelt copper? Nature, or natural selection, is a blind force, not an intellectual "planner" who deals with abstruse concepts like bigger and better stone or bronze-headed clubs. Certainly not — and even more unthinkable — in order to allow Man to invent language, speech, writing, mathematics, engineering, and science!

It is entirely off-limits for classical evolutionary processes on Earth to produce a brain of this immense caliber.

Hence, every brain jump from the earliest Hominids of a million years ago, to Erectus' already double-sized brain to the mighty modern brain is sheer, unmitigated, incredible *overendowment.*

Natural selection stopped short of overendowing any other species in any way, so as to keep the "survival race" on a fair and even keel. Nature does not have "favorites." Why, then, did natural selection make this one great and wholly unbelievable overendowment in one sole case, and present mankind with a brain of *ten times* the capacity needed for daily survival?

We could lay a bet of a million to one that the evolutionists cannot, and never will, give a *scientifically* satisfactory and foolproof answer.

On the other hand, there are dozens of authorities who will openly declare that Man is the great "Misfit of Evolution."

One such statement goes, "Man is a mathematical improbability. [Earth] has produced a current crop of perhaps a million species [of all creatures]. Of them, one may be loosely described as sapient [intelligent].... Were we not so evident [real], an impartial observer would be forced to conclude that we could not and do not exist."[11]

No mincing of words there!

Man is a "mathematical improbability" and should "not exist" under evolutionary law. Therefore, Man only becomes "probable" if we look for the origin of his magnificent mind out in space, where the starmen came from.

Perhaps the true clincher is this further statement by the same authority: "New in humans [their brains] are such areas as the speech center in the third convolution of the temporal lobe [Broca's area], and close to it the center for knowledge and its practical application, which is important in technical skills."[12]

Two *new* areas that exist in no other earthly animal's brain, not even in rudimentary form. And those areas have little to do with brute survival, for how could *speech, abstract knowledge, and technical skill* in any way aid Man in defending himself against predators, in gathering nuts to eat, in hunting down game?

What is the real "necessity" to Man's bare survival in discovering the law of gravity, tabulating the chemical elements, inventing the radio and combustion engine, in utilizing atomic power?

Any brain capable of achieving those brobdignagian feats simply could not come out of Evolution's prime concept — survival of the fittest. For those things did not in the least "fit" mankind for the primitive battle of life.

They only added a *postsurvival* kind of life of infinite grandeur to human existence.

If evolutionists are still stubborn and insist there must be some evolutionary explanation, we might quietly point out that a million other creatures — and dozens close to Man in general physical terms — did not evolve this sort of superbrain. Why should *one* species, and only one, gain this unparalleled mental ability denied to every other living creature?

Mankind is then, in a sense, the "chosen species." But not chosen by Evolution, which cannot overendow, but by Starman, who could.

As a matter of fact, we believe the anthropologists are wrong in lumping modern Man *(Homo sapiens sapiens),* as only one species out of others, in the genus *Homo. (Homo sapiens sapiens* classifies Man as a creature who thinks and also *knows* he thinks.)

A genus is a group of animals with mutual characteristics of a general type, a subdivision of a broader *class.* Within the genus are the various *species.* Different members of a genus cannot interbreed, only the individual specimens of a single species.

Now, not only can Man not interbreed with apes (a different genus), but it is doubtful if today's *Homo sapiens* could have crossbred fertilely with *Homo erectus.* Modern humans might not even be able to breed with Neanderthal Man, although Cro-Magnon Man (who is also *Homo sapiens sapiens)* of 35,000 B.C. definitely would have been mutually fertile with current humans.

Take this interbreeding factor, add to it the "isolated splendor" of Man's incomparable brain, plus all the physiological changes from *Homo erectus* to *Homo neanderthalensis,* and it is then our contention that modern Man should be in a *separate genus* of his own, not merely one of several species within the genus *homo.*

Man might well be promoted to his own sole genus as *sapiens supremis* (or any suitable term), in which the "sapiens," meaning *intelligence,* automatically lifts him out of the *Homo* genus that includes poor-brained *Erectus* and places him in his own niche, never to be confused anthropologically with his lesser relatives.

Neither *Homo erectus* nor Neanderthal Man could ever have broken down the atom into protons and electrons, or even invented the battle-ax.

But above and beyond all that, we believe mankind should be elevated to a new genus for another cogent reason — *because he is not purely earthly in origin.* If he is Hybrid Man with part parentage from starmen, as we maintain, then certainly he cannot fit into any ordinary genus produced exclusively on this Earth.

Man's genus name could then quite appropriately be *sapiens stellar.*

14

Cerebral Clues

Tremendous advances have been made in laboratories throughout the world since the termination of World War II. The details of these advances need not be mentioned, but certain fields have seen fantastic developments.

First, of course, is the program of space exploration. Then come the completely new fields that include magneto-hydrodynamics, the laser, Project Deep-Sea Drilling, open-heart surgery and heart transplants, color television, tape recorders, the transistor, and a host of hardly lesser science marvels. It is an "explosion" of science technology.

It is apparent that in every field of human endeavor, a real effort is being put forth today to make giant strides forward on all scientific fronts.

It is also true in medicine and in one special branch of medicine — the study of the brain. In England, where there was ample reason to study brain damage due to war injuries, a number of laboratories have recently struck "pay dirt" in the highly specialized field of electroencephalography.[1] A brief review of what has been done in this field since World War II will enable us to appreciate more fully the truly startling revelations that have been uncovered in the last few years, and that relate directly to our Hybrid Man theory.

First, the standard electroencephalographic (or EEG) techniques were extended infinitely further by the development of a device termed an "averager."

In the usual technique, a pen was made to trace out the variations in the cranial-current's intensity occurring between two electrodes placed at various locations on the exterior skin of the live human skull. A graph resulted that was "jerky," having a great number of vibrations occurring in it within a few seconds.

In the standard EEG recording five such complete setups operated five pens, and the paper tape record that resulted produced a completely individualistic pattern of five "traces." There was no way of correlating these five records until the "averager" was invented. This device manages to determine the total current amplitudes occurring in any given moment of time in all five pens simultaneously.

The "averager," then, produces a record that is entirely unlike the usual electroencephalogram. These records, taken from the brains of many individuals, produced some startling new discoveries when analyzed.

First, it was found that each individual has a typical "vibration rate." Each brain has pulses of current traveling through it that are slow when compared to the rapid variations described in the old EEG setup.

It was found eventually that each brain produces four wavelengths of pulsations. Delta waves (0 to 4 hertz wavelength) occur in infants and sleeping adults. Theta pulses (4-8 hz.) are associated with creative moods, fantasizing, and daydreaming. Alpha waves (8-13 hz.) represent tranquility with eyes closed and lack of visual imagery. Beta waves (13-26 hz.) are released during times of tension and anxiety, also during intense concentration.

Second, it was found that the brain changes its pulse rate when the eyes are closed, during light sleep, and at other stages of slumber.

Finally, it was found that this pulse rate could be used to actually determine whether or not an individual was *imagining* something! The very act of "imagining" could be accurately detected, simply by noting when Theta waves radiated from the brain during the waking state.

The measurement of such an exotic faculty was further enhanced by a newly discovered technique known as "flicker," where an extremely bright light is flashed repeatedly and rhythmically in front of the patient's eyes. This flashing or pulsing is synchronized, exactly, with the slow Theta pulse occurring in the patient's brain.

Entirely new discoveries about the brain resulted from the use of the flicker technique. The exact location in our brain of the mental screen (the screen of "imagination" on which we project the picture in our "mind's eye") was determined, and the probable method by which these pictures are produced was revealed.

Television tubes and radar screens display characteristics similar to the human brain's ideation activities.

In conventional TV, the "trace" or moving electron-beam starts at one edge of the screen, the upper corner, then proceeds across from side to side. On each pass, it drops downward a tiny fraction of an inch. This, in receiving sets of the United States, occurs 550 times a second before the trace has reached the bottom of the screen. It then flicks back to the upper corner to start all over again.

In radar, however, there is a beam that is pivoted at the center of a round screen, which sweeps like the hands of a clock, around and around, "painting" the picture upon the phosphor of the tube face.

It has been established without question that the human brain operates like a radar set, and the mental screen upon which we project our imaginary pictures operates like a radar screen — in short, there is a radial "sweep" arrangement.[2] It was further established that such an arrangement does not exist in any other mammal brains on Earth.

It is exclusive to Man.

Let us return for a moment to two of those mysterious pulsations, the Alpha and Theta pulses that occur in the human brain. Researchers were astonished to discover that the speed with which the radar sweep went around the human radar screen was exactly the same speed possessed by the Alpha and Theta rhythms.

Again we repeat that the data most important to this book's study is the statement that Man is the *only mammal* with such a "radar" brain. Restated, this means that the most careful research *has failed to discover anything more than a faint trace of the ability to imagine things in the minds of any animal except Man.*

Thus, humans are the only creatures who can plan ahead, imagine possibilities, and discard those deemed unwise. No other creature can mentally create such vast mechanisms of future actions before the time to carry them out — except Man. No other creature can imagine a walk in the woods or conjure up the dear face of a loved one long departed.

This leads us again to a familiar point that we have made before, for this amazing discovery fits in very well with this book's basic contention that Man is a hybrid and that his marvelous mind came from outer space.

Just how does the human brain "visualize" or see clear-cut images on the mind's "screen"? Much more research will have to be done before that miraculous ability can be pinned down.

Scientists have determined, however, that certain areas of the brain have control over such mental imagery. When those areas are stimulated by the touch of a fine wire through which a mild electric current is projected, mental images leap vividly into the subject's mind. Images are conjured up from either past memories or from recent events in that person's life. There seems to be some complex "feedback" system that taps such "stored" images and releases them to sensory visualization centers.

This ability to visualize mentally is abundantly possessed by Man but is only fleetingiy displayed by the higher apes, as determined by ingenious scientific experiments with chimps. Unfortunately, it is impossible to determine by skeletal remains alone whether any manlike creature in Man's ancestry did or did not possess the means to visualize.

Did *Homo erectus* think in "pictures" too? It is rather dubious, because it seems to be a function of brain *quality* that is involved.

No one has yet been able to deduce brain quality with any degree of exactitude from skeletal remains, but the strong probability is that the brain structures of Erectus and possibly of Neanderthal Man were both inferior to modern Man's, to the extent that mental imagery was either absent or of sporadic occurrence.

In fact, we will make the educated guess that the full-blown ability to "see inside the brain" did not come along until *Homo sapiens* came along, which would include Cro-Magnon Man as well as modern Man.

It is well known that as long as 15,000 or 20,000 years ago, Cro-Magnon Man painted exquisite pictures of animals and objects on cave walls. Since he could not very well drag a woolly mammoth down into the caves, he must have depended on his memory to draw the creatures. But to do the scenes with such remarkable excellence and in faithful detail — and in *color* — the Cro-Magnon "old masters" must have relied on vivid mental images carried along within their brains.

The above pioneering brain research has blossomed into a new mental therapy for the ill, and, for the healthy, it offers a new way of achieving mind-expansion without the use of dangerous drugs like LSD.[3]

The new therapy technique is called "biofeedback," meaning that the subject is shown his brain waves in action via the electroencephalograph or EEG machine. His brain waves can either be visually reproduced on a screen as a series of wave motions, or as sound vibrations of a certain pitch. The wave-pattern changes before the patient's eyes or the pitch to his ears as his brain switches from one to another of the four types of mental waves that always emanate alternately from the human brain, day and night, waking or sleeping.

The Alpha waves are the most fascinating, in that they usually come into being when the subject goes to sleep. But now experimenters have "coached" their subjects to produce the Alpha pulses in the waking state. Some inner control mechanism in the brain is triggered off to do this, after intense practice.

This Alpha-pacing, as such research is called, has given psychiatrists a new therapeutic tool for relieving disturbed patients. Once they are taught to *consciously* produce the Alpha rhythm while awake, they go into a state of relaxation or half-sleep that is somewhat akin to hypnosis. In this state, their anxieties and other mental aberrations can be more easily treated by the doctor.

But further research indicates the Alpha rhythm is far more versatile and is indirectly related to creativity, pleasure, and meditation. It looks promising that when this brain-wave-control technique is perfected, it will offer a cure for insomnia, bring more happiness or content, improve memory, and in general increase mental and physical health. In short, it may become a sort of "mental medicine" quite as potent as those used in chemotherapy.

And this newly discovered "biofeedback" mechanism of the human brain is again something that could never follow from the limited species-improvements offered by natural selection.

It could only come from a hybrid brain tailored by the starmen to perform the EEG wonders.

Now let us take up another aspect of Man's mental makeup that is taken for granted in the human race, yet is so remarkable when one stops to think of it that we can only marvel at the phenomenon.

Namely, human genius.

Where does it come from? And how can humans be so diverse in mental attainments that one person can be a dozen or a hundred times more intelligent (in the intellectual sense) than the average Man on the street?

True geniuses, such as Einstein (with his probable 200 IQ) occur so rarely in the human race that they seem to have little or no relationship to the common laws of heredity.

Digging into the laws of genetics, however, brings out one rather odd bit of information regarding recessive genes. This is the fact that recessive genes can, under certain circumstances, persist in a family under such conditions that many, many generations will show no trace of that particular recessive characteristic.[4] Then, due to some marriage by pure chance with another carrier, it may show up many generations later.

For example, there are many people (mainly women) who are carriers of recessive genes for color blindness, but they show no trace of it themselves.[5] Also, blue eyes are due to a recessive gene, while brown eyes have the backing of a dominant gene; hence, there are many more dark-eyed people on Earth than light-eyed.

Getting back to our topic, true genius does display some of the strange occurrence phenomena as to rarity that are displayed by recessive genes. So could it be that true genius is — when it occurs — the extremely rare "cropping up" of a characteristic given to us long ago by our *outer-space ancestors?* Even if that is not the answer, Evolution doesn't have any answer at all.

Let us first of all recall the concepts of Alfred Wallace, codiscoverer of Evolution along with Darwin, over 100 years ago. Wallace stated quite flatly: "Exceptional intellectual activity cannot by any stretch of the imagination have become part of Man's mental make-up through the process of natural selection — for natural selection never overendows a species with any particularly desirable characteristic."[6]

This is another example of the principle of overendowment that we dealt with in the last chapter. Genius is the *greatest possible* overendowment factor of all, as Wallace clearly saw a century ago.

Therefore, we see that this great man (himself a genius!) tends to support our basic concept, even if only by implication. He contends that Man "is a contrary small exception to the orderly workings of the theory of natural selection."

He meant "small" only in comparison to the immense number of other species of animals who did faithfully follow evolutionary laws.

Wallace's statement about "exceptional intellectual activity" (genius, in a word) is our springboard for another concept that may be among the most clear and unequivocal items of evidence that the Hybrid Man theory is correct.

It is the rather shocking concept that in general, Man's forebears were *more* intelligent than modern Man! We mean *earthly men* of B.C. times. And that the rate of occurrence of genius then was much higher than now.

But, because there were so few of such mental giants, and so many average people came along at a constantly increasing ratio, the "genius gene" was incessantly and continuously "diluted" in the racial gene-pool.

Today, with the enormous burgeoning of human population into multibillion quantities unknown to those early days, that dilution has made it very difficult for the genius-gene to crop up in our times and among our people, so that mental masterminds are rarer per capita than the fabled dodo, even though they may total up to a sizable sum.

Is this indigestible in your mind? Do you believe that people today are "smarter" on the average than people of B.C. times? How can we twist it around and claim those "ignorant, backward, half-civilized" people of ancient times had more brainpower than we can boast of?

But ponder this. Studies have been made in which sober scientists present that very view — that the incidence of genius and of high-caliber minds was proportionately greater in olden times than today. It is too complex to give all the intricate data, but some of the renowned figures of earliest times, since history was recorded, stand out as supreme thinkers who may be unmatched today.

We must not be misled by the flowery writings of B.C. times, nor smile at the "ignorance" shown of the simplest principles of modern science. The point is what great advances in human thought and behavior and ethics — all the higher and more spiritual attributes of mankind — were first inaugurated in those long-gone days. We must look behind the obsolete language-expressions and "funny" wordings to the great golden nuggets of primary thought and principles that they formulated, to our everlasting benefit.

To many impartial scholars, a brief excursion into the past of art, poetry, literature, and government has served to show that we have reason to suspect that some of the geniuses of the past were greatly superior to our best present-day geniuses. (Even in the field of science and technology, amazing archeological finds show that the battery and electrical current were known in ancient Babylon, the telescope in Assyria, and the blast furnace in India.)

The incredibly beautiful poetry of the ancient poet Sappho, to some minds has never been equalled.[7]

Certainly it is true that statues of the best Greek periods cannot be surpassed today by some of our best sculptors.

The basic concepts of government, first deduced by the Romans and their contemporaries, still serve today, 2,000 years later, as models for the best democratic (republic) governmental systems in the world.

The ringing style and clear purposeful prose of writers who lived long before Caesar's time serve today to fasten firmly in men's minds concepts of morality that many of us these days would have great difficulty in formulating.[8]

In ancient Greece, many fundamentals of science were discovered by sheer deduction. Thales taught that the stars are made of the same matter as Earth. Epicurus proclaimed there was a plurality of inhabited worlds that were similar to Earth in all ways. The atom was known to the Greeks, as were the circumference of the Earth and the fact that it was round, the principles of basic optics, the principle of specific density of matter (Archimedes and his famous golden crown in the bath), the basic mechanical instruments, the fact that the moon was a small, round world too, and many other scientific principles.

And all without the huge laboratories and elaborate electronic apparatus we have today. Surely that was *genius* of the first magnitude shining through.

To go even further back, the great piles of mammoth bones in Europe show conclusively that ancient Man constructed most ingenious means of capturing those monsters. In fact, he probably hunted them to extinction.[9]

We see it is possible that genius — respected as it is today — is inferior perhaps to the genius that conceived the design of the great Pyramid of Cheops or discovered the wheel. We also see that genius may have been much more common per capita in ancient days than it is at present.

This would explain the marvelous cave artwork at Altamira, Spain, and the incredible persistence of the caveman living on the fringes of the glaciers during the Ice Ages in Europe.[10] It would also explain the marvelous flint-flaking techniques that we know existed in prehistoric times, and which no one can master today, oddly enough.[11]

Genius could easily be, as we have seen, an evidence that Man is a hybrid. Certainly, it offers a startlingly logical explanation for what we know about high-quality intelligence.

Why is this to be considered strong evidence of the hybridization of mankind? *It comes out of the fact that no other animal displays the slightest sign of genius.*

In his famed book, Desmond Morris goes through the process of how the human baby rapidly learns to think and then goes on to gain one other mental skill — "Other images are born [in the baby's brain] — flowers, houses, animals, boats, cars. These are heights the young chimp can never, it seems, attain. After the peak has been reached . . . the animal continues to grow [physically] but its pictures [in the brain] do not. *Perhaps one day a chimp genius will be found, but it seems unlikely.*" (Italics added.)[12]

An ape da Vinci, for instance, would be so far above his fellows that he would learn to read and write like humans, at least in rudimentary terms. This ape genius — who has never yet appeared on Earth — would astound scientists by his feats, such as counting to ten or using a typewriter intelligibly even if clumsily, or fixing a broken toy.

The complete absence of shining intellects among the primates or any other species of animal — no genius horses or dogs or cats are known either — must make all of us ask in surprise why the human race alone produces outstanding individuals far above the common herd in mental powers.

It seems there can be only one explanation — the introduction long ago of extraneous superintellect genes into the mainstream of human life. Only this can account for a Ptolemy, Galileo, Newton, Edison, Einstein, and all the other great brains that have graced mankind's history.

And only great-brained men from extraterrestrial sources could have injected those supermind genes into the racial bloodstream of mankind on Earth. Otherwise, science and biology simply have no explanation for genius except to call it a "fortunate" mixture of genes and chromosomes, but one that violates the laws of heredity.

And why doesn't that happen to other animals?

A supposed evolutionary process that takes place *only* with humans, and excludes all other species, is highly suspect. It goes entirely against natural selection as defined by Darwin.

And look at the Bible, which gives us a brainteaser that has its roots in some extraordinary biological event in prehistory— "There were giants in the earth in those days; and also after that, when the sons of God came in unto the daughters of men, and they bore children unto them, the same became mighty men which were of old, men of renown" (Genesis 6:2-4).

What could be plainer? As we asked before, who could the "sons of God" be but extraterrestrial visitors? And when they mated with the "daughters of men" and bore them children, *those children became "mighty men, of renown."*

That biblical quotation alone is enough to place something like the blessing of divine truth on the Hybrid Man theory.

If not, how can biblical scholars and theologists possibly interpret that verse in any other sense-making way? And it is quite noticeable that this scriptural bombshell is shunned, or passed off glibly, and never fully analyzed in any sermon in church. The religionists tend to consider such enigmatic verses as "imaginative" passages of garbled import, written when the inspired authors were less than "inspired."

But what if those words are truly "divine" (truthful) writings straight from "headquarters"?

Certainly all religious people, if they are sincere in wanting to understand the truths buried in the scriptures, should deeply ponder those words and wonder if not only science but all theology has been preaching a false doctrine about the origin of humanity. Preachers and scientists have been woefully wrong before. Are they once again abysmally wrong, or blind to the truth? If so, it is indeed a "cardinal sin" any way you look at it.

To return to the subject of genius in men, we find another hybridization clue in science's study of the human brain's structure.

The cerebrum, or upper portion of Man's brain, is huge in proportion to the rest of the "primitive" cerebellum inherited from our animal ancestry. And surrounding the cerebrum is the accordion-pleated cortex, an "envelope" that produces all thoughts and abstract ideas. As recent authorities put it:

> The cortex is not only the seat of intelligence, it is also, and perhaps more significantly, the association center of Man's brain. ... Among animals, many patterns of action are nearly automatic, performed by instinct or through previous conditioning. In Man, for the most part, these patterns are performed consciously. ...This use of the brain results in what is known as reasoned behavior, a mental phenomenon that only Man is capable of because only he has the large cortex that is necessary in order to achieve it.[13]

Now, it is not only a popular notion but a scientific fact that we humans only use a *part* of our full brainpower. Some say we use one-tenth and leave nine-tenths fallow. Others say one-third and two-thirds. But in any case, the full or even nearly full use of the brain probably results in what we call genius.

But if the *average* human brain is already an overendowment, as we have seen, then what can we call genius but a super-overendowment! The laws of natural selection are here so utterly violated that no evolutionist can possibly deny it.

The next pregnant question is: Where did that enormous cerebrum cortex, which gives us overendowment piled on overendowment, come from?

If it cannot conceivably be a product of earthly Evolution, it must have come from a nonearthly source in outer space.

Surely anyone reading this can add that obvious two and two and get the simple and inexorable answer: that our magnificent thinking apparatus came from another world. That our great cortex was biogenetically bestowed on Hybrid Man by his Starman colonizers.

We are almost tempted to say, *We rest our case.* But we won't because our case is far from through! There is more, much more, to add to the circumstantial proof of our Hybrid Theory in the rest of this book.

Genius may in another way be an indication that Man is a Hybrid. For in the mystery of genius, why is it that we cannot produce it whenever we choose? We can breed cats with no tails, dogs as big as small horses, and rabbits that weigh ninety pounds. We cannot, however, breed geniuses in our own, our very own, human race!

It has been tried. Time after time, in ancient times as well as modern, men and women of surpassing intellect have married in high expectation, only to find that their children were either quite ordinary or quite intelligent — but not geniuses.

This points out quite plainly that human breeding, in relation to its mental attributes, does *not follow the Mendelian laws* that are a corollary of natural selection.

We can predict or anticipate blue eyes, color blindness, and perhaps light or dark hair — but not where and when genius will appear in which children. This indicates the genius-gene is not Evolution-born, where it would operate in a "normal" manner in the human race, but is instead an alien gene that randomly pushes to the surface at odd and unpredictable times.

One of the authors, Max H. Flindt, has come up with his own special outlook on this matter of the quality of the human mind.

We have seen, he says, that each person is a mixture of physical and mental traits, a mixture whose complexities we have so far not seen clearly. But we can suspect that there is an *order* in these complexities.

That is, just as a list of chemical elements can be arranged in an extremely useful table (Periodic Table of the Elements, as per Mendeleev), we may be able to place each person living today in a "niche" or "category," both physically and mentally, to make up a grand Periodic Table of Human Beings.

And further, just as we combine two elements from their precise table of properties to form a predicted compound, might we not similarly use our Periodic Table of Human Beings so that a couple, male and female, could produce offspring who are guaranteed geniuses in advance?

A breathtaking thought! But don't smile. Some modern geneticists are boldly stating that in time, we will be able to manipulate the genes in wholesale fashion to produce any desired "kind" of humans with the precision of an automated baking machine turning out pies. They shy clear, quite naturally, from stating *what* kind of "planned humans" would be best to turn out, but surely no one would object to producing an increased number of pure geniuses.

Looking at how one Einstein completely overturned science for the better, within the past half-century, we can almost visualize how much a dozen Einsteins — per year! — would advance civilization.

And yet, perhaps there is a warning in this. The genius we specifically aim for should be in the fields of the humanities, not science-technology. It almost seems as if the starmen slipped a bit and infused too much of the technology gene into us, and not enough of the social gene.

That is, we need true leaders toward a better world, statesmen of far vision, social geniuses, human-relationship experts, philosophical masterminds, peace-promoters — every kind of humanitarian mind.

The human race has overbalanced the scales and rushed too far ahead into an automated and mechanistic "paradise" that is growing into a spiritual hell, because people are at odds with one another and lack sympathetic communication.

Can the Periodic Table of Human Beings, used with judicious wisdom, miraculously bring forth on this world men of Christlike genius, who will use ten-tenths of their awesome minds to guide the human race away from possible cataclysm?

And if we are indeed a Hybrid colony of the unseen starmen, who may still be our silent watchdogs today (see last chapter), are they striving as best they can to somehow promote biogenetic science on Earth and thus open up the path for us to better the world by producing better minds?

15

Mental Clues

From the sublime to the unsublime. In fact, from the greatness of the genius mind to the tragic state of a mind that is ill. That is our next foray into the mental mysteries of humanity as a whole.

It is quite possible that one disorder of Man's mind — schizophrenia — may be key evidence that Man is a Hybrid. Schizophrenia literally means "split mind." *Split mind?*

What is there about the human intellect that could cause an investigator or physician to label any mental illness as having "split" the mind? Actually, the medical term schizophrenia describes quite appropriately what does happen to its victim. He splits, mentally, and gives evidence of being only partly a rational human being, as far as his mind is concerned, and becomes a personality of dual nature.

Further, as we shall soon see, there are some schizophrenics who give evidence of the behavior patterns of prehistoric Man — in short, ape-man. Just as genius is a possible evidence of the superintelligent outer-space ancestors of Man, schizophrenia is a striking parallel evidence of Man's earthbound ancestral forms.

189

A schizophrenic may simply be showing that he is part Starman and part Hominid. Thus, the very symptoms of schizophrenia are credible evidence that Man is a Hybrid.

Why? Simply because animals who are products of straight Evolution never show evidence of schizophrenia whatsoever (as established by animal psychologists in many unique experiments).

Approximately 0.85 percent of the United States population is affected, at some time or other in their lives, by this cerebral malady. This means that about one out of 130 citizens becomes a victim.

It has been estimated that before the new tranquilizers were introduced in America, more than 45 percent of all mental-hospital patients were long-term schizophrenics. In a recent year, it was calculated that more than 250,000 people in the United States were under treatment for this unfortunate affliction. [1]

Schizophrenia is not only the single most common mental illness, it is also the most puzzling. What actually causes schizophrenia is one of the major mysteries of medicine. [2] Many theories are current about the origin of the disease and it has been said, not entirely in jest, that there are as many theories about schizophrenia as there are psychiatrists.

But, as yet, no single theory has received the unqualified endorsement of even 50 percent of the practicing psychiatrists. And the symptoms of this psychosis were first described long before 1900. Obviously, therefore, although tranquilizers are doing wonders as an alleviating treatment for schizophrenia, we still lack a clear picture as to the real reason why people get this mind disease.

Through the years, some very unusual things have been discovered about schizophrenia.

For instance, it has been found that many victims of this disease have some very peculiar body hair patterns. [3] More specifically, men who are prone to this disease display feminine body-hair patterns, and women victims often display the converse.

Schizophrenic patients oftentimes show evidence of small hearts and other slight but noticeable physical abnormalities. [4] Yet no one has been able to prove to the satisfaction of the general psychiatric profession that physical changes occur in the *brains* of schizophrenics.

There is one other bit of evidence regarding the victims of this disease—some advanced patients, hopeless victims beyond the reach of medical help, display thinking patterns that resemble exactly those displayed by animals.

This is how it is described (paraphrased, not verbatim):

> A patient who has not spoken for years wants to have her hair combed. She will run her fingers through her hair (which she would not do if it were combed), and the attendant will correctly interpret her wish and comb her hair. This is called an "as if" action, and characterizes the thinking of lower animal forms. Dogs, for instance, upon looking at a piece of meat, will lick their chops *as if* they had already eaten a piece of the meat. Similarly, a mental patient will make flat, circular, sweeping motions with her hands while looking at a wrinkled rug — obviously making motions that she could make only if the rug were perfectly smooth on the floor, and expressing, by this means, her wish that someone would smooth out the rug. Similarly, animals, apes included, will make motions that can be made only *after some prized goal is obtained,* and thereby express the wish that the goal were obtained. This "as if" thinking is seen so often in schizophrenia that I believe it is atavistic and represents regression to some prehistoric thought-processes.

We shall see later how that phase "prehistoric thought-processes" hits closer to the mark than they know!

We are now ready to formulate a theory — a theory that may explain why schizophrenics get this disease. Let us grant that mankind, unknown to himself, is a Hybrid — partly of Earth origin and partly of outer-space origin. It may be possible that a certain small fraction of our population is, in a sense, *imperfectly* hybridized.

That is to say, these individuals may not be perfectly "homogenized" in their two diverse biological heritages from earthly Hominid and alien Starman.

Does this also help to explain the mystery of the microcephalic idiot who may have the small head and brain of our early Hominid ancestors? And does it explain the fact that some schizophrenics have abnormal body-hair patterns related to ancient furry coats? And, finally, is their mental apparatus as scrambled and awry as their small hearts and otherwise defective physiques? This applies only to those schizophrenics who have physical defects but would also apply in general to the majority of schizophrenics who are physically normal but mentally abnormal.

The questions above enable us to begin to make some sense out of the confusing picture. It is easy to suppose that these people may have a defective integration between the "beast" (Hominid) and the genius (Starman) in their brain as an inherent aspect from hybridization in prehistoric times.

This explanation seems to make sense, for it is well known that schizophrenics are often very intelligent and can function well in life, providing they are not placed in positions of excessive strain or responsibility that may make them "split" mentally.[5]

To many people, the above possible explanation for the origin of schizophrenia may seem to be of little use to humankind. But if the theory is correct, we can see immediately that some fascinating possibilities open up for the possible biochemical treatment of schizophrenia; second, for a new approach in the psychiatric treatment of this disease; and, above all, for "relief from stigma" that is typified by the epithet "kook."

Someone more proficient in this area than the authors may be able to formulate a radically new and successful course of therapy based on the above premise. It could possibly result in a "miracle" treatment, with a good chance of recovery for many schizophrenics now regarded as hopeless cases, *if it is understood by the doctor that the patient has a mind "split" between his Hominid and his Starman heritages.*

Still more significant, as possible proof of the Hybrid theory, is that very recent medical research strongly indicates how schizophrenia may be *inherited* through genes, rather than being the result of bad environment and emotional traumas.[6] A roundup of opinion among researchers states that "with respect to the mode of genetic transmission (through the generations), some investigators advocated a single-gene theory involving dominance....Some have advocated a theory of recessiveness... others a double-gene mechanism."

Isn't that a clear gene-linkage with the past hybridization of mankind?

That would go back to where Starman instilled his "brilliance gene" into the humanoid bloodline, which already of course held the "dimwitted gene" of low Hominid intelligence. And today, still carrying those two genes, some unfortunate humans are alternately governed by *both* of them to display their dichotomy in mentality.

Thus, we see that the "schizophrenia genes" of the medical researchers may well be the twin genes of beasthood and brainhood, acting in our Hybrid brain cells since ancient times to turn modern victims quite literally into "split personalities."

Like anthropology and its missing link, medical and psychological science has found schizophrenia a "hot potato" that leaves them nonplussed. Nobody can be left "nonplussed" by the clear-cut Jekyll-Hyde gene explanation under our Hybrid theory.

Want to know if your birthday falls on a Sunday, in the year 1992? Charles and George (last name withheld) can tell you in a split second — and be right. Yet the two young brothers have been in a California institute for the mentally retarded since age nine. They are low-IQ idiots in all average mental activities except one — they are mathematical prodigies.

They are called "idiot geniuses" by psychiatrists, and that brings us to a new category of mental phenomena displayed by the human mind.

How can a person be both an idiot and a genius?

Actually, they are not true geniuses except in one sole direction — the weird ability they have for using instant mental calculations of the most complex kind, while yet being unable to add two and two! Their cranial "talent" works only along one narrow groove.

Here's what they can do:

1. Tell instantly when any given date in any year ahead for twenty centuries will fall on a Sunday.

2. Snap out without hesitation that February 15, 2002, will be on a Friday, and that August 28, 1951, was a Saturday.

3. Tell you the birth date of any famous man in history and how old he would be if still alive today after many centuries.

4. Recall almost any day in their own lives and state whether it was cloudy, rainy, or sunny. They *never* miss.

Baffled scientists call them "walking calculators." But the amazing paradox is that the pair can neither add nor subtract, multiply nor divide any *ordinary* sums in arithmetic! You can stick them on adding one apple to one pear — but not on what dates Monday will fall on for all the years from today to A.D. 3000.

When asked how they do it, the two childlike men will give a lopsided drooling smile and say, "It's in my head." And psychiatrists admit that they have no better or more scientific answer to this near-incredible mental warp that crops up at rare times in human births and brains.

But we, the authors of this book, think *we* have an answer. And one that is a major backup for our Hybrid Man theory.

We call it the *Theory of Simultaneous Regression.* It proves once again that the concept of Man being a hybrid and a colony can be used — without strain — to solve many strange and baffling mysteries in human life.

One related aspect to the idiot-genius riddle is the strange fact that extremely ugly people have frequently proven to be of surpassing intelligence — so intelligent that their names are graven forever in human history.

Socrates was such an individual. He was a frog-faced, repulsive character whose greatest delight in life was a good intellectual argument.

When the "normal" Theory of Evolution is examined, it can be seen that by deduction, the most intelligent people should be the *least* apelike and, therefore, the most handsome of individuals. In fact, many fine intellectuals who were handsome and pleasing in appearance have drifted across the pages of history. Hollywood provides many excellent examples of high intelligence combined with extraordinary good looks.

But how can we equate this with the jarring note of the occasional *ugly* duckling in history who towered above his contemporaries in sheer intellect?

Among the ugly ducklings were men like Abraham Lincoln, Irwin S. Cobb, and Socrates as outstanding examples. These were men who were so ugly that they were actually objects of curiosity, while their contributions to mankind's wisdom, letters, laws, and sciences have been so great that their names will always command respect and honor.

Furthermore, it is difficult to equate intelligence with gigantic stature. But Lincoln was a giant for his day.[7] France's De Gaulle was also an enormous man of great height,[8] who, at an age when most other men had been retired for ten years or more, was pulling France up to powerful heights in the world community of nations.

He and the others seem not to fit Shakespeare's immortal lines: "Surely the good Lord would not put his most precious jewels into a tower four stories high."

Is it possible to devise a theory to explain these "apemen" and "giants" who, despite their physical freakishness have high IQs and enormous capacity for synthesis, organization, and creativity?

In our opinion, these strange geniuses can only be explained by starting with the assumption that Man is a Hybrid who occasionally has "throwbacks" or regressive types occurring in his progeny.

And, on rare occasions, humans produce a kind of individual that may be called a *"simultaneous regression type."* That is, they are both *mental* and *physical* throw-backs at the same time. It admirably explains Lincoln being superintelligent, ugly, and of enormous physical stature. He could most definitely have been a product of regression, for his *mind* was closer to that of our outer-space ancestors, and at the same time, his *body* was closer to the giant apes of the past.[9]

His case is a very vivid reminder of a previously quoted verse in Genesis: "There were giants in the earth in those days;... the same became mighty men of old, men of renown." Then there are the words of the famous anthropologist, Weidenrich: "I believe that giants are ranged somewhere in the human line — in the pre-history of Man."

If it is assumed that this argument provides a logical explanation for the ugly-geniuses and giant-geniuses who have so enriched the intellectual heritage of mankind, then we can at the same time reiterate that such "mixed" geniuses are arguments *in favor of Man's being a Hybrid.*

For, if Man is the product of *normal* or conventional Evolution, a regressive type of individual *would never, never have high intelligence.*

Evolution simply cannot work "backwards" that way.

It is the assumption that intelligence *superior* to modern Man's is ranged somewhere in Man's *past* that permits us to explain the ugly genius and the mental giant (both ways) of history. At the same time, it permits us to view with equanimity the current concept that the unusually intelligent people who are also handsome, superior types are but normal products of an exceptional advance in the evolutionary development of mankind.

It is the *exceptions* that prove the rule — the Hybrid Man theory.

This fledgling theory of simultaneous regression also permits that previous perplexing mystery of mankind to be explained — the idiot-geniuses.

It is important first to delve deeper into the unbelievable abilities of these idiot-geniuses, so that we see how impossible it is for that fantastic mental performance to come out of classic Evolution. A few lines from a textbook on psychology will be examined and this will lead us back to our idiot-genius enigma.

> Arithmetical prodigies have been found among the ranks of the feebleminded. ... A favorite feat is to determine the number of minutes a person has lived, from a knowledge of his age or date of birth (without paper and pencil). Multiplication of three place numbers, naming square roots and cube roots of four place numbers have also been executed within a few seconds.[10]

Seconds! If any of you have ever worked out cube roots of four-place numbers, *with pencil and paper,* you know how laborious and time-consuming such calculations are.

And again: [11]

> Henry Mondeaux, the untutored son of a poor woodcutter, is a famous example of remarkable arithmetic ability in an otherwise dull person. In his childhood, he received no instruction, but was sent to tend sheep at the age of 12. ... He worked out for his own use many special devices and aids to computations. After long exercise at these calculations, he offered to tell people the number of seconds in their ages. At this time a schoolmaster became interested in him and offered to instruct him. Unfortunately the boy had a very poor memory for names and addresses and he spent nearly a month searching the city before he was able to locate his benefactor. . . . He demonstrated his ability to solve [the following]:

"There is a fountain containing an unknown quantity of water; around it stand people with vessels capable of containing a certain unknown quantity. They draw at the following rate: the first takes 100 quarts and 1/13 of the remainder; the second takes 200 quarts and 1/13 of the remainder; the third takes 300 quarts and 1/13 of the remainder and so on until the fountain is emptied."

Mondeaux gave the correct answer to this question in a few seconds.

Here again is the strange mixture of incredible ability in one line of human endeavor coupled with quite the opposite in other areas, namely, idiot-like or apelike mental processes combined with "calculating genius." And/or with physical anomalies.

As Socrates, gifted beyond belief in philosophy, was froglike in appearance, so Mondeaux, the "lightning calculator," took almost a month to find his benefactor—a schoolteacher—in the city!

Again, the theory of simultaneous regression, easily supportable by findings from genetics, can explain Henri Mondeaux.

To be explicit, his incredible mathematical ability would be a product of regression to this ability in Man's outer-space ancestors, while his lack of intelligence in all other areas was a parallel regression to the level of intelligence of Man's apelike ancestors.

Many other mysteries of mankind can be understood and interpreted through this theory of simultaneous regression. It is actually a corollary of the main theory that Man is a Hybrid — a mental phenomenon that does not take us by surprise but, indeed, is *expected* if modern Man's mind is a "melting pot" of two minds, earthly and nonearthly.

Hence, we claim — quite reasonably, we think — that idiot-geniuses, ugly-geniuses, giant-geniuses, and all such weird physical/mental anomalies are a *direct consequence and proof* of the Hybrid Man theory.

It is not only some forms of mental illness, genius, and idiocy, combined with certain unusual physical characteristics, that are strange aspects of the human psyche. Beyond those are still further wonders of the human mentality on an even higher and more inexplicable plane.

First of these is the possibility that *racial memory* exists within us all, deeply buried and seldom, if ever, seeing the light of conscious memory in most individuals.

So little research has been done in this area — mostly by reason of biologists refusing to take the subject seriously because it smacks of "mysticism" — that there is little to present here. Nevertheless, it may be that many so-called cases of "reincarnation" believed in by various occult groups and Eastern philosophies are really manifestations of racial memory from ancient times, carried within the person's memory bank in his brain.

The visions of a "former life" may merely be the sudden dredging up of those fragmentary and fleeting memories that could not have happened in his own life — but could have happened to his ancestors and been passed along to him unknowingly as an evanescent memory.

Some cases of supposed reincarnation have been investigated so thoroughly that there can be little doubt that the person has had "extranormal" access to a body of facts and events that occurred before his time, sometimes centuries ago.

If such cases are authentic, they seem to bolster the validity of paranormal phenomena, ESP, parapsychology, and all those elusive fields of mental mysteries that science is helpless to deal with. And that scientists usually sweep under the carpet for not fitting into current theory of "things as they are."

Or things as the hard-nosed scientist *thinks* they are.

No, we are not mounting a defense of psychic phenomena. Rather, we are going to take certain inexplicable experiences called "paranormal" and lop off the "para," switching them from the realm of the unexplainable and "unscientific" into the area of rational acceptability. In short, we will give a nonoccult explanation for reincarnation in its various exotic forms, and certain types of "retrocognition" (seeing in the past) if they occur *before* the percipient was born.

In short, we are postulating that memories of past lives, vivid visions of past disasters many years before the "clairvoyant" person lived, and even the "inspiration" for great new ideas or scientific discoveries may come from racial memory.

Memory that we inherited from the *starmen*, mind you, when they injected their memory-genes into the gene pool of the entire human-race-to-be of early times.

A best-selling archeologist in both Germany and America embellishes this basic idea in his own way but to the same end.[12] He believes that brilliant scientific discoveries are culled from an all-embracing pool of "age-old knowledge." He also calls it "cosmic memory," which was brought to us by what the ancients called the "gods" who descended from heaven and taught primitive mankind many great wonders of civilization.

But this knowledge became lost through time and mis-chance and the march of many "dark ages" until "At certain fortunate moments the barriers separating us from the primitive memory fall. Then the driving forces brought to light again [in certain human minds by the stored-up knowledge from the starmen] became active in us."

The result is a Galileo inventing the telescope and advancing astronomy in one great leap, a Newton discovering or rediscovering the laws of gravity, an Einstein formulating the brain-bending concept of Relativity.

The above author has one very strong point to back up his contentions.

He hammers it home by saying, "Is it only a coincidence that printing and clockmaking, that the car and the airplane, that the laws of gravity, and the functioning of the genetic code, were invented and discovered *almost simultaneously. . .* in different parts of the world?"

Further examples are countless and often startling. Two astronomers, J. C. Adams of England and U. J. Leverrier of France, both worked out the position of the undiscovered planet Neptune almost on the same day and hour, advising where telescopes should be pointed.

The cotton gin was invented by two men separately and led to bitter court battles as to who was first and deserved the patent rights.

And need we point out one of the most conspicuous of all such "double" discoveries — *the Theory of Evolution itself!*

Darwin and Wallace may both have tapped the racial memory-bank within their brains — or the "cosmic consciousness," or whatever one may name it — at precisely the same moment. The starmen, products of other-world Evolution themselves, well knew the subject inside out and that knowledge could have lodged in the memory-cells of their progeny, including the whole human race and all its thinkers to come.

Scientists often state or admit that their great discovery came in a flash of "intuition" or as a "hunch" out of nowhere. They are awed and puzzled themselves at the sudden "inspiration" that swept through their minds, often while they were not even thinking of the subject. Or, as in the case of Friedrich August Kekulé, the famed nineteenth-century chemist, the brilliant idea of the "benzene ring" for organic compounds came to him in a "dream" at night.

We suggest that all such strange mental phenomena involving great ideas are nothing more than race memory, in which a rare pathway in one Man's brain is suddenly opened into the memory cells that hold the ancient inherited knowledge of our starmen sires long ago.

Many vivid dreams are also reported by people, wherein they seem to be savage, hairy cavemen, battling fierce extinct beasts like dinosaurs. Rather than pure subconscious imagination, we think those also are an example of race memory, only in this case, the recollections (by dreams) revert back to the other side of our hybrid makeup — to the racial memory of the Hominids with whom the starmen mated.

Another dream is reported so universally, as we know from psychiatric records and experimental "dream labs," that it goes beyond the bounds of mere coincidence. In fact, *you* have probably had this dream yourself — a dream of flying or floating effortlessly in the air, or of soaring like an eagle high over people and cities.

Now if it is so widespread among humans, where would we get such a *strange* dream? After all, we have nothing in our personal or racial history that could furnish the kernel for a flying dream — we have never passed through an evolutionary stage of being birds or flying mammals of any sort. The act of flying (without aircraft of course, which never take part in those dreams) with our own physical bodies — and always without wings or props of any sort — is utterly *alien* to our physical or mental natures.

A sudden clue to this ubiquitous phenomenon has come recently with the space age. Many people who first saw the motion pictures of astronauts in orbit, *floating in zero-g*, were startled, for it was exactly like their dreams of floating and slow-motion flying. With that clue, we can link it up to a very significant and ancient race-memory — *that of flying through space, in a spacecraft, where weightlessness goes on for days, months, or even years.* And from where else could this race memory come than our starmen ancestors, who spent much time in space travel?

A peculiar, "out-of-place" dream of flying common to most humans . . . and a postulated origin for our race from our space-flying star-sires. The two fit together so perfectly they almost clap together resoundingly. Millions of years of spaceflight and adaptation of the starmen to zero-g weightlessness not only worked its way into their gene pool but was then transmitted into our earthly gene pool in the guise of a strange racial memory that manifests itself only in our dreams. Everyone knows how "weird" and "fantastic" his flying dream seems, even while he's dreaming it.

And so, the theory of Hybrid Man can not only solve scientific secrets about Man's origin, but also explain quite nonmystically a sizable body of psychic phenomena coming out of racial memory but misinterpreted by paranormal researchers as "reincarnation," "retrocognition," and "out-of-the-body experiences" (astral projection through time and space which are often reported quite like the above "flying" dreams).

And again we submit that the concept of Hybrid humanity is the *simplest* explanation for the anomalies in both fields. According to the principle of Occam's razor — always to choose the least complicated explanation out of many alternatives — the theory of Hybrid mankind should be taken more seriously than skeptics might want to.

To get back to race memory — once implanted in the human brain, any memory, however trivial, is *never forgotten* (the consensus of psychiatrists and psychologists today). Thus, the ancients passed their memory of how Evolution worked, as told by the starmen, along to future generations through patterns of memory genes.

It is hardly a stretch of imagination to say that if the "memory" of how to form a human baby is implanted in the ovum or indelibly impressed on the chromosome pattern within the egg cell, then why could not a *memory* from ancient times also be transmitted in the same way? This requires no magic or occultism or wild imagination to make it possible as well as highly logical.

It so happens it is *not* imagination at all, as recently proved by scientific work right in the laboratory. Briefly, researchers in a unique experiment first trained worms (planariums) how to seek light when placed in darkness in a simple maze. Then they chopped up or even ground up the worms into a mash, which they fed to other living worms. Presto — the new worms did not blunder around helplessly in the maze but uncannily found the light with little trouble.

Yet they had *not* been trained. How could they "know" which way to go?

The researchers calmly announced that there was only one answer — the new worms had "eaten memories" from the chopped-up worms! To be more explicit, the cells of the mashed worms must have held some indestructible gene/chromosome (DNA) pattern of memory of how to lick the maze, and the new worms gained that knowledge by simple "digestion" of the memory-cell pattern of the dead worms.

If that isn't weird enough (in scientific eyes), the researchers also bred the worms who possessed the maze know-how, and their progeny, too, were maze experts! We are moved to proclaim (that is the only immodest word) that the above experiments are direct and undeniable *proof* that there *is* such a thing as racial memory, theorized for a long time but heretofore stubbornly denied by orthodox science.

We spelled out the above in rather pedantic and plodding terms in order to leave no doubt in the reader's mind that science itself has backed up the existence of racial memory. The authors of this book did not "invent" it.

The enormous implications of a universal race memory can well be left to your imagination — that within us all lurk deeply buried memories of tremendous knowledge implanted into the human gene-pool by the superscientific starmen, as part of our mental "heritage." At rare and glorious times, one among us somehow blunders through the phylogenic "amnesia curtain" and remembers something terrific that he joyously announces as his own genius, not knowing the truth.

It may be that all, or most, major scientific discoveries and great new ideas in any area of human life are in reality memory-gifts from the all-wise starmen. We need an "and/or" here — and/or the ideas come out of genius brains that are again an inherited "gift" from the same source.

Remember how we previously pointed out that the "rate" of genius in the human race has gone down steadily since ancient times, when people were more directly exposed to our star-sires' great knowledge? It may be that today we are only gleaning the leavings, through racial memory, of the great secrets of the universe. Our science technology is just a veneer of materialistic child's play.

What we do *not* yet seem able to tap out of racial memory are the golden roads to peace and plenty and the brotherhood of Man. Let us not be deceived by the gloss and glitter surrounding us when inside, our souls are hollow and afraid and abysmally ignorant.

The concept of racial memory immediately leads us into perhaps the greatest of all mysteries of the human mind. A mystery of several parts though all are related.

Where, in short, does Man get his *curiosity* that makes him want to find out what makes things tick? His restless drive for *more knowledge,* even if of a materialistic nature? His *ambitions to build a "better world"* even if his progress is slow and erratic toward that goal? His need, hunger if you will, for *religion?*

And, most vital of all, his *exploratory* instinct that is even now leading him off his home-planet into the space darkness, plus his *sense of destiny* that makes him dream of a shining goal awaiting him, somewhere?

If we take the exploratory attribute alone, we see how really great the gulf is between the primates and Man.

All the apes live together in small bands, never being solitary animals like leopards or tigers. These bands or "tribes" have rigid territorial rules about anybody wandering away alone, where they would be helpless prey to predators.

The ape-child is never allowed to roam freely and explore the world, so to speak. Not even the close-by world beyond his tribe's narrow jurisdiction. Nor does the apeling's limited brain have the capacity to see anything to explore for, beyond the necessities of eating, surviving, and procreating.[13]

Remember, that is all Evolution asks for, or has bred into the species.

The Man-child, however, is an ape of a different sort entirely.

We all know how even a baby will crawl to explore any odd or exciting thing it sees. True, young chimps in captivity will also display a certain amount of curiosity and pick up a brightly-colored toy or reach for a dangling balloon. But their attention span is very short, so that after a few pawings they lose all interest. And things such as color pictures in a book or the strange little human models inside a doll's house, leave the ape-child completely uninterested. He has no mental reach for the *complex,* like the human child's high-powered brain.

All through childhood, the urge is there to seek out the new and the unknown, as apes never *never* do. When chimps are given a set of building blocks, they will clumsily build crude structures for a short time, then tire of it and go to something else. The human child *keeps going,* finding ever new and more fascinating towers to build and knock down (so he can build again).

This is a simplified example but it clearly and unequivocally emphasizes this key point: *where apes leave off, humans begin.*

And all of that keep-at-it drive to take the world apart does not and *cannot* come out of Evolution. Natural selection simply cannot overendow a species with not only a "top-heavy" brain but also an incredible inner desire to learn things never known in nature — radio, cars, atomic power come immediately to mind. They are the result of Man's exploratory instinct.

How could nature build *that* into him?

Now, where do we get this unique and truly unearthly feature in our makeup?

We cannot say that our big brain alone egged us on, for the dolphin, whale, and elephant all have bigger brain-sizes and nobody has yet seen a dolphin in orbit, an elephant using a computer, or a whale teaching Einstein's theory.

Like a slot-machine hitting the jackpot, the answer falls into place with a bang if we merely think of our star-borne ancestors who, after achieving a supercivilization far beyond ours, *began exploring the universe in spacecraft.*

Ship after ship, crew after crew — and gene after gene — the grand *exploratory* heritage infused the entire race, forevermore.

Perhaps this phase lasted millions of years for the starmen, long enough for natural Evolution (which probably *did* operate on their world) to instill the seek-the-universe factor in their DNA/RNA/gene/chromosome system.

Hence, when the starmen visited Earth long ago and "created" hybridized mankind, we automatically inherited this greatest of all human attributes — *the restless and eternal drive to find out everything, see every existing object, and go everywhere.*

We submit that this answer is far more understandable and sense-making than evolutionary double-talk regarding how man's tool-making hand stimulated his brain — or was it the other way around? They are never sure, nor how much descending from the trees to the ground, to walk on two feet and leave the hands free, entered into the picture. Meaning, actually, that they are way off the track and are playing with phantoms instead of reality. Their Occam's razor is not sharp enough to cut through such entangled Gordian knots.

Besides, for this quantum leap from the nonexploratory ape to the space-exploring human to occur in a short million or two years of slow brain-evolution (a tick in the clock of natural selection), is sheer belief in superstition.

Scientifically, it must be rejected out of hand.

All those strange and esoteric mental "quirks" listed before — curiosity, quest for knowledge, ambitions for a better world, sense of destiny, need for religion, as well as the exploration urge — exist in every one of us, but no ape or lower animal can possibly share even one of them.

Why do we alone have such grandiose drives, ambitions, and yearnings?

No precept of Evolution or natural selection or survival of the fittest can even remotely account for the rise of those mental strivings in the human mind. You cannot start with ape-minds that are completely without intellect and get to human minds with their sublime thinking powers.

It's a non sequitur that a dozen Darwins could never cram into an evolutionary framework.

16

UFO Clues

Are the Unidentified Flying Objects (UFOs) real? Otherwise known as flying saucers?

We make the immediate point that whether or not these strange craft exist makes no actual difference to our theory of Hybrid Man, which is rooted solidly in anthropological, archaeological, anatomical, and other scientific data. Other people's theories of Man's possible extraterrestrial origins start with lengthy attempts to first prove the UFOs are from outer space and then go on to explain how mankind got on Earth. This book's approach, on the contrary, was to first establish that humans simply cannot be purely creatures of earthly evolution, and we will *now* go into the flying saucer phenomenon.

Be it admitted, however, that if UFOs prove to be bona fide vehicles from outer space, *it would be the strongest clue of all to the validity of our Hybrid Man theory.* In fact, not just a clue but virtual *proof.* The entire flying saucer phenomenon fits into the concept of Man as a Hybrid and a colony like a hand in a glove. For, if the flying saucer stories are true, then:

207

1. The extraordinary care with which the alleged pilots of these craft have evaded close contact or collisions with pilots in earthly aircraft and with humans in general is compatible with the concept of Man as a colony whose purpose at present is deliberately being kept from him.[1]

2. The unusual and vastly superior propulsion systems that the flying saucers seem to possess would support the supposition that man's outer-space ancestors have developed, through millions of years of scientific research, greatly superior power sources and space drives.[2]

3. The patient way in which the flying saucers are reported to practice surveillance of Man, his works, his vehicles, and his newest nuclear wonders also fits the concept that open contact will not be permitted between earthman and his ancestral race until Man evolves or progresses sufficiently to warrant trust.[3]

4. These flying saucers are supposed to require their occupants to endure incredible g-forces. Their designers, then, must know engineering principles that are so far ahead of anything we practice today that, scientifically speaking, it would be child's play for them to hybridize a planet and produce intelligent men out of brute-witted ape-men.[4]

5. The most important point is that the flying saucers' occupants are not too concerned about humans as yet being suspicious of their existence so long as they don't pin it down. This one basic fact has thunderous implications. It could mean that these outer-space intelligences will *choose* the time when contact can occur. Such actions would indicate that the starmen are going to reveal themselves in gradual ways so that panic and worldwide mental shock will be avoided. This sounds like true sympathy and *solicitude* toward *us — quite like wise masters for their colony.*

The conclusion is obvious. If flying saucers exist, they, and everything that is known about them, perfectly and neatly fit the theory that Man is a Hybrid and a colony.

But until those mysterious objects darting in our skies are detected by scientists for what they are (if ever), or reveal themselves openly as extraterrestrials (ETs), we can only say they may *someday* clinch the theory of colony Earth and Hybrid Man.

UFOs, or so-called flying saucers (paradoxically, of every conceivable shape besides the saucer-like disk), are not a recent phenomenon at all. Diligent UFOlogists (a branch of science that may someday become sanctioned) have dug into records far past and found innumerable references to unidentified aeroforms that read just like the present-day sightings of UFOs.[5] The Bible is particularly rich in such UFO lore, according to certain scholars,[6] but even Greek, Roman, and earlier literature mention "suns" and "moons" and "sickles"[7] that awed people looking into their night skies thousands of years ago.

Ezekiel's "flaming chariot" in the Bible is often cited by UFO researchers as an unmistakably described flying saucer. When this was stated in the best seller by Erich von Däniken *(Chariots of the Gods?),* a certain engineer at NASA laughed. He was a topnotch engineer of rockets and aircraft, and he told his wife it was a crackpot idea. To prove it, he read over the passages in the Bible telling about the flying phenomenon in detail. To Joseph Blumrich's surprise, the more he read, the more he began to see the basic engineering data for a true flying spacecraft. He thereupon wrote a whole book about it.[8] Blumrich was convinced that UFOs or spacecraft had indeed visited the biblical people as well as others in ancient times.

As a matter of fact, it is very likely that Neanderthal Man and the first Hominids two million years ago must also have spied unknown shining bodies in the sky and even seen them land, if our theory is correct. For the starmen who molded the human race genetically through hybridization must have visited Earth almost continually, in order to carry out their great human-creating experiments in their world-sized biological laboratory.

So even if UFOs were not reported today, we would have to "invent" flying saucers. After all, how else could our alien sires reach Earth except with spacecraft of some sort?

As a brief summary, the modern phase of UFOs began in the United States in 1947, when a businessman named Kenneth Arnold was flying his private plane in Washington state and was amazed to spy nine crescent-shaped objects speeding near Mt. Rainier and skipping along like "saucers" being sailed across water.[9] The press devised the name "flying saucers," and the controversy was on. The great controversy over whether they were real or illusionary still goes on to this moment, with great passion on both sides between the believers and skeptics. The latter include almost all "hard-nosed" scientists.

Ironically, as we have seen earlier in the book, the greater majority of scientists, including astronomers, today believe the universe is teeming with inhabited worlds and intelligent beings, human or otherwise. Wild horses, however could not drag out of them the acknowledgment that there is any connection between their belief and the sightings of alleged flying saucers. In the author's belief, those scientists are stubbornly failing or refusing to add a glaring two and two. But among scientific minds, there are a few who have achieved the enlightened answer of four.

One such was Ivan Sanderson (deceased 1972), noted zoologist, who, in a book surveying the entire UFO phenomenon, gives the speculations of earnest students of the field.[10] He lists the possibilities that mankind may not be a sole product of earthly evolution but may instead have been "seeded" on Earth by ETs, that superior intelligences may have consistently "interfered" with our history, and that we may actually be "owned" by other-world creatures who came and surreptitiously took over Earth long, long ago.

That basic idea, curiously enough, was stated by the famed Charles Fort, indefatigable collector of strange mysteries unexplained by science.[11] In the early 1900s, he listed many UFOs long before they were called flying saucers, and he dropped this sly little bombshell: "I think we [humans] are property."[12]

As we, the authors, acknowledged before, this general concept that Man may have an extraterrestrial origin was mentioned by others before us. "Mentioned" is the right word, since none of them attempted in any scientific way to *back up* their contention.

In that way, this book differs from them all by doing something for the *first time,* we believe — *examining factual data about mankind that removes this concept from the realm of a pure mental exercise and lifts it up by solid data into the category of legitimate scientific enquiry.* It is (if the simile can be forgiven) the "missing link" between UFO speculation and scientifically acceptable theory.

Another man of high scientific caliber who came to believe in UFOs as interstellar spacecraft was the late Wilbert B. Smith of Canada. During his directorship of Project Magnet, designed to investigate UFO anomalies, he came after long study to firm conclusions regarding them, including the fact that they "colonized" Earth. He first states unequivocally that the flying saucers are real, then adds significantly: "We may summarize the entire flying saucer picture as follows. We [the human race] have arrived at a time in our development when we must make a final choice between right and wrong. The [UFO] people from elsewhere are much concerned about the choice which we will make... partly because *we are their blood brothers* [italics added] and they are truly concerned with our welfare."[13] Quite obviously, Wilbert Smith had no doubt that the aliens were somehow responsible for implanting the human race on Earth.[14] Yet neither did he give any sort of tangible proof that his beliefs were true, and scientists have ignored him.

Two mainline scientists of international reputations have also voiced the possibility of ET visitations to Earth, but only in the far past, discrediting the UFOs of today. They are Dr. Carl Sagan, head of Planetary Sciences at Cornell, and Dr. S. I. Shklovski, noted Soviet scientist, who collaborated on a book, *Intelligent Life in the Universe.*[15] In it is this remarkably frank passage by Dr. Sagan, stating that he had come upon a legend that seemed to be a "genuine contact" with ETs. He adds, "It is of special interest because it relates to the origin of Sumerian civilization."[16]

As mentioned before, that event is one of the greatest mysteries in archeology and anthropology — if Cro-Magnon Man (modern Man) already existed in 40,000 B.C., why did it take him until 10,000 B.C. to achieve even rudimentary civilization, *30,000 years later?* Thus, the great *suddenness* with which civilization arose has always startled archeologists, and they have nothing but lame answers that are no answers at all.

Carl Sagan gives a much more rational and believable answer when he goes on to say, "Sumer was an early — perhaps the first — civilization in the contemporary sense on the planet Earth. ... Taken at face value the legend suggests that contact occurred between human beings and a non-human civilization of immense powers."

What else can a nonhuman civilization mean than a nonearthly one that exists on another world in space? Dr. Sagan even goes on to give the Sumerian description of the ETs and the craft they came in, also the many "wonders" they possessed, then admits *that this may not be myth but an actual historical event.* [17]

Sagan then cites one of those myths. "Sumerian civilization is depicted by the descendents of the Sumerians themselves to be of non-human origin. A succession of strange creatures appears.... Their only apparent purpose is to instruct mankind." He goes on to say that the strange creatures, called Oannes and other names, are always described as "endowed with reason," or as powerful "beings," as "semi-demons" and "personages" — but never as *gods.* Thus there was no religious obscurity or mythical fantasy mixed in with these writings, and they sound exactly like plain down-to-earth history. And it is originally stated in the legends that they always came from the sky!

That sounds precisely like the ancestral starmen arriving to help out his creations and teach the human race about civilization.

It is our firm contention in this book, of course, that the *only* true explanation for the rise of civilization and, indeed, of *Man himself,* is a gift from the starmen who hybridized Man and colonized Earth eons in the past. But Dr. Sagan is rather reluctant to endorse fully any ET theory. The foremost scientific exponent of UFOs in the United States, if not in the world, is the nuclear scientist Stanton T. Friedman. His forthright declarations about UFOs make no concession to "maybe" or "perhaps." To establish the reality of UFOs, as opposed to the opposition's arguments denying their physical existence, he says: [18]

Every large-scale scientific study of UFOs —there are at least four —has produced a substantial number of observations by competent observers of objects having definite size, shape, texture, and most important, flight characteristics indicating a) These are manufactured objects, b) They are under intelligent control, c) That the combination of physical description and flight behavior, as observed and described by witnesses all over the world, rule out terrestrial origin.

Contrary to the government's and the air force's public attitude that UFOs are in a limbo of scientific exile, Friedman declares that:

"Recent polls clearly show that a majority — silent though it may be — of engineers and scientists involved in research and development activities *do* believe that UFOs exist[19] and that the government has not told us all it knows. And that the Condon Report conclusions were *not* definite. A full 8% of these professional people believe *they* have observed a UFO, with another 14% thinking they may have. Half of the poll respondents — all professional engineers and scientists — believe that some UFOs originate in outer space!"

Friedman goes right on to hammer at the famous, or infamous, Condon Report of 1969. [20]

According to a special UFO subcommittee of the prestigious American Institute of Aeronautics and Astronautics (formerly the American Rocket Society) 30% of the 117 cases studied by the Condon committee could not be either identified, nor rejected for lack of information. These cases included three sightings by orbiting astronauts, and a number of combined radar-visual cases — some lasting for over an hour and involving more than six highly trained witnesses.

It may or may not be generally known that many of the most obdurate scientists who scorn the "UFO myth" still reject the Condon Report as "unscientific investigation" that was heavily biased from the start against all flying saucer reports.

Friedman also scornfully denounces Project Cyclops, the proposed effort backed up by international scientists to spend some $6 billion (repeat, $6 *billion)* to set up an enormous array of radio-telescopes in order to "tune in" the stars for messages from intelligent worlds.[21] Friedman makes the sparks fly as he says:

> "The really outrageous notion is that serious consideration is being given to spend billions on the possibility of tuning in to another civilization [in outer space] ... and no consideration is being given to getting data on the thousands of reported UFOs observed here as landing." His punch line is, "If we are interested in contacting extraterrestrials, as the very existence of Project Cyclops implies, *then why not try to contact UFO pilots?"*

Earlier in this book, the authors, too, were shaking their heads in bewilderment, wondering why scientists — if they are so anxious to get in touch with nonearthly creatures — do not concentrate intensely on solving the UFO mystery (which is right in front of their noses), on the simple possibility that they *might* be piloted by those very nonearthly beings they would love to trade formulas with. At least, how could they lose?

The abortive Condon Report cost some $600,000. A somewhat larger yet modest fund of say $5 million or $10 million could probably once and for all settle the flying saucer question and might conceivably result in breakthrough communications with UFOnauts. Surely, as Friedman so vehemently cries, that would be much more sensible than committing ourselves to an outlay of *600 times* that much money to aim a radio-telescope complex at a thousand random stars — and most likely miss the ones in between that are inhabited. It almost seems as if the scientific establishment has gone senile and can no longer make rational decisions on matters of cosmological importance.

Finally, Friedman makes a suggestion that suddenly throws great illumination on the whole UFO debate.[22] He mentions that as early as September 1970, "I suggested that a better term than UFO would be EEM — Earth Excursion Module. The analogy between the reported actions and behavior of our own Lunar Excursion Modules and their oddly dressed pilots, and the many reported UFOs on the ground... is a real one."

With telling logic he further expands on this:

In both cases we have strangely shaped — compared to airplanes, balloons, or helicopters — craft able to land in unprepared out-of-the-way places with no assistance from people at the landing sites. In both cases the pilots look weird by normal standards, though they all appear to be "humanoid." In each case, the pilots have been observed by reliable witnesses [NASA, in the case of our lunarnauts] to seek out and gather specimens, to pick up artifacts, and to apparently gambol aimlessly in what appears to be a childish fashion. The duration of the stay is limited and in each case the humanoids finally re-enter their Excursion Modules and take off again, without local assistance and without leaving someone behind.

The haunting similarity between our astronauts with their LEMs, and the aliens with their EEMs, continues beyond mere coincidence: "In both cases, the Excursion Modules have been observed to rendezvous with 'mother ships' and to apparently take off for another heavenly body at high speed. In both cases the reported mother-ships look nothing like conventional airplanes or rockets used to boost our spaceships into orbit."

We think Stanton T. Friedman has made his point.

For the record, we must include another aspect of the UFO mystery highly scorned by orthodox science, but which nevertheless should not be dismissed too lightly. Namely, ESP or telepathic communications that certain people claim to receive from the UFO occupants, sometimes referred to as the "Space Brothers."[23]

The arresting thing about many of these cases is that the recipients of the "voices" are *not* avowed psychics and never claimed to be such. They are sane, normal, everyday people who suddenly hear "voices within their minds." At first they think they are going insane but are finally gripped by the "authenticity" of the voice whose messages seem to "ring true." Probably many people never reveal this kind of deep, dark secret for fear of ridicule or worse, but those bold enough to set down the messages have a tremendous story to tell, which, if true, is proof positive that the UFOs are ridden by ETs. And some key messages back up the Earth-colony and Hybrid Man concept to an astounding degree.

We are not going to claim that such paranormal evidence is evidence at all. But our theory, which involves an original human race millions of years old, would hardly preclude the development of ESP abilities among them. In fact, it would almost seem to be another *inevitable* result, through an unguessable stretch of time, of the *mental* evolution of our starmen ancestors.

Perhaps this explains another great riddle among humans — the "mental voices" heard by famed people through history, including Joan of Arc and many religious saints that the churchhood does not condemn as insane, believing instead they have heard the "Word of God." That would be the past-age interpretation, but could the "Word of God" actually be from the UFOnauts? Most of their messages to the "contactees" of UFOlogy, whether those who ride in their spacecraft or those who merely receive ESP, are on a high plane of idealism, sounding quite "spiritual" in tone. [24]

More pertinent, however, than ESP contacts are what seem to be *personal* interactions between humans and starmen when they meet on the ground, and this has been apparently going on all through history right up to the present day. In each wave of saucer reports, there are a certain number of landing cases, and some percentage of the landing cases involve direct confrontations with the starmen with whom talk is exchanged. It is almost as though the aliens are "checking up" on their colony of Hybrid people, by obtaining scattered "samplings" of how things are going on Earth.

But most significant, as far as this book is concerned, are the reports of *sexual* encounters with starmen. Many of these reports cannot be derided, because of their exhaustive documentation by doctors.

One case stands out as a "classic," the seduction of Antonio Villas-Boas of Brazil by a four-foot-tall beauty in her flying saucer.[25] Briefly, the young farmer was hustled aboard the saucer by "little men" or humanoids, and was locked in a room naked. Also naked was the diminutive seductress with white skin and slanted eyes who entered and proceeded to make unmistakable advances to Antonio. They twice had intercourse, which the Brazilian said was quite "normal" by earthly standards.

The later investigators were struck by one gesture the girl made, according to Antonio, after intercourse. She patted her abdomen and pointed upward at the stars. *Her apparent meaning was that the child resulting from the union would be born on another world in outer space.*

The reader will instantly see how this reverberates back through many previous chapters dealing with the postulated interbreeding between the starmen and Hominids or early Homo-humans. One can readily surmise, from the case above, that the starmen are still keeping a watch on how their Hybrid humans came out, and whether they remain sexually compatible with the original race. Or are the starmen still experimenting and "improving" the human stock by continued matings that will introduce new and better characteristics into the human gene-pool?

For the record, the late Dr. Olavo Fontes, a distinguished Brazilian doctor, personally interviewed Antonio and, after checking all details carefully, pronounced his story absolutely true. Psychiatrists also examined Antonio to give him a clean bill of health, mentally.[26]

Dozens of other cases of alleged sexual contact with aliens are on record, including women as well as men. Because of the intimate nature of such alien/human coital contacts, the people involved are anonymous except in the guarded files of various private organizations of good reputation that investigate all UFO reports.

It is estimated, however, that at least ten times more sex cases are never reported at all, quite understandably. What man or woman wishes to publicize or even reveal in confidence their sex experiences, when the other party is not another earthly man or woman but a male or female from outer space? Hence, we do not know just how many of these clandestine sex affairs are secretly being currently carried out by the starmen, year after year. We who are writing this book suspect it would create a worldwide "scandal" if the truth were known.

John A. Keel, among the foremost UFO investigators in the world, has interviewed hundreds of people involved in UFO encounters and states that he has an undisclosed number of such sexual UFO contact cases in his files.[27] It must be a large number, because he puts it that he uncovered "sexual encounter" cases in several states, concentrated around college campuses. He remarks further that there is often a sort of paranormal aspect to these cases, deliberately fostered by the UFO-people. "Essentially," he says, "these sexual encounters follow the patterns of the well-known incubus-succubus phenomenon found in religious and psychic lore." It is a known fact that even in nonsexual contact cases, the witness seems befuddled later as if the aliens had hypnotized him to "forget it all." He sometimes cannot account for a "lost" hour or two during the encounter.

One wonders, therefore, if most human specimens chosen for sexual experiments have similarly been "brainwashed" into not even realizing they underwent some sort of sex contact with beings from another world? It might be a widespread biogenetic sex-program practiced by the starmen today for purposes we can only guess at.

Dr. Berthold Schwartz of New Jersey, a psychiatrist who runs down UFO reports on his own, has studied cases in which the witness' genitals were affected after contact with UFOnauts, usually in the form of rashes or pimples around the sex organs.[28]

"Obviously sex and the sexual system," observes John A. Keel, "plays a mysterious role in these [UFO] manifestations." He has been quietly conducting an extensive survey into the matter, he says, "hoping to develop a rational hypothesis before bringing such a delicate matter into the open."

With all the sex-advice books on the market today, we might only half-facetiously suggest a new one — *Sex, Outer-Space Style.*

Yet all these sex fun and games in which the starmen indulge (but presumably for more serious purposes!) should not surprise us if we recall the chapter on "Sex Clues," in which it was pointed out that our space sires are even "sexier than the human race."

In context with this subject, it is an established fact that more than 100,000 people utterly vanish from Earth each year.[29] No trace is ever found by missing persons bureaus nor by the best detective hunts. Many UFOlogists surmise that these people are *abducted* by the starmen and whisked away from Earth alive. What their fate is, we don't know, but from certain hints in both contactee writings and ESP messages from UFOs, the "victims" need not be pitied. Some are allegedly taken to the home world or worlds of the starmen to live a new life in a semi-utopian society. Perhaps they are "guinea pigs" but only in the sense of what their reactions are to such advanced civilizations. The starmen colonizers may be constantly testing out the state of the human mind to see when and if their earthly colonists can be ready to accept the shocking truth — that we humans are always under intelligent surveillance. Also to find out, perhaps, when the human psyche will be matured enough so that Earth and its denizens can be introduced to the vast brotherhood of civilized worlds throughout the galaxy.

We might bring in the UFO "flap" that occurred in 1973-74. Utterly confounding the air force, which abandoned its Project Blue Book because UFOs seemed more mythical than real, and also dismaying the Condon committee, which thought it had written off the flying saucers as something akin to poppycock, a great series of sightings swept the United States. Far too many impeccable and credible witnesses — including state governors, senators, pilots, mayors, police chiefs, scientists and other dignitaries — reported seeing UFOs for the authorities to ignore.[30]

One wonders if the government, sooner or later, will not be forced into launching another scientific investigation, hopefully better than that of the Pentagon or University of Colorado.

One final look at the UFO controversy, to see if it can be resolved affirmatively or not and how valid this book's thesis is. One of the authors, Otto O. Binder, published a book in which he listed the main corroborative points that well sum up the grand concept of Earth being a deliberately planted colony of hybrid humans, in a galactic project going back millions of years.[31]

With some changes and additions, they are:

✰ The many legends, from all over Earth among widely separated cultures, of "skymen" descending like gods and benefiting or guiding mankind.

✰ The fact that Man himself is a misfit in the scheme of classical Darwinian evolution.

✰ The vast prevalence of dwarfs, kobolds, trolls, pixies, fairies, gnomes, and other "little men" in human myth and literature, sounding very much like the many reported landings today of "little humanoids" three or four feet tall.

✰ The Villas-Boas sex-seduction case, and those of other men and women, indicating biosexual experimentation still being carried out today by the saucermen.

✰ The many "contactee" stories in which (if taken at face value and not yet proven utter hoaxes or hallucinations) the saucermen often claim to have visited Earth for untold eons, having a "vested interest" in the human race.

✰ The perennial disappearance of thousands of people from Earth annually — as well as many animals — who could quite logically (with no other explanation available) have been spirited away by UFOs.

✰ The many ships through the centuries, and modern planes, which have just as mysteriously vanished from Earth, tying in with the extraordinary number lost in the notorious Bermuda Triangle, which is haunted by UFOs.[32]

✰ The long and endless list of saucer sightings (even if clothed in obscure language of old) that goes back to the first Sumerian and Egyptian written records,[33] and undoubtedly could be continued back to Hominid times millions of years ago.

✰ The unsolved astronomical sightings through telescopes, since the Seventeenth century, of gigantic objects in space crossing the sun or moon's disk and disobeying the laws of celestial mechanics for natural bodies, thus proving they are artificial and powered craft.[34]

☆ The Bible, richest source of UFOs in disguised language as "chariots of fire" and "glowing clouds," with visitations of "angels" (probably starmen).

☆ The single significant biblical statement — that the Sons of God took unto themselves wives from the daughters of Earth.[35]

☆ Hieroglyphics, carvings, and cave paintings of prehistoric times depicting obvious "astronauts" and spacecraft.[36]

☆ The fantastic feats of ancient engineering — pyramids, giant statues, colossal stone temples — that were impossible for the primitive man to construct with Stone Age technology.[37]

☆ The at least 1 million "earths" or habitable worlds that scientists concede must exist in our galaxy, from which the starmen could therefore have come.

☆ The possibility of faster-than-light speeds, so that spacecraft from remote suns could reach Earth.

☆ The very sudden uprise of civilization in Sumeria, and the universal legends of "sky people" bringing knowledge to Earth.

☆ The highly advanced astronomical knowledge of ancient peoples — Chaldeans and Mayans, particularly — who had no telescopes.

☆ The point-by-point analysis of how "slow motion" evolution could never have produced big-brained man in the short time between ape-men and humans.

☆ The strong possibility that giants and monster-men really existed and were the abortive results of the star-men's interbreeding program.

☆ The "life gap," wherein no life existed in pre-Cambrian times, as if living microorganisms were "seeded" on Earth.

☆ The peculiar fact that desert species of plants have no fossil history at all, as if "imported" to Earth.

☆ All the impressive list of physiological and anatomical attributes that are unique to Man and could never have come out of classical evolution.

☆ The startling Piri Reis map, copied from ancient cartographic charts that only flying machines could have made, as early as 10,000 B.C.[38]

☆ The giant UFO "landing fields" observable only from the air, dating back to ancient times.[39]

✮ The pattern of worldwide surveillance of our planet by UFOs, including people, cars, planes, ships, and orbiting vehicles.

✮ The pattern of "little humanoids" from landed saucers[40] who are seen gathering specimens of plants, rocks, even animals.

✮ The "green fireballs" of 1947-52 seen in the Southwest near our atomic installations, as if the saucermen are "watchdogs" against the outbreak of nuclear war.[41]

✮ The inexplicable "waves" of UFO sightings — 1952-54, 1957-61, 1966-67, 1973-74, which may be "preconditioning" exercises to prepare earth people for the eventual appearance of the starmen in public.

Add to all this man's insatiable curiosity, exploration instincts, religious feelings, and amazing sense of destiny, and we have an enormous mass of anomalies and mysteries about man's body and psyche that science cannot explain in the least.

Only the theory of Hybrid Man and colony Earth can.

We seem exposed today to a vast unknown that Man's mind has not yet encompassed. We are perhaps on the verge of the greatest revelations known in history. We may learn, soon perhaps, that we are only one tiny part of a Grand Family of humans stretching to the remotest star.

If so, it should be met with revel and joy to know that we are citizens not of one world, but of the great and wondrous universe.

We rest our case.

Mankind is a Child of the Stars.

Notes

Introduction

1. Norman MacBeth, *Darwin Retried,* Gambit Inc., Boston, 1971.
2. *Ibid.,* p. 149.
3. Lynn Rose, "The Censorship of Velikovsky's Interdisciplinary Synthesis," *Pensée,* May 1972, p. 30.
4. *Ibid., p.* 44.
5. *Ibid., p.* 30.

Chapter 1

1. *Life Magazine,* October 19, 1949, p. 113.
2. *Science News,* August 19, 1972, p. 117.
3. *Ibid.,* September 25, 1971, p. 204.
4. *Ibid.*
5. International Bible Students Association, *Did Man Get Here by Evolution or By Creation?* Watchtower Bible & Tract Society, 1967, p. 41.
6. *Ibid.,* p. 42.
7. A. Bean, *The Races of Man,* The University Society, chap. 8.
8. *Life Magazine,* op. cit.
9. *Ibid.*
10. *The Universal Standard Encyclopedia,* vol. 6, Funk & Wagnalls, Unicorn, New York, 1962, p. 2245.
11. Charles Darwin, *The Descent of Man,* Hurst & Co., New York, p. 624—.
12. *Ibid.,* p. 64.
13. Loren Eisley, *Darwin's Century,* Doubleday, Anchor Books, Garden City, N.Y., p. 309.
14. *Early Man,* Life Nature Library series Time-Life Books, New York, 1971, p. 52.
15. Stewart Edward White, *The Unobstructed Universe,* E. P.

Dutton, New York, 1940, p. 90.

16. Ivan Sanderson, ed., "Pursuit," *Journal of S.I.T.U.,* Columbia, NJ., January 1972, p. 11.

17. *Saga,* Gambi Publications, Brooklyn N.Y., June 1970, p. 25.

18. *The Primates,* Life Nature Library series, Time-Life Books, New York, 1971, p. 177.

19. *Early Man,* op. cit., p. 176.

20. Otto O. Binder, *Flying Saucers Are Watching Us,* Belmont Books, New York, 1968, p. 121.

21. Eric Norman, *Gods, Demons and UFO's,* Lancer Books, New York, 1970, p.12.

Chapter 2

1. Such eminent scientists as Professor Roland Puccetti, Willy Ley, Dr. Robert Bieri, and Dr. Joseph Kraus, along with others, have developed this "universal human" theory by scientific logic.

2. *Science News,* July 14, 1973, p. 30.

3. "Directed Panspermia," a paper by Dr. Francis H. C. Crick, molecular biologist of Cambridge, and L. E. Lorgel, Salk Institute for Biological Studies, San Diego.

4. *Science News,* May 11, 1974, p. 301.

5. *Ibid.,* November 27, 1971, p. 357.

6. *Ibid.,* June 5, 1971, p. 383.

7. *Ibid.,* June 26, 1971, p. 435.

8. Harlow Shapley, *Of Stars and Men,* Beacon Press, Boston, 1958, p. 85.

9. *Science News,* March 27, 1971, p. 210.

10. *Ibid.,* June 26, 1971, p. 435.

11. Shapley, op. cit., p. 144.

12. I. S. Shklovski and Carl Sagan, *Intelligent Life in the Universe,* Holden-Day Inc., San Francisco, 1966.

13. *National Enquirer,* August 20, 1972, p. 30.

14. Otto O. Binder, *"Are the Russians Secretly in Direct Communication With UFO's?"* UFO Report, Saga, Spring 1974.

15. *Ibid*

Chapter 3

1. *Science News,* August 26, 1972, p. 137.

2. *Ibid.,* May 13, p. 313.

3. *Ibid.,* June 24, 1971, p. 64.
4. *Ibid.,* March 27, 1971, p. 210.
5. Earl C. Slipher, *Mars,* Sky Publishing Corporation, Cambridge, Mass., 1962, p. 29.
6. Ross E. Hutchins, *Plants Without Leaves,* Dodd, Mead & Co., New York, 1966, pp. 84-95.
7. *Science News,* June 24, 1972. p. 405.
8. *Ibid.,* August 12, 1972, p. 105.
9. *Ibid.,* January 22,1972, p. 55.
10. *Ibid.,* June 24, 1972, p. 405.
11. *Ibid.*

Chapter 4

1. *Evolution,* Life Nature Library series, Time-Life Books, New York, 1971, p. 149.
2. Ernest A. Hooton, *Up From The Ape,* rev. ed., Macmillan, New York, 1947, pp. 394-395, 630-631. (Also, Sir Arthur Keith, *The Antiquity of Man,* J. B. Lippincott Co., Philadelphia, 1925.)
3. *Early Man,* Life Nature Library series, Time-Life Books, New York, 1971, p. 47.
4. *Science News,* September 2, 1972, p. 152.
5. *Ibid.*
6. Maitland A. Edey, *The Missing Link,* Time-Life Books, New York, 1972, p. 52.
7. *Ibid.,* p. 143.
8. *Ibid.,* p. 144.
9. *Ibid.,* p. 146.
10. *Science News,* op. cit.
11. *Ibid.*
12. B. Ernst & T. J. E. De Vries, eds., *Atlas of the Universe,* Thos. Nelson & Sons, New York, p. 131.

Chapter 5

1. Desmond Morris, *The Naked Ape,* Dell Books (paperback), New York, 1967, p. 18.
2. George Price, *The Phantom of Organic Evolution,* Revel Co. Ltd., London, 1924, p. 91.
3. Norman Macbeth, *Darwin Retried,* Gambit Inc., Boston, 1971, p. 121.

4. *Ibid.*, p. 140.
5. *Early Man,* Life Nature Library series, Time-Life Books, New York, 1971, p. 51.
6. *The Primates,* Life Nature Library series, Time-Life Books, New York, 1971, p. 179.
7. Morris, op. cit., p. 35.
8. *Ibid.*, p. 35.
9. *Science News,* November 18, 1972, p. 324.
10. Macbeth, op. cit., p. 159.
11. *Ibid.*, p. 160.

Chapter 6

1. *Early Man,* Life Nature Library series, Time-Life Books, 1971, p. 107.
2. *Ibid.*, p. 126.
3. Norman Macbeth, *Darwin Retried,* Gambit Inc., Boston, 1971.
4. *Ibid.*, p. 46.
5. *Ibid.*
6. *Ibid.*
7. *Ibid.*, p. 44.
8. *Ibid.*, p. 48.
9. *Ibid.*, p. 95.
10. *Ibid.*, p. 77.
11. *Ibid.*, p. 50.
12. *Ibid.*, p. 94.
13. *Ibid.*, Chapter 7.
14. *Early Man,* op. cit., p. 52.
15. Ernest A. Hooton, *Up From The Ape,* rev. ed., Macmillan, New York, 1947. p. 448.
16. *Early Man,* op. cit., p. 54.
17. *Ibid.*
18. *Ibid.*

Chapter 7

1. *Nature,* February 11, 1911, vol. 85, #2155, p.59.
2. Desmond Morris, *The Naked Ape,* Dell Books (paperback), New York, 1967.
3. Charles Darwin, *The Descent of Man,* 2nd ed., Hurst & Co., New York, 1874 and later, pp. 623—25.
4. Morris, op. cit.
5. Darwin, op. cit., p. 627.

6. *Man From the Farthest Past,* Smithsonian Institution Series, 1930, p. 173.
7. Spector, *Handbook of Biological Data,* W. B. Saunders Company. (It is pointed out that, though the brain is only 2.2% of the body weight, 14% of all blood-flow goes to the brain.)
8. Morris, op. cit., p. 38.

Chapter 8

1. *Scientific American,* #211, October 1964, pp. 78—86.
2. *Ibid.*
3. B. Ernst & T. J. E. De Vries, eds., *Atlas of the Universe,* Thos. Nelson & Sons, New York, p. 200.
4. Earl C. Slypher, *Mars,* Sky Publishing Corp., Cambridge, Mass., and Northland Press, Flagstaff, Ariz., 1962, pp. 31, 120.
5. John Lewis, *Anthropology Made Simple,* Doubleday, New York, p. 30.
6. There is one sole freakish exception to the rule: Along with Man, the extinct animal *homalodotherium* had no diastemata.
7. A. L. Kroeber, *Anthropology,* Harcourt Brace, New York, 1948, pp 12—13. (Also See William K. Gregory, *The Evolution of Human Dentition,* Williams & Wilkins Publishers, Baltimore, 1922, pp. 370—73.)
8. Desmond Morris, *The Naked Ape,* Dell Books (paperback), New York, 1967, p. 58.
9. *Ibid.,* p. 57.

Chapter 9

1. *Today's Education,* October 1970, p. 88.
2. Anne Morgan, *Kinship of Animals & Man,* McGraw-Hill, New York, 1955, pp.180—82.
3. *Ibid.*
4. *Life Before Man,* The Emergence of Man series, Time-Life Books, New York, 1972, p. 14.
5. *Ibid.,* p. 15.
6. Norman Macbeth, *Darwin Retried,* Gambit Inc., Boston, 1971, p.74.
7. *Ibid.,* p. 89.
8. *Ibid.,* p. 156.

9.   *Ibid.*, p. 101.
10. International Bible Students Association, *Did Man Get Here by Evolution or by Creation?* Watchtower Bible & Tract Society, New York, 1967, p. 35.
11. Macbeth, op. cit., p.. 106.

Chapter 10

1.   Desmond Morris, *The Naked Ape,* Dell Books (paperback), New York, 1967, p. 53.
2.   *Ibid.*
3.   *Ibid.*, p. 46.
4.   *Ibid.*, p. 53.
5.   *Ibid.*, p. 62.
6.   *Ibid.*, p. 68.
7.   Ernest A. Hooton, *Up From the Ape*, rev. ed., Macmillan, New York, 1947, p. 40.
8.   Private communication from George Higer, who has dissected these animals, excepting the whale.
9.   *Ibid.* (In seaport towns of England, one may occasionally see an old salt walking with a cane made from the penis bone of a large whale.)
10. Morris, op. cit., p. 67.
11. *Ibid.*, p. 9.

Chapter 11

1.   Leslie B. Arey, *Developmental Anatomy,* W. B. Saunders Co., p. 120.
2.   Williams, *Obstetrics,* 12th ed., p. 131.
3.   N. J. Berrill, *Man's Emerging Mind,* Oldbourne Science Library, London, p. 293.
4.   Loren Eisley, *Darwin's Century,* Doubleday, Anchor Books, Garden City, L.I., pp. 279, 368.
5.   *The Primates,* Life Nature Library series, Time-Life Books, New York, 1971, p. 183.
6.   Desmond Morris, *The Naked Ape,* Dell Books (paperback), New York. 1967, pp. 92.
7.   Schunk, *The History of Man,* Chilton Pubs., Philadelphia, pp. 228, 234. (See also, Weston La Barre, *The Human Animal,* The University of Chicago Press, p. 54.)
8.   Norman Macbeth, *Darwin Retried,* Gambit Inc., Boston, 1971, pp. 32, 162.

Chapter 12

1. Norman Macbeth, *Darwin Retried,* Gambit Inc., Boston, 1971, p. 141.
2. *Ibid.*, 89.
3. *Ibid.*, 103.
4. *Ibid.*
5. International Bible Students Association, *Did Man Get Here by Evolution or by Creation?*, Watchtower Bible & Tract Society, New York. 1967, p. 10.
6. Jean Sendy, *The Coming of the Gods*, Berkley Medallion (paperback), New York, 1973, p. 41.
7. *The Universal Standard Encyclopedia,* Unicorn Publishers, New York, 1955, vol. 23, p. 8679.
8. *Man From the Farthest Past,* Smithsonian Institution Series, Vol. 7, p. 17.
9. *Life,* November 10, 1972, p. 78.
10. Theodosius Dobzhansky, *Evolution, Genetics and Man,* John Wiley & Sons, New York, 1957, p. 337.
11. *Science News,* June 12, 1971, p. 402.
12. *The Primates,* Life Nature Library series, Time-Life Books, New York, 1971, p. 11.
13. Desmond Morris, *The Naked Ape,* Dell Books (paperback), 1967, p. 54.
14. G. G. Simpson, *Life of the Past,* Yale University Press (paperback), New Haven, 1953, p. 59.
15. Loren Eisley, *Darwin's Century,* Doubleday Anchor Books Garden City, L.I., p. 313.
16. Gustav Schenk, *The History of Man,* Chilton, Philadelphia, p. 103.

Chapter 13

1. Erich von Däniken, *Gods from Outer Space,* G. P. Putnam's Sons, New York, 1970, p. 25.
2. *Ibid.*, p. 24.
3. Loren Eisley, *Darwin's Century,* Doubleday Anchor Books, Garden City, L.I., p. 279.
4. *Evolution,* Life Nature Library series, Time-Life Books, New York, 1970, p. 149.

5. Carelton S. Coon and Edward E. Hunt, Jr., eds., *Anthropology, A to Z,* Grosset & Dunlap, New York, p. 79.
6. Eisley, op. cit., p. 285.
7. *Early Man,* Life Nature Library series, Time-Life Books, New York, 1971, p. 178.
8. Arthur Koestler, *"Man—One of Evolution's Mistakes?"* New York Times Magazine, October 19, 1969, p. 112.
9. *Life Before Man,* Emergence of Man series, Time-Life Books, New York, 1972, p. 19.
10. *Early* Man, op. cit., p. 108.
11. Robert Audrey, *African Genesis,* Delta Publications, New York, p. 330.
12. *Ibid.,* p. 36.

Chapter 14

1. Charles Darwin, *The Descent of Man,* 2nd ed., Hurst & Co., New York, 1874 and later, pp. 623—25.
2. *Scientific American,* #211, October 1964, pp. 78—86.
3. *Science News,* November 6, 1971, pp. 314—16.
4. F. A. E. Crew, *Organic Inheritance in Man,* Oliver & Boyd Ltd., London, 1927, pp. 134—35.
5. *Ibid.,* p. 205.
6. Loren Eisley, *Darwin's Century,* Doubleday Anchor Books, Garden City, L.I., New York, pp. 308—3 14.
7. *Ibid.*
8. *The Universal Standard Encyclopedia,* op. cit., vol. 3, p. 848.
9. A. L. Kroeber, *Anthropology,* Harcourt, Brace & Co., New York, 1923, p. 412. (See also *Early Life,* Life Nature Library series.) Twenty-five thousand prehistoric stone implements and a thousand mammoth skeletons were found at Predmost.
10. *Man From the Farthest Past,* Smithsonian Institution Series, Inc., Washington, D.C., 1934, Vol. 7, p. 67.
11. Otis T. Mason, *The Origins of Invention,* MIT Press, pp. 136—37.
12. Desmond Morris, *The Naked Ape,* Dell Books (paperback), New York, 1967, p. 110.
13. *Life Before Man,* Emergence of Man series, Time-Life Books, New York, 1972, p. 19.

Chapter 15

1. *The Universal Standard Encyclopedia,* Unicorn Publishers, New York, 1955, vol. 19, pp. 6904—905. (Also, *Encyclopedia Britannica,* 1964 ed., vol. 20, p. 70, and vol. 11, p. 744.)
2. *The Universal Standard Encyclopedia, ibid.*
3. Sylvano Arresta, *American Handbook on Psychiatry,* Basic Books, New York, 1959, vol. 1, pp. 486—87.
4. *Ibid.*
5. Karl A. Menninger, *The Human Mind,* 3rd ed., Alfred A. Knopf, New York, 1946, pp. 93—107.
6. *Science News,* July 22, 1972, p. 58.
7. *Encyclopedia Americana,* 1946 ed. vol. 17, p. 410. (Lincoln was 6 feet 4 inches, when the average height was considerably less than today.)
8. *Ibid.,* vol. 8, p. 594. (During World War II, De Gaulle was the tallest officer in the entire French army.)
9. Lord Charnwood, *Abraham Lincoln,* Garden City Pub. Co., N.Y. (copyright 1917 by Henry Holt & Co.) pp. 7—8.
10. Anne Anastasi, *Differential Psychology,* Macmillan, New York, 1937, pp. 265, 267.
11. *Ibid.,* pp. 267—68.
12. Erich von Däniken, *Gods from Outer Space,* G. P. Putnam's Sons, New York, 1970, pp. 67—68.
13. Desmond Morris, *The Naked Ape,* Dell Books (paperback), New York. 1967, chap. 3.

Chapter 16

1. Points like this are contained in a variety of books about UFOs or flying saucers. The reader is urged to consult any good reference work in "UFOlogy." A full list of references is available from the U.S. Government Printing Office; Lynn E. Catoe, *UFOs and Related Subjects,* An Annotated Bibliography, Library of Congress (AFOSR 68—1656, Washington, D.C., 1969).
2. Aimée Michel, *The Truth About Flying Saucers,* Criterion Books, New York, 1956, pp. 197 ff. (See also, Leonard G. Cramp, *Space, Gravity and the Flying Saucer,* British

Book Center, New York, 1955, pp. 56 ff.)

3. Otto O. Binder, *Flying Saucers Are Watching Us*, Belmont Books (paperback), New York, 1969, pp. 162, 163.
4. Cramp, op. cit.
5. Harold T. Wilkins, *Flying Saucers on the Attack*, Ace Books (paperback), New York, 1954, pp. 156 ff.
6. Morris K. Jessup, *UFO's and the Bible*, Saucerian Books (paperback), Clarksburg, W. Va., 1965.
7. Wilkins, op. cit.
8. Josef Blumrich, *The Spaceships of Ezekiel*, Bantam Books, New York, 1974.
9. Brinsley le poer Trench, *The Flying Saucer Story*, Neville Spearman Ltd., London, 1966, p. 24.
10. Ivan T. Sanderson, *Uninvited Visitors*, Cowles Education Corp., New York, 1967, p. 159.
11. *The Books of Charles Fort*, omnibus prepared by the Fortean Society, Henry Holt & Co., New York, 1941, p. 163.
12. *Ibid.*, p. 163.
13. Wilbert B. Smith, *The Boys From Topside*, Timothy Green Beckley, ed., Saucerian Books (paperback), Clarksburg, W. Va., pp. 13 ff.
14. *Ibid.*, p. 29.
15. Carl Sagan and S. I. Shklovski, *Intelligent Life in the Universe*, Holden-Day Inc., San Francisco, Calif., 1966.
16. *Ibid.*, p. 445.
17. *Ibid.*, p. 456.
18. *UFO Preview*, pamphlet of the California UFO Research Institute, Lawndale, Calif., December 1971, p. 2.
19. *Ibid.*
20. *Ibid.*
21. *Ibid.*, October 1971, p. 2.
22. *"UFOs, Myth and Mystery,"* paper presented by Stanton T. Friedman at 1971 Midwest UFO Conference, St. Louis, Mo., June 12, 1971, p. 4.
23. Bryant and Helen Reeve, *Flying Saucer Pilgrimage*, Palmer Publications (paperback), Amherst, Wis., 1965.
24. *Ibid.*
25. Coral and Jim Lorenzen, *Flying Saucer Occupants*, Signet Books (paperback), New York, 1967, pp. 42 ff.
26. *Ibid.*
27. *Anomaly: A Journal of Forteana*, edited and published by John A. Keel, New York, #7, Fall 1971, p. 117.
28. Keel, op. cit.
29. Otto O. Binder. *"UFO's Own Earth—and All Mankind,"* Saga, December 1971, p. 94.

30. These UFO sightings by VIPs, from August 1973 on, are reported in many newspapers of the time, also by UPI and AP releases.
31. Otto O. Binder, *Flying Saucers Are Watching Us*, Belmont Books (paperback), New York, 1969, pp. 175 ff.
32. Ivan T. Sanderson, *Invisible Residents*, World Publishing Co., New York, 1970, pp. 99 ff.
33. Carl Sagan and S.I. Shklovski, op. cit., p. 461.
34. Wilkins, op. cit., pp. 217 ff.
35. *Genesis* 6:4.
36. Erich von Däniken, *Gold of the Gods*, G. P. Putnam's Sons, New York, 1973, various chapters.
37. Binder, op. cit. (book), pp. 93 ff.
38. *Ibid.*, p. 151.
39. Mossis K. Jessup, *The Expanding Case For the UFO*, Citadel Press, New York, 1957, p. 240.
40. Otto O. Binder, *What We Really Know About Flying Saucers*, Fawcett Publications (paperback), New York. 1968, various chapters.
41. Reeve, op. cit., p. 143.

A. Africanus, 56, 165
Aborigines, Australian, 94
Abortions, spontaneous, in
    humans,136
Abraham Lincoln (Charnwood),
    232n.
Acceleration during space travel,
    98, 137
Acquisitions by species, 91
Adams, JC .,199-200
Adolescence in humans,141
African Genesis (Audrey), 230n.
African Hominids, 55, 56 *see* also
    Hominids
Africanus Boisei, 56
A. Habilis, 57, 57
Air Force, U S 213 219-21
Algae, fossils of, 3
Alphabets, 113
Alpha Centauri (star), 28
Alpha waves, 176,179
Altamira, Spain, cave paintings at,
    183
American Handbook on Psychiatry
    (Arrests) 231n., 232n
American institute of Aeronautics
    and Astronautics 213
American Rocket Society, 30,213
Amino acids, 22
Amphibians, evolution of, 147
Anastasi, Anne, 232n.
Anatomy, *see* Physiology
Ancient civilizations, 181-83,203,
    220-21
    see also Civilization
Animals,
    classification of, 53,173-74
    copulation among, 122
    instincts in, 185
    psychology of, 190-91
Anomalies of evolution, 61-62,
    73-74, 83
Anomaly: A Journal of Forteana
    (Keel) 233n,
Anthropoids,
    brains of, 150
    evolution of, 164
    female, 127
    hands of, 104
    learning processes in, 141
    tool use by, 85-87
Anthropology, 47-53, 54-56, 76
    107, 164-67, 193, 211

bipedalism and, 156-57
evolution and, 137
physical, 91, 105, 133, 138,
    158-62, 165-174
race and, 82-83
tool use and, 83-86
Anthropology (Kroeber), 229n.,
    231n.
Anthropology, A to Z (Coon and
    Hunt), 231n.
Anthropology Made Simple
    (Lewis), 228n
Anthropomorphism in evolution,
    79-80
Antimatter, 29
Antiquity of Man, The (Keith),
    226n.
Apes (Pongids), 53, 60, 61-2, 65-
    66, 84
    brain of, 115, 145-48, 150,
        153, 162, 165, 171, 178, 205
    childhood of, 140-41, 204-05
    evolution from, 22, 57, 58,
        164-66
    female, 124-25, 127-28
    genius in, 183-4
    hair on, 94-96, 127
    humans compared with, 6, 17,
        54, 64-65, 67, 92, 94-95, 104,
        108, 122-25, 127-28,144,170-
        71, 153, 171
    intelligence of, 149, 150, 153,
        171
    language of, 112
    learning processes in, 149-50
    macaque, 65, 158
    newborn, 140-41, 206-07
    nursing by, 125
    orgasms in, 123
    pregnancy in, 125
    reproduction in, 122-23,135,
        136
    sexuality of, 122-23, 127-28
    society of, 140-41, 206
    taste in, 114
    thumbs of, 158
    tool use by, 85
    vision of, 115
    vocalization in, 111
Appendix in humans, 105
Aquatic mammals, 93, 98, 99
    see also Dolphins; Whales
Archeology, 120

Galileo, 185, 201
Ganymede (satellite of Jupiter),
    38
Genes,
    for genius, 181-182, 187-88
    manipulation of, 66, 68-69, 78,
      112, 114, 118, 119, 121, 137,
      140, 142, 167, 187
    memory and, 204-05
    racial memory and. 204-05
    recessive, 181
    schizophrenia and, 194
    starpeople and, 185, 187-8, 201,
      207, 208, 219
Genetics, DNA code of, 24, 118
    genius and, 181-182, 187-8
    idiot-geniuses and, 199
    manipulation of, 66, 68-69, 78,
      112, 114, 118, 119, 121, 137,
      140, 142, 167, 187
    Mendeian laws of, 187
    mutations and, 118-19, 152
    vision and, 117
Genius,
    in apes, 184-5
    in humans, 180-188, 195-200,
      205
Genus, 54, 161, 173-74
George, 194-5
Gibbons, 61, 91
Gilgamesh (deity), ii
Ginkgo trees, 64
God,
    evolution and, 82
    starpeople and, 97, 121, 218
Gods, Demons and UFO's
    (Norman), 225n.
Gods from Outer Space (von
    Däniken), 231n, 232n.
Gold of the Godz(von Däniken),
    233n.
Goldschmidt. Richard B., 116
Gorillas, 61, 65, 83, 84, 91
    brain of, 162
    penis of, 133, 134
    reproduction in, 136
    teeth of, 107
Government in ancient Roman
    civilization, 183
Great apes, 61-62, 84, 147
Greece, ancient civilization of,
    14, 183-4
Greek literature, Unidentified

Flying Objects in, 211
Greenberg J. Mayo, 25
Gregory, William K. 229n,
Gross, VemoilL.. 17
Growth of the Brain, The
    (Donaldson), 228n.

Habilis, 57, 58, 67
Hair,
    of apes, 94-96, 127
    of humans, 89, 92-97, 99, 191
    of mammals, 93, 95, 113
    of monkeys. 94-95
    muscles and, 113
    of primates, 94-95
    schizophrenia and, 191
Handbook of Biological Data
    (Spector), 228n,
Hands,
    anthropoid, 104
    hominid, 156
    human, 85, 103-05, 155-60
Hardin, 116-17
Hawks, 115
Healing of human skin, 105
Heat,
    ape females in, 124-25
    human females in, 123, 124
Henoch, iii-iv
Heredity, 181-182, 185
    Mendelian laws of, 187
    schizophrenia and, 194
Higer, George, 230n.
Higher primates, see Primates,
    higher
Hindbrain, 152
Hippopotamuses, brain of, 155
History 01 Man, The (Schenk),
    230n, 231n.
Holy Land, spread of humans
    from, 79
Homalodotherium, 228n.
Hominids, 6, 8, 9, 51, 53-58, 60,
    61-63, 65-71, 73, 84, 99, 94,
    159, 163
    brain of, 150, 156, 157, 160,
      161, 164, 168-69, 171, 172
    childhood of, 142
    female, 142
    hands of, 156
    hunting by, 142, 171
    male, 142

Roman civilization, 14, 183
Roman literature, Unidentified
Flying Objects in, 211
Rose, Lynn, 235n.
Rosenberg, Gunther, 16-17

Sagan, Carl, 30, 31, 37-38, 169,
213, 214, 225n, 233n.
Sanderson, Ivan T., 212, 225n,
233n.
Sapiens stellar, 174
Sapiens supremis, 174
Sappho, 183
Satellites,
of Earth, 33
of Jupiter, 38
of Saturn, 38
Saturn,
atmosphere of, 38
life on, 42
Schenk, Gustav, 230n, 231n. -
Schiaparelli, Giovanni, 43, 45
Schizophrenia, 190-94
Schwartz, Berthold, 221
Science,
expansion of, 175
racial memory and
discoveries of, 201, 205
sex and the development of,
129
Scientific community, iii, 166
Scopes, John T., 1
Seals, 99
Self-evolution, 118
Sendy, Jean, 230n.
Senses,
sight, 89, 114-18, 120
taste, 114
touch, 104
Sewall Wright Effect, 71
Sexoloy, 132
Sexuality,
of apes, 122-25, 127-28
of baboons, 122
civilization and, 124, 129
evolution and, 127, 128
of humans, 122-34
of primates, 122-23, 127-28
of starpeople, 108-12, 132-34,
219
Shakespeare. William, 167, 196
Shapley, Harlow, 9, 27-29,225n.

Shklovski, I.S., 231, 225n.,233n.
Shrews, tree, 158
Siberial meteorite (1908),29-30
Sidney (kangaroo), 156
Simpson, G.G., 64, 79, 230n.
Simultaneous regression,
theory of, 195, 197-99
Skin of humans,
colors of, 83-4
low healing rate of, 105
muscles and, 113
sensitivity of, 89, 104
Skulls,
fossils of. 74-5
human, 4, 5. 8-9, 51-2
Neanderthal Man, 75, 165
Swanscombe Man, 74
Sleep, brain waves during, 176,
180
Slypher, Earl C., 226n., 228n,
Smiles by humans, 108
Smith, Wilbert B., 213, 233n.
Society,
ape, 140-41, 206
baboon, 183
see also Civilization
Socrates, 196, 199
Sonar in dolphins, 153
*Space, Gravity and the Flying
Saucer* (Cramp), 232n.
Space probes,
Mariners, 43, 45, 46
of Mars, 43-46
Pioneer, iii, 38
of Venus, 38, 39
Viking, 42
Spaceships of Ezekiel, The (Blum-
rich), 232n,
Space travel,
conditions during, 98, 137,
210
of starpeople, 34-36, 98-
99,136-37, 166, 203,207-8,
209-22
by Unidentified Flying
Objects, 29,33, 41, 209-22
Sparrows, brain of, 162
Special creation, theory of, 81-82
Speciation, 72
Species, 54, 83, 142, 173-4
Spector, 228n.
Speech in humans, 89, 111-12
brain center for, 173

About the Authors

MAX H. FLINDT

Born in 1915 in San Jose, California. The son of pioneer science-fiction writer, Homer Eon Flint. Ardent studies in chemistry, physics, biology, paleontology, and anthropology led him to a life dedicated to independent scientific research. Former posts include that of Senior Laboratory Technician under Nobelists Dr. Edward Teller, Dr. Glenn Seaborg, and Dr. Melvin Calvin at Lawrence Radiation Laboratory, Berkeley, California; Laboratory Analyst in Research at Lockheed, where he engaged in highly classified space research; and research on human blood anomalies under the late Professor Emeritus Percival Baumberger of Stanford University.

Flindt is the first to scientifically document from biological evidence the possibility that mankind may be a hybrid from a prehistoric union of terrestrial humanoids and starmen, which is this book's main thesis. He privately published a pamphlet entitled "On Tiptoe Beyond Darwin" (Copyright 1962), which was later expanded to short book length (Copyright 1965). The present book is a greatly expanded version, with much additional scientific data to further substantiate this concept.

If you wish to correspond with Max about this book, please forward all correspondence to:

Max H. Flindt
344 San Luis Ave.
Los Altos, CA
94024-4023
Please enclose a SASE for reply.
or E-mail - Karen@ozarkmt.com Attn: Max H. Flindt

OTTO O. BINDER

Born 1911, Bessemer, Michigan. Three years college: City College of Chicago. University of Illinois, Northwestern University; majored in chemical engineering.

First published story, 1932 (fiction). Over 3 million words published in fiction, including science fiction. Over forty books published, including *Victory in Space, Careers in Space,* and such astronomical texts as *The Moon, The Planets, Riddles of Astronomy,* all for school circulation. Under NASA contract in 1966 wrote the Mercury, Gemini, and Apollo Programs in chart form for educational purposes.

Two UFO books published: *Flying Saucers Are Watching Us,* Belmont Books, 1969 (re-issued in 1971); *What We Really Know About UFOs,* Fawcett Gold Medal Books, 1968.

Over 300 articles (nonfiction) published in national magazines, on science subjects and UFOs. Articles for science yearbooks on chemistry, astronomy, physics, and biology.

Member of original American Rocket Society, American Interplanetary Society, National Spaceflight Association, Aerospace Writers Association, and so on.

Founder and editor of *Space World* magazine, 1959-63, subscribed to by high schools, colleges, and professional people.

Wrote for juvenile market: *Golden Book of Jets, Book of Space Travel, Book of Atomic Energy,* and so on.

Syndicated strip, *Our Space Age,* ran for nine years in some 250 U.S. newspapers and in such foreign countries as Spain, Holland, Brazil, Argentina, Mexico, and others.

Biographical sources: *Pilgrims Through Space and Time* by J. O. Bailey, Argus, 1947; *The Immortal Storm* by Sam Moskowitz, ASFO, 1954; in *Editor and Publisher,* September 10, 1960; *Bergen Record* write-up, Hackensack, NJ., March 11, 1961; *New York Journal American,* January 1, 1961;

Contemporary Authors, Gale Research, Detroit 1962-67; *Working Press of the Nation,* National Research Bureau, Chicago, IL, 1969 to date.

Awarded honorary Master's Degree in astronautical science by NASA in 1963, with teaching certificate.

Major writing since 1965 in the field of UFOlogy: books, articles, analyses, statistics. Exponent of ET (ExtraTerrestrial) theory for UFOs, along with Dr. J. Mien Hynek, Dr. Jacques Vallee, and Stanton T. Friedman (nuclear scientist).

Latest contribution in the field to research for Max H. Flindt's theory of Hybrid Man and colony earth.

Otto O. Binder died in 1974 after the 1st printing of *Mankind - Child of the Stars.*

Other Books Published
by
Ozark Mountain Publishing

For more information about any of the above titles, or other
titles in our catalog, write or visit our web site.

P.O. Box 332
West Fork, AR 72774
WWW.OZARKMT.COM
1-800-935-0045 / 1-800-230-0312

Wholesale Inquiries Welcome